MORE GREAT RACEHORSES OF THE WORLD

Roger Mortimer
and
Peter Willett

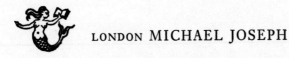

LONDON MICHAEL JOSEPH

First published in Great Britain by
MICHAEL JOSEPH LTD
52 Bedford Square
London, W.C.1
1972

7181 1032 3

Set and printed in Great Britain by
Ebenezer Baylis & Son Ltd., The Trinity Press, Worcester, and London
in Ehrhardt eleven on twelve point
and bound by James Burn at Esher, Surrey

CONTENTS

1*

Acknowledgments

The authors wish to thank the following for permission to quote from their publications: J. A. Allen & Co. Ltd., London, for an extract from *Men and Horses I Have Known* by George Lambton; Pelham Books Ltd., London, for an extract from *Racing with the Gods* by Marcus Marsh; Hodder & Stoughton Ltd., London, for an extract from *My Story* by Gordon Richards.

Acknowledgments are also due to the following for permission to reproduce photographs in which they hold the copyright:

R. Anscomb for plates 26 and 29; *The Blood-Horse*, Lexington, Kentucky, for plate 20; *The British Racehorse* for plates 2, 3, 4, 6, 8, 10, 11, 16, 17, 19, 22 and 23; W. W. Rouch & Co. Ltd., for plates 5, 7, 9, 12, 13, 14, 15, 18, 21, 24 and 30; Mike Sirico for plate 28.

FOREWORD

The selection of great racehorses is a controversial matter. Every racing man has his own ideas of the greatest horses he has seen, heard of or read about, and the authors are conscious of the fact that they are bound to offend the susceptibilities of some readers by the omission of certain thoroughbred heroes and the inclusion of others. They do not claim to have incorporated all the greatest racehorses of the world. They do claim that all the horses included have, for one reason or another, just cause to be considered great.

The horses included possessed qualities which appealed strongly to the authors; it is hoped that they will appeal equally to the readers.

The foaling date of each horse is indicated in brackets in the relevant chapter heading.

Blink Bonny (1854)

Four fillies only have achieved the wonderful double of winning the Derby and the Oaks. They are Sir Charles Bunbury's Eleanor (1801), Mr. W. I'Anson's Blink Bonny (1857), the Chevalier Ginistrelli's Signorinetta (1908) and Mr. E. Hulton's Fifinella (1916). Blink Bonny had been winter favourite for the Derby at a time when ante-post betting was really heavy, yet her starting price was 20–1. Her Derby time, 2 minutes 45 seconds, was then a record for the race. It was 11 1/5th seconds slower than Mahmoud's time in 1936.

Bred, owned and trained by Mr. William I'Anson, a Scotsman who had settled at Malton in Yorkshire, Blink Bonny was a bay filly by Melbourne out of Queen Mary, by Gladiator. She stood 15 hands 2½ inches with a neat, lean head, a longish neck and the best of shoulders. Melbourne had sired the great West Australian, winner of the "Triple Crown" in 1853. Queen Mary was out of an unnamed mare by the Derby winner Plenipotentiary. On St. Leger day 1844 the yearlings sold at Doncaster included Mendicant and Queen Mary. A buyer from Scotland, a certain Mr. Ramsay, was on the lookout for a nice filly and took a fancy to both these two. In the end he bought Queen Mary for 300 guineas. Mr. John Gully bought Mendicant, who won the Oaks and bred the 1858 Derby winner Beadsman. Queen Mary not only bred Blink Bonny, but was the grandam of the Derby winner Blair Athol and also of the St. Leger winner Caller Ou. It was apparently owing to the successes of a horse called Braxey that Mr. I'Anson determined to acquire Queen Mary. By then, though, she had disappeared into the wilds of Scotland and it proved extremely difficult to discover where she was. When he finally tracked her down, Mr. I'Anson was able to buy her for £30.

I'Anson was one of the old-fashioned sort and did not believe in wrapping up two-year-olds, even good ones, in cottonwool. He reckoned the best policy for Blink Bonny was plenty of work at home and plenty of racing, too. In fact he later admitted he had never in his life worked a two-year-old harder. She ran eleven times her first season. She was third in her first two races, the Zetland Stakes at York and the Mostyn Stakes at Chester; later she was third in the Convivial Produce Stakes at York in August. She won the Sapling Stakes at Manchester, the Bishop Burton Stakes at Beverley, the Tyro Stakes at Newcastle, the Produce Stakes at Liverpool, the Bentinck Memorial Stakes at Goodwood, the Gimcrack Stakes at York, and the Filly Stakes and a Sweepstakes at Doncaster. Prize money was not lavish in those days and these eight victories only earned just over £2,000. During the season Lord Londesborough wanted to buy her for £3,000 and I'Anson was prepared to accept the offer provided he could continue to train her. That did not suit his lordship so I'Anson bumped the price up to £4,000 which was more than Lord Londesborough was prepared to pay. Subsequently that season I'Anson turned down offers of £5,000 and £6,000.

It was an unfortunate characteristic of Melbourne's stock that they frequently had trouble with their teeth. Late in the autumn Blink Bonny was afflicted with this in an exceptionally severe form, suffering great pain that caused continual paroxysms, and losing condition to such an extent that she was reduced to a mere bag of bones. It was impossible to feed her with corn and for weeks all she could eat was a little green stuff. Nevertheless, she retained her position as winter favourite for the Derby. In the spring she began to pick up and I'Anson thought she was good enough to win the One Thousand Guineas even if she was only half fit. He overestimated her capabilities. Favourite at 5–4 on, she finished a poor fifth of eight behind the north country filly Imperieuse, trained at Malton by the famous John Scott.

The public were equally dismayed at Newmarket by Blink Bonny's wretched appearance and her lamentable performance. Her Derby price drifted to 1,000–30 and this was freely available at the start of Epsom week. In fact it had been taken for granted that she would not run in the Derby and when it was known for certain that she was being permitted to take her chance, covering money forced her price down to 20–1.

Favourite for the Derby at 4–1 was Mr. J. S. Douglas's Tournament who was giving George Fordham his first Derby mount. Tournament, however, sweated up profusely when he was being saddled and his chance could hardly have been improved by a delay of an hour at the start, the cause of which was a total lack of discipline on the part of certain jockeys. Other fancied runners were Lord Zetland's Skirmisher and Mr. T. Parr's M.D. The pace, for those days, was a fast one and Tournament and Skirmisher were both in trouble before Tattenham Corner was reached. The Danebury candidate Anton led into the straight and he was still in front approaching the distance, followed by Arsenal, Blink Bonny and M.D. At that point M.D. was going the best but just as his supporters were starting to cheer him home, he broke down badly and his chance had gone.

In the meantime a tremendous finish was just building up. Anton had given all he had, but Blink Bonny, ridden by Charlton, Black Tommy, Strathnaver and Adamas were almost in line and it was difficult indeed to separate them as they flashed past the post. The verdict of the judge was that Blink Bonny had won by a neck from Black Tommy, with Adamas a short head away third and Strathnaver a neck behind Adamas. A length and a half covered the first seven horses to finish.

Black Tommy was a 200–1 outsider, owned by a certain Mr. Drinkald and apparently at Epsom saddled by Mr. Drinkald's valet. Despite his starting price, the colt was not a little fancied by his owner who had backed him at extreme odds to win a fortune, one of his bets being £20,000 to a coat, waistcoat and hat. Mr. Drinkald was convinced Black Tommy had won. "Thank God I've won the Derby!" he exclaimed, and then added a trifle ungenerously, "and not a soul is on but myself." When Blink Bonny was declared the winner Mr. Drinkald could hardly believe it and a friend who was with him described in gruesome detail how Mr. Drinkald turned a nasty shade of green and gasped for breath as if he had been dealt a heavy blow just below the heart. It must indeed have been a moment of cruel disappointment. Incidentally, those who lost their money on Tournament had the chance to get it back when he won the Stewards Cup at Goodwood in July with 7 st. on his back.

Although Blink Bonny had had a hard race in the Derby, she seemed none the worse for it and it was decided to let her run in the Oaks two days later. Again ridden by Charlton, a Yorkshire jockey, she won very easily indeed. Undoubtedly her ability to stand up to the exacting demands made on her was assisted by her temperament, as she had the most placid and kindly of dispositions. After Epsom she was given a walk-over in a Sweepstakes at Ascot and then won the Bentinck Memorial Stakes at Goodwood and the Lancashire Oaks at Liverpool.

Not surprisingly she started a hot favourite at 5–4 for the St. Leger but to the chagrin of her backers she could do no more than finish fourth behind the One Thousand Guineas' winner Imperieuse. Some ugly rumours had in fact been circulating about her and a rough section of the Doncaster crowd sought vengeance on I'Anson, who might well have been lynched in front of the weighing room but for the effective intervention of the famous pugilist, Tom Sayers.

The situation was not perceptibly improved when two days later Blink Bonny carried off the Park Hill Stakes over the St. Leger course in a faster time than that recorded by Imperieuse in the St. Leger.

There is little doubt that Charlton pulled Blink Bonny in the St. Leger. I'Anson, who had backed his filly to the tune of £3,000, was not implicated in the plot. The instigator was John Jackson, an influential Yorkshire bookmaker, tough, quickwitted and entirely without scruples. He was not the first member of his profession, nor the last by a very long way, to specialize in the corruption of jockeys and his death at a comparatively early age was no loss to the Turf. Jackson himself had backed Imperieuse heavily and had laid Blink Bonny, confident that Charlton would not hesitate to betray his employer if offered sufficient money to do so. That confidence was not misplaced. I'Anson had been warned of the plot but believed in the integrity of Charlton and decided to stand by him; with dire result.

Blink Bonny's only race as a four-year-old was the Bentinck Memorial at Goodwood in which she ran so badly that she had to be pulled up. Unfortunately she died at the early age of eight and her fame as a brood mare rests on the achievements of her remarkable son Blair Athol.

Bred by I'Anson, Blair Athol, by Stockwell, was a rangy chestnut with a white face and a flaxen tail. He took a long time to come to hand and never ran as a two-year-old but I'Anson held a very high opinion of him and refused an offer of 7,000 guineas from John Jackson. This refusal convinced Jackson that Blair Athol must be something out of the ordinary and accordingly he backed Blair Athol heavily at a long price to win the Derby. This action on the part of Jackson proved to have profound significance the following year.

As a three-year-old Blair Athol, like Blink Bonny, suffered from bad teeth, but when that trouble had been successfully cleared up he fell a victim to intermittent lameness, the source of which the vet was unable to diagnose. Quite by chance a friend of I'Anson's over-heard a conversation in the barber's shop at Malton and thereby discovered that Blair Athol's lad had been bribed to prevent Blair Athol from running in the Derby and was in the habit of kicking him savagely in the genitals from time to time. A confession was extracted from the culprit who was then given a tremendous thrash-ing and thrown out of the yard. The lameness then swiftly disappeared.

That was not the end of the worries concerning Blair Athol and the Derby. A number of leading bookmakers had backed Lord Glasgow's General Peel, winner of the Two Thousand Guineas, to win a very large sum in the Derby. They wanted to stop Blair Athol running at Epsom and to back him for the St. Leger instead. A conference of those involved was held and Jackson managed to persuade those present that Blair Athol be permitted to run, despite the fierce opposition of Messrs. Steel and Hargreaves, the latter of whom, described by a contemporary as "a lucky, screaming gentle-man with a large face and pink eyes", was a repulsive villain who had made a fortune through the nobbling of Ratan in the notorious 1844 Derby.

Blair Athol had never run before the Derby but his ability was no secret to the public and the officers of two cavalry regiments backed him to win £23,000. He triumphed at Epsom by two lengths, Jackson winning £40,000 and I'Anson £15,000. In the Grand Prix de Paris, in which his rider was not a little intimidated by the vicious hostility of the French crowd, Blair Athol was defeated but he subsequently won the St. Leger. He was a great success as a stallion and was four times champion sire.

Blink Bonny holds one record in racing history that is unlikely to be equalled. She is the only filly to have won the Derby and to have bred a Derby winner herself. On her death her skeleton was set up in the museum at York.

Shotover (1879)

The year 1882 is famous in English racing history as a truly remarkable one for three-year-old fillies. All the classic races were won by fillies, and fillies occupied the first three places in the St. Leger. If Shotover is selected here as the representative of these great fillies, it is because of the significance of her victories—she won the Two Thousand Guineas and the Derby—and not because she could necessarily claim to be the best.

In 1881 Lord Falmouth's Dutch Oven, by Dutch Skater out of a very fast mare called Cantiniere, had won nine races including the Dewhurst Plate. That great trainer George Lambton recorded: "She had a glorious bang tail which she carried very high; when she galloped, it floated behind her like the flag of a ship."

Nellie, by Hermit, was a beautiful filly owned by Mr. Leopold de Rothschild. She was always coming up against Dutch Oven and these two good fillies ran wonderfully true to form. Receiving 7 lb., Nellie beat Dutch Oven by three parts of a length in the Prince of Wales's Stakes at York. At level weights in the Rous Memorial Stakes at Newmarket, Dutch Oven beat her rival by a neck, and the following week in the Clearwell Stakes she gave her 3 lb. and won by a head.

Lord Rosebery's Kermesse, by Cremorne, was a long, low filly, very dark brown, almost black, in colour. She won five races including the Middle Park Plate. Her only defeat was when she and St. Marguerite dead-heated for second place in the Richmond Stakes at Goodwood behind Dutch Oven, Kermesse conceding the winner 4 lb.

Lord Stamford's Geheimniss, by Rosicrucian, was a filly with a superb action that won all her seven races with ease. The Hermit filly St. Marguerite, owned by "Mr. Manton", the "nom de course" of the Duchess of Montrose, was as handsome as the others and won four good races. In addition there was another very handsome filly by Hermit, the Duke of Westminster's Shotover. Shotover's two-year-old record, though, did not begin to compare with those of the other fillies mentioned. Somewhat delicate in constitution and slow to come to hand, she did not run until the autumn and then she failed to win a race.

Chestnut in colour, Shotover was bred by Mr. Henry Chaplin (later Viscount Chaplin) and was out of a mare called Stray Shot, who had won over two miles and whose grandam was the Oaks winner Mendicant, dam of the Derby winner Beadsman. When Shotover came up for sale as a yearling, Robert Peck, who was then training for the Duke of Westminster, bought her on the Duke's behalf for 1,500 guineas. The Duke did not take to her much and Peck agreed to take her over himself at the price he had originally given. Later, though, the Duke changed his mind and bought her back from Peck.

Shotover did not run as a two-year-old till October. Starting at 50–1, she was unplaced behind Kermesse in the Middle Park. She was then second in the Prendergast Stakes at Newmarket but failed to secure a place in a nursery when carrying only 7 st. 6 lb. She was still very backward and had really been raced chiefly with the object of giving her experience. At the end of the season Peck retired and the Duke's horses joined John Porter's stable at Kingsclere. Thus Shotover became the stable companion of Geheimniss.

During the winter Shotover made quite exceptional physical progress and in the spring she shaped so well at home that Porter had visions of her taking on the colts, who were not a distinguished collection, in the Two Thousand Guineas and beating them. Accordingly Shotover was tried at Kingsclere on April 18th. The result of the trial was somewhat inconclusive, leaving Porter more hopeful than confident. However, ridden by Tom Cannon and starting at 10–1, she won the Two Thousand Guineas very smoothly by two lengths from Lord Bradford's Quicklime. As she had had anything but a hard race, it was decided to run her again two days later in the One Thousand Guineas. Unfortunately she had taken more out of herself than had seemed apparent. A red-hot favourite at 4–1 on, she was beaten a neck by St. Marguerite with Nellie a head away third. Thus the first three in that race were all daughters of Hermit.

Shotover picked up nicely before the Derby in which she started at 11–2, a hot favourite being Mr. H. Rymill's Bruce, a See Saw colt trained at Ilsley in Berkshire. As a two-year-old Bruce had won all his four races—the Windsor Castle Stakes at Ascot, the King John Stakes at Egham, the Rous Plate at Doncaster and the Criterion Stakes at Newmarket. As a three-year-old he did not run before Epsom, but he had been very well galloped at home and Berkshire was on him to a man. He was a great favourite with the public, too, and was heartily cheered at Epsom as he cantered past the stands to the start.

Unfortunately for all concerned, Bruce was ridden by Sammy Mordan, who had partnered him in all his races as a two-year-old. This curious, lisping little man, who habitually referred to himself in the third person, was not only a very indifferent rider but possessed the conceit and self-satisfaction sometimes found in second-rate and third-rate jockeys. Moreover, it is by no means certain that he was honest. Undoubtedly a number of well-informed persons had their suspicions about him in this particular race. A prominent bookmaker, who was inclined to be cautious as a rule, persistently opposed Bruce in the market and laid him without hesitation at a point above the odds. He won so much money over Bruce's defeat that he was able to have built for himself a huge and hideous house just outside London.

Whether he was trying or not, Mordan rode a lamentable race in the Derby. He set off in front from the start and was in the lead coming down the hill. At Tattenham Corner he lost lengths by going wide, subsequently excusing himself on the grounds that Bruce had been frightened by a sheet of paper blown across the course. In the last two furlongs Bruce began to tire and he was quite unable to withstand a perfectly timed challenge by Tom Cannon on Shotover, who won by three-quarters of a length from Quicklime with Sachem a bad third. Bruce ought to have occupied third place but Mordan rounded off a nice afternoon's work by easing him up near the finish. Mr. Rymill took his defeat in most sporting fashion and there is no record of him having taken just vengeance on his deplorable jockey. It only remains to add that Bruce, ridden by Fred Archer, won the Grand Prix de Paris. He sustained a leg injury soon afterwards that put an end to his racing career.

Shotover remains to this day the only filly to have won the Two Thousand Guineas and the Derby. In 1912 Tagalie won the One Thousand Guineas and the Derby. Dutch Oven finished seventh behind Shotover at Epsom. She had not done well physically in the spring and her turn was to come later in the year. There was no question of running Shotover in the Oaks as Porter was convinced that the race could be safely left to Geheimniss and his confidence was fully justified by the result as she won with ease from St. Marguerite and Nellie.

At Royal Ascot, Shotover won the Ascot Derby and the Triennial Stakes. Geheimniss, having won over $1\frac{1}{2}$ miles at Epsom, was required to compete in the five furlong Fern Hill Stakes and went under by a short head to the two-year-old Narcissa. Kermesse in the meantime was recovering from two pasterns she split in the spring and she was unable to race before the autumn.

By Goodwood, Dutch Oven was returning to her best and was confidently expected to win the Sussex Stakes on the Wednesday. Unfortunately old Mat Dawson, thinking the race was on the Thursday gave her a strong gallop over a mile on the Wednesday morning and probably because of this she was beaten.

At York, Dutch Oven won the Yorkshire Oaks in a canter. She was pulled out again two days later for the Great Yorkshire Stakes but could only finish a modest third behind the front-running Peppermint and Nellie. She appeared to be a non-stayer in that race and drifted out to 40–1 for the St. Leger.

The Duke of Westminster had second claim that year on Fred Archer's services and it seemed probable that Archer would be free to ride Shotover in the St. Leger. Almost at the last moment, though, Lord Falmouth, exercising his right, decreed that Archer must ride Dutch Oven. Archer then asked Lord Falmouth if he could be liberated to partner Geheimniss, by then reckoned Shotover's superior, at Doncaster. To this request Lord Falmouth replied: "If I give you to the Duke you will have to ride Shotover, so you might as well be beaten on Dutch Oven as Shotover." According to John Porter, if Lord Falmouth had released Archer, the Duke would have permitted him to ride Geheimniss "because everyone at Kingsclere knew she was the better of the two".

A furlong from home Geheimniss, ridden by C. Loates, looked like winning the St. Leger quite easily but all of a sudden Dutch Oven appeared from nowhere, swept past her and won by a length and a half. Shotover, who, like Geheimniss, did not really stay the distance, was four lengths away third. Not altogether surprisingly, there were a number of suspicious-minded individuals who thought Archer had pulled Dutch Oven at Goodwood and at York but he would hardly have made strenuous efforts to get off riding the filly had he thought she possessed a serious chance of winning the St. Leger.

Two days after the St. Leger Shotover won the Park Hill Stakes over the full St. Leger distance, her deficiency in respect of stamina being offset by the mediocre nature of the opposition. At Newmarket in October she ran a most gallant race in the Select Stakes, only failing by a length to concede 10 lb. to Kermesse and Nellie who dead-heated for first place.

Shotover remained in training in 1883 but her zest for racing had gone and after several failures she retired to the stud, where she was not an outstanding success, her best winners being Orion and Bullingdon. She died at Eaton in 1898 and is buried there in good company between Lily Agnes, dam of Ormonde, and Ornament, dam of Sceptre.

There are still elderly persons living at Kingsclere who were told by their parents or grandparents of the great celebrations there after Shotover and Geheimniss had landed the Epsom double. A gigantic picnic was held on the Downs and everyone in the village and in neighbouring hamlets was entertained. A huge meal was served in two enormous marquees and there was every sort of festivity. Hundreds of balloons in the colours of the Duke of Westminster and of Lord Stamford were released and the party ended with a magnificent firework display. As John Porter rightly said: "Who can say we were not justified in rejoicing?"

Iroquois (1881)

In the first sixty years or so of the last century, it was taken for granted, at any rate in this country, that the British thoroughbred reigned supreme. The first big jolt to national self-esteem in this particular sphere came in 1865 when Count F. de Lagrange's French-bred Gladiateur won the Two Thousand Guineas, the Derby and the St. Leger. In his own country he carried off the Grand Prix de Paris amid scenes of the wildest enthusiasm, while in 1866 he returned to England to win the Ascot Gold Cup by a matter of forty lengths. No wonder he became known as "The Avenger of Waterloo". It was no advertisement for British sportsmanship that after the St. Leger the runner-up's owner, a Mr. Graham who had been a wrestler and who had made a fortune out of the production of gin, objected, with no valid evidence to support him, to Gladiateur on the grounds that the French colt was really a four-year-old.

The next blow administered to the pride of the British racing world took place in 1881 when the American colt Iroquois won the Derby.

Iroquois was bred by Mr. Aristides Welch at the Erdenheim Stud, Chestnut Hill, near Philadelphia and was by Leamington out of Maggie B.B., by Australian out of Madeline, by Boston. Leamington had been imported from England and was by the St. Leger winner Faugh-a-Ballagh, a full brother to Birdcatcher. The maternal grandsire of Iroquois had been imported from England, too, while, through Boston, Maggie B.B. traced back to the first English Derby winner, Diomed, who was exported to America and exercised immense influence on bloodstock breeding there.

Iroquois was acquired by Mr. Pierre Lorillard, the American tobacco millionaire, a leading figure on the American turf and a man keen to demonstrate to the English racing world the swiftly

improving status of the American thoroughbred. He made a recon-
naissance of English racing in 1879 and created quite a sensation by
winning with the six-year-old Parole the City and Suburban and the
Great Metropolitan on successive days at the Epsom Spring Meeting, those races being of far greater significance than they are today
when they rate as very ordinary handicaps.

Iroquois had come to England as a yearling in 1879 and was
installed at Newmarket in the stable of Mr. Lorillard's American
trainer, Jacob Pincus. In those days the average Englishman, who
had seldom been out of his own country in his life, was liable to be
almost aggressively insular and intolerant, viewing foreigners, and
any way of life that was alien to his own, with ridicule and fairly
good-natured contempt. At Newmarket Pincus, a character in his
way, became very much liked but no one was disposed to take him
at all seriously, just as the Italian owner-trainer, the Chevalier
Ginistrelli, was looked on at Newmarket as a bit of a joke. Both
Pincus and Ginistrelli, though, had the last laugh, Ginistrelli
winning the Derby and the Oaks in 1908 with his remarkable filly
Signorinetta.

Pincus, for his part, made no secret of the fact that he thought
English training methods both crude and inefficient. He was a
fervent believer in the clock and the time test and placed no reliance
at all on a system of trials by weight. He never succeeded in making
any converts at Newmarket but at least he proved conclusively that
he knew his own job.

Iroquois, a very handsome brown colt with a beautiful action,
was not kept in cottonwool as a two-year-old, and Pincus, who
greatly annoyed the local touts by having his string out at four
o'clock in the morning, made him "sweat for the brass". He ran
twelve times in all and won four races, his most important successes
being in the Chesterfield Stakes at Newmarket and the Lavant
Stakes at Goodwood. The race, though, that earned him the most
credit was the July Stakes at Newmarket in which he ran Lord
Falmouth's Bal Gal to a head. Bal Gal was a brilliant two-year-old
and won eight of her nine races including the Champagne Stakes at
Doncaster, her solitary defeat being at the end of the season, when
she had probably trained off, in the Middle Park Plate.

Iroquois wintered well but he was amiss for some weeks in the
spring. Perhaps, like a good many other American-bred thoroughbreds, he detested the persistent north-easterly winds that are apt to

sweep across Newmarket Heath in March and at the beginning of April. At all events, he carried a lot of flesh and was palpably backward when he took the field for the Two Thousand Guineas at the end of April. Quite unfancied and virtually unbacked, he amazed and delighted Pincus by finishing second, beaten three lengths, to Peregrine, who actually belonged to the Duke of Westminster but because of the recent death of the Duchess ran in the name of Mr. Grosvenor. Peregrine was making the first appearance of his career, and on account of the ease with which he won, there was a tendency to regard him as a colt of quite exceptional merit. He was therefore made a short-priced favourite for the Derby.

One man who entertained a rather less exalted view of Peregrine was that great jockey and shrewd judge of form, Fred Archer. From what he had seen of Iroquois in the Two Thousand Guineas, he thought Iroquois had a great chance of beating Peregrine in the Derby. Accordingly he paid a call on Jacob Pincus and asked for the ride on Iroquois at Epsom. Naturally Mr. Lorillard and Pincus were only too delighted to secure the services of the outstanding rider of the day.

At the Newmarket Second Spring Meeting it was hoped to subject Iroquois to a proper racecourse test but he had only a solitary opponent when winning the ten furlong Newmarket Stakes, while he was given a walk-over in the Burwell Stakes. Pincus, however, was giving him a lot of work, so much in fact that the whisper went round Newmarket that Iroquois was being galloped into the ground and was sure to be stale by the time he got to Epsom. In the paddock on Derby day Iroquois did in fact look extremely light and the paddock critics, shaking their heads, pronounced him over-trained. In reality he was trained to the minute. Pincus was confident, Archer supremely so.

Peregrine, ridden by Webb, was a firm favourite at 6–5, Iroquois second favourite at 11–2. The field of fifteen included two other American horses, Don Fulano and Marshal Macdonald, both owned by Mr. J. R. Keene. It was one of the hottest Derby days on record and the paddock was almost deserted since everyone was seeking such shade as the few trees and the hedges provided. Mr. Lorillard himself was not present, but his wife was there with a strong American contingent.

The early stages of the race call for no comment. At Tattenham Corner the leader was Lord Rosebery's Voluptuary, who three years later, ridden by Mr. E. P. Wilson, won the Grand National Steeple-chase. A quarter of a mile from home Voluptuary was in trouble and was headed by Scobell, Town Moor and Cumberland. Almost immediately these three were joined by the favourite.

At this point Webb elected to draw his whip and gave Peregrine "one for the road". Peregrine resented this strongly and at once veered sharply to the right away from the rails. Archer had been tracking the favourite and this was his opportunity. He at once steered Iroquois through the gap and challenged Peregrine, who, despite his swerve, had shaken off his other three rivals. A short, sharp struggle then ensued, Iroquois obtaining the mastery with about a hundred yards to go to win rather cleverly by a neck. Town Moor was third.

Although the race had been won by a "foreigner", the victory was a remarkably popular one, largely no doubt because the winner had been ridden by Fred Archer and accordingly had been very heavily backed. When the code word "Iropertow" (1st Iroquois, 2nd Peregrine, 3rd Town Moor) reached the western end of the Atlantic cable, there were scenes of the wildest enthusiasm. Business was suspended on Wall Street and the Stock Exchange reverberated to outbursts of cheering. No section of the American nation was more delighted than that very substantial one composed of persons of Irish descent. These, for the most part, regarded England as their deadly enemy and were overjoyed at this blow to English arrogance and self-esteem.

Great events on the Turf in those days were liable to inspire a deluge of verse. The success of Iroquois was recorded in the following lines:

> Flushed red are American faces!
> Hurrah for old Leamington's son!
> You'll show the pale Briton how races
> Across the Atlantic are won.
> Dash on as if life was at venture,
> And news shall unloosen the cork
> From seas of champagne at Newmarket
> And oceans of "fizz" at New York!

Mr. Lorillard himself had received the good news at the Jerome Jockey Club grounds and was able to receive there the congratulations of many of his friends. National pride was so stimulated that a suggestion was seriously mooted to place a bronze statue of Iroquois in the Central Park, New York. Archer himself was approached by an American who wanted to take him on tour in the United States and offered him £10,000 before starting.

Still in great form, Iroquois won the Prince of Wales's Stakes and the St. James's Palace Stakes at Royal Ascot. In the autumn he won the St. Leger at the surprisingly good price, in view of his record, of 2–1. The word had gone round at Newmarket that he was "a dead 'un" and that accounted for this rare and unintended generosity on the part of the bookmakers. Probably the rumour was due to the local touts failing to comprehend the training methods of Pincus. In October he ran below form in the Champion Stakes at Newmarket, finishing third behind the 1880 Derby winner Bend Or and Scobell, but he was pulled out again two days later for the Newmarket Derby and won with ease. The following year he had training troubles and never ran. He finished his career in 1883 when he beat his old rival Scobell in the Stockbridge Cup. A really good horse at his best, he had done much to place the American thoroughbred fairly and squarely on the map. The next American-bred colt to win the Derby and St. Leger was Never Say Die in 1954.

Iroquois retired to the stud at the Bellmead Farm, Tennessee. He was far from being a failure but he hardly fulfilled the very high hopes that had been placed in him. He died in 1899.

Curiously, there was probably an even better American three-year-old than Iroquois in England in 1881. This was Mr. J. R. Keene's Foxhall, who might conceivably have earned the "Triple Crown" had he been entered for the classics. As it was, he won the Grand Prix de Paris, the Cesarewitch, and then the Cambridgeshire with 9 st. on his back, a very big weight for a three-year-old in that highly competitive nine-furlong handicap. The following year he won the Ascot Gold Cup.

La Flèche (1889)

Baron de Hirsch's La Flèche was one of the greatest fillies of English racing history. Her victories included the One Thousand Guineas, the Oaks, the St. Leger, the Cambridgeshire, the Ascot Gold Cup and the Champion Stakes. What is more, she ought to have won the Derby as well.

Baron Maurice de Hirsch was a German Jew, born in Munich in 1831. He increased the wealth he had inherited by large contracts for the construction of railways in Germany, Belgium, Holland, Russia and Turkey. In addition, he was sensible enough to marry a rich wife. After the Franco-Prussian war he settled in Paris. The Baron's dearly loved only son Lucien was a frequent visitor to England. He made many friends there, some of whom were members of the racing world, and he himself started a small stud in England in 1884. To the bitter sorrow of his father, he died in 1887. It was because his son had been so fond of England that the Baron decided to come to England himself, and largely because of his son's enthusiasm for the sport, he took up racing. The Prince of Wales, later King Edward VII, could never be accused of entertaining any vulgar anti-semitic sentiments and a number of rich German Jews figured among his closest friends and associates. When the Baron took up racing in 1889, he was introduced to the famous John Porter of Kingsclere by the Prince. Porter was then the Prince's trainer and he became forthwith the Baron's trainer too.

The Baron electrified the sporting world in 1890 by paying 5,500 guineas at the Hampton Court Yearling Sale for a filly by St. Simon out of Quiver, by Toxophilite, and thus a full sister to the Duke of Portland's Oaks and St. Leger winner Memoir. At the sale, the Baron sat on the box of a coach with the Prince of Wales while Lord Marcus Beresford, the Prince's racing manager, stood on the roof of the coach and did the bidding. The price was unprecedented at that time and Mr. Edmund Tattersall was sufficiently moved to call for three hearty cheers for the Baron and the Hampton Court Stud. These were apparently accorded in unrestrained fashion.

The filly, a bay that was named La Flèche, never stood more than 15 hands 3 inches and was lean and wiry in appearance, being distinctly of the greyhound type. She had, though, a beautiful, intelligent head and the best of feet and legs. When she was looking as well as she possibly could, it was an indication that she was not at her best; she produced her peak form when she was ragged and thin. Richard Marsh, who trained her after the age of three, recalled that when she won the Liverpool Cup with 9 st. 6 lb. he was so ashamed of her appearance that he did not remove her sheet till the last possible moment. When she won the Cambridgeshire with 8 st. 10 lb. as a three-year-old, she carried a winter coat like a woolly bear. She was all "use", with wide hips, a tough physique, and a faultless action. Above all, she loved racing.

La Flèche joined John Porter's stable at the same time as a colt that was also to prove an outstanding winner, the Duke of Westminster's Orme. As a two-year-old, La Flèche was unbeaten, winning the Chesterfield Stakes at Newmarket, the Lavant Stakes and the Molecomb Stakes at Goodwood, and the Champagne Stakes at Doncaster. In the Chesterfield Stakes she beat Bona Vista, winner of the Two Thousand Guineas the following season. In the Champagne Stakes she finished many lengths in front of Sir Hugo, destined to beat her in the 1892 Derby.

In the meantime Orme won the Richmond Stakes and the Prince of Wales's Stakes at Goodwood; the Middle Park Plate, the Dewhurst Plate and the Home-bred Foal Stakes, all at Newmarket. His only defeat was in the seven furlong Lancashire Plate at Manchester, an £11,000 event for two-, three- and four-year-olds. Orme was second to the four-year-old filly Signorina, who later bred the famous Signorinetta, winner of the Derby and the Oaks.

The opinion at Kingsclere at the end of 1891 was that there was very little indeed between La Flèche and Orme, the filly being rated perhaps a shade the superior.

This is not the place to tell of the manner in which Orme, heavily backed in the ante-post market for the Derby, was poisoned in April the following year. For several days his life was in grave danger but his robust constitution eventually pulled him through. Porter had good grounds for suspecting one of his own employees and frankly discounted the theory of Loeffler, the Newmarket horse dentist, who declared that the trouble was solely due to a badly infected tooth. Orme of course had to miss the Derby but he and his owner were given a memorable reception when Orme returned to the racecourse to win the 1¼ miles Eclipse Stakes at Sandown in July.

Meanwhile La Flèche thrived. In fact she did so well in the early months of the year that it was deemed unnecessary to try her before the One Thousand Guineas. Starting at 2–1 on, she won with any amount in hand from The Smew and Adoration.

La Flèche's next target was the Derby. She gave every possible satisfaction between Newmarket and Epsom and in the Derby she started a red-hot favourite at 11–10. Second favourite at 100–9 was the French colt Rueil, who won the Grand Prix de Paris shortly afterwards. The Two Thousand Guineas winner Bona Vista was on offer at 100–8.

La Flèche was ridden by George Barret, a very good rider at his best but unfortunately just beginning to display traces of incipient insanity. Wildly over-confident, he lay an absurdly long way out of his ground in the early stages, shouting to, and gesticulating at, the other jockeys in the race. At Tattenham Corner he was still many lengths behind the leaders. He then seemed at last to appreciate the gravity of the situation and set off in hot pursuit. It was all too late, though, and La Flèche, running on with great courage, failed by three parts of a length to catch Lord Bradford's 40–1 outsider Sir Hugo, by Wisdom out of Manœuvre.

> Surprise of surprises! A great shout arises,
> Proclaiming to all that the fav'rite is done,
> Wisdom's chef d'œuvre, the son of Manœuvre,
> Lord Bradford's Sir Hugo the Derby has won.

There can be little doubt that, ridden with just adequate competence, La Flèche would have won comfortably. It must have been a bitter experience for Baron de Hirsch and the situation was exacerbated by the intense rivalry existing inside the stable between the supporters of La Flèche and those of Orme. In fact the Orme partisans were sufficiently ill-mannered to express quite openly their entire satisfaction at La Flèche's defeat. The Kingsclere stable was certainly not a happy or united one in 1892.

Two days later La Flèche, again partnered by Barret, turned out for the Oaks. She had not recovered from her gruelling race in the Derby and only scraped home by a head from The Smew, whom she had beaten with such ease in the One Thousand Guineas.

At Goodwood Orme won the Sussex Stakes, La Flèche the Nassau Stakes, and in September these two formidable companions met in the St. Leger. Orme, ridden by Barret, was favourite at 11–10 on, while La Flèche, Jack Watts up, started at 7–2. La Flèche won the race very comfortably by two lengths from Sir Hugo with Orme unplaced. There had been sinister rumours that the bookmakers had bribed Barret to stop Orme and in the parade ring the Duke of Westminster informed Barret that his riding would be watched with the closest attention. Furious at the insinuation, Barret set off in front on Orme and rode him into the ground. Possibly Orme could never have stayed the distance; he had little chance to do so as the race was run.

Orme won four more races that season, all at Newmarket—the Great Foal Stakes, the Champion Stakes, the Limekiln Stakes and the Subscription Stakes. In the ten furlong Free Handicap he failed to give 16 lb. to Diabolo but as this was his third race in three days, there was some excuse for his defeat. As for La Flèche, she won the £7,900 Lancashire Plate at Manchester and then three races at Newmarket, the Grand Duke Michael Stakes, the Newmarket Oaks and the Cambridgeshire.

In the Cambridgeshire La Flèche carried the stiff weight for a three-year-old filly of 8 st. 10 lb. In a field of twenty-eight she was giving weight to all her opponents bar Buccaneer, winner of the City and Suburban and the Ascot Gold Cup; and Miss Dollar, whose 10 lb. penalty for winning the Duke of York Handicap brought her weight up to 8 st. 11 lb.

Before the Cambridgeshire Porter gave only the lightest of preparations to La Flèche who had already gone in her coat. Interfering friends of the Baron went to him and complained that Porter was not training the filly properly. Porter was told by the Baron to continue to use his own judgment. If in fact Porter had worked the filly hard, she would probably have gone "right over the top", and had the Baron ordered a different sort of preparation, Porter would have told him without hesitation to take his horses elsewhere. Favourite at 7–2, La Flèche ran with her usual zest and courage to win by a length and a half from General Owen Williams's Pensioner, to whom she was conceding 34 lb.

At the end of a materially successful but somewhat worrying and unhappy season, Porter was informed that the horses of the Prince of Wales were being transferred to Richard Marsh. They were accompanied by all the Baron's horses, too. There were many tensions within the stable and not the least of the troubles was that Porter, extremely able and exceptionally conscientious, had little sense of humour and did not appreciate the occasionally barbed witticisms of Lord Marcus Beresford. A year later the Baron asked Porter to take his horses back again but Porter replied that his stable was full.

In all probability La Flèche was never quite so good again after her three-year-old career though Marsh always rated her the best mare he ever trained. She had in fact been covered by Morion in the spring of 1893 and did not run until the Eclipse Stakes in July. She was not at her best then though, for her, she looked particularly well; and furthermore she was sexually amiss, showing that the mating had been a barren one. She could only finish third to Orme and Medicis. In the Gordon Stakes at Goodwood she again met Orme, who this time gave her 7 lb. and beat her by a neck. In the Lancashire Plate at Manchester she ran well but was beaten into third place behind the Duke of Portland's Raeburn and the 1893 "Triple Crown" winner Isinglass. Raeburn, third in the Derby, was receiving 10 lb. from Isinglass, who met with the solitary defeat of his entire career on this occasion.

By the autumn La Flèche looked light and mean but in fact she was running into form. She won the ten furlong Lowther Stakes at Newmarket and after failing in the Cambridgeshire with 9 st. 7 lb., she won the Liverpool Autumn Cup at Aintree, then a race of considerable significance, with 9 st. 6 lb. Finally she was given the virtually impossible task of carrying 9 st. 11 lb. in the Manchester November Handicap and not surprisingly failed to finish in the leading three.

There were further triumphs in store for La Flèche in 1894. In those days good horses were expected to be versatile over matters of distance and her very first race of the season was the $2\frac{1}{2}$ mile Ascot Gold Cup which she duly won. Even the top-class mares and fillies were required to be tough and resilient and the very next day La Flèche was pulled out for the $1\frac{1}{2}$ mile Hardwicke Stakes. She was, however, still feeling the affects of her exertions in the Cup and she was beaten half a length by Ravensbury, second in the Derby the previous year. In the autumn she failed under top weight in the Prince Edward Handicap at Manchester but ended her racing career in style with a victory in the ten furlong Champion Stakes at Newmarket. She had run twenty-four times and had won sixteen races worth £34,703. Three of her defeats were in handicaps in which she was carrying big weights. Only bad luck, or more accurately the incompetence of her rider, had prevented her from winning the Derby and thus equalling the achievement of Sceptre who won four of the five classic races in 1902. Her remarkable versatility is shown by the fact that she won over five furlongs, six furlongs, a mile, nine furlongs, ten furlongs, eleven furlongs, a mile and a half, a mile and three-quarters and two miles and a half.

Baron de Hirsch died in 1896 and La Flèche was sold to Sir Tatton Sykes at the Newmarket July Sales for 12,600 guineas. The best of the colts she produced was John O'Gaunt, by Isinglass. John O'Gaunt's parents, therefore, had won six classics and two Ascot Gold Cups between them. John O'Gaunt himself only won one race, but ridden by an amateur, Mr. George Thursby, he was second in the 1904 Derby to St. Amant. In due course he sired the St. Leger winner Swynford, who in his turn sired the Derby winner Sansovino and that outstanding sire Blandford. Of La Flèche's daughters, Baroness La Flèche, by Ladas, was dam of the One Thousand Guineas winner Cinna. At the stud Cinna produced two colts by Son-in-Law, Beau Père and Mr. Standfast. Neither was of much account on the racecourse but both were highly successful sires in America and New Zealand. Beau Père's stock did very well in Australia, too.

It was mentioned earlier that La Flèche was a full sister to the Duke of Portland's Memoir, who numbered the Oaks and the St. Leger among her successes. Their dam, Quiver, was by Toxophilite and it was this fact that greatly influenced the Duke of Portland's decision to buy the most famous of all Australian horses, Carbine, since Carbine's sire, Musket, was by Toxophilite. It was hoped that Carbine would "nick" with St. Simon mares but that theory proved somewhat unsuccessful.

A half-sister to La Flèche was Maid Marian, by Hampton. She was the dam of Polymelus, winner of over £16,000 in stakes and five times champion sire.

Isinglass (1890)

The last two decades of the nineteenth century were one of the golden ages—another was the nineteen-thirties—of the British Turf, when the racing scene was dignified by five winners of the Triple Crown and by other great horses, like St. Simon and Orme, who did not win a Classic race. Isinglass was one of the Triple Crown winners, and in at least one not unimportant respect, prize money earnings, he surpassed Ormonde, Common, Galtee More and Flying Fox, the other winners of the Two Thousand Guineas, the Derby and the St. Leger during the period. The eleven victories of Isinglass accumulated £57,455, a record which withstood all prize money increases in Great Britain for nearly sixty years until at last it was broken by Tulyar in 1952.

If Isinglass had won the same races in 1971—an impossibility since his career covered four seasons, but nonetheless a meaningful criterion—he would have earned £172,750, or almost precisely three times as much, from nine victories. Two of the races he won, a two-year-old maiden plate at the Newmarket Second Spring Meeting and the Newmarket Stakes as a three-year-old, have no counterparts in the modern racing calendar. Moreover richly endowed international races like the King George VI and Queen Elizabeth Stakes and the Prix de l'Arc de Triomphe, which yielded Mill Reef the sum of £136,757 in 1971, had not been founded in the days of Isinglass though they, or corresponding events, must have fallen to him on all public form, if they had been in existence. He made virtually a clean sweep of the principal English races available to him and dominated his contemporaries regardless of age and distance.

The histories of the most illustrious figures on the Turf, both human and equine, tend to become encrusted with romantic legend which do not stand up to critical examination. So it is with the breeding of Isinglass. Tradition has it that James Machell sold Isinglass's dam Dead Lock as practically useless, but wanted to buy her back when one of her offspring, Gervas, began to win races. For a long time, so the legend tells, he was unable to trace her, but one day a farmer drove into his yard in search of a carthorse stallion and he recognized the mare between the shafts as Dead Lock. He promptly bought her, sent her to Isonomy and so bred the Triple Crown winner of 1893.

The truth is different and more prosaic, though the origins of Isinglass were certainly improbable enough for one of the really great horses of all time. Dead Lock was by the St. Leger winner Wenlock, but sprang from a female line which for a hundred years before and at no time since her day has produced an animal with a tithe of the ability of Isinglass. Dead Lock was a half-sister to three small winners, but never ran herself and was purchased for 19 guineas by Machell when Lord Alington weeded her out of his stud about the year 1881. Machell mated her to his own stallion Blue Blood, an almost complete failure at stud, and so bred a colt called House of Lords, who was equally useless and was cut and sent to Italy. Her next foal was Gervas, by Trappist, but before Gervas could show winning form Machell had sold her, and she passed through the hands of Mr. Tatton Willoughby, a brother of Lord Middleton, and Colonel Eyre before Machell bought her back. Even then Machell did not keep her long, but passed her on, in foal to Isonomy, to Mr. (later Colonel) Harry McCalmont a year later. The foal she was carrying was Islington, a minor winner. Two years later she returned to Isonomy and this time the product was Isinglass. The mating was arranged just in time, for a year later Isonomy was dead.

James Machell was one of the strangest and most flamboyant characters that have animated the British Turf. He began life as an infantry soldier, but resigned his commission at the age of twenty-four in order to indulge and cultivate his undoubted flair for all things to do with racing. He was a fine judge of a horse; some people believed that he was an even better judge of a chaser than a flat racer. In the course of time he came to combine the roles that in modern times would be described as owner-breeder, professional backer, bloodstock agent and racing manager. Such was his reputation for racing expertise that he was invited to buy and manage horses and act as racing mentor for a number of wealthy young men, and the fact that most of them left the Turf poorer than when they arrived was due not so much to following his advice but to failing to do so.

Harry McCalmont was one of Machell's employers who did not lose his money. He was a thorough sportsman who served in the Boer War, went into Parliament and died, in 1902, when still in the prime of life. By the time that McCalmont took up racing Machell was in his fifties, very experienced and forthright in his expressions of opinion, hot-tempered and a martyr to gout. If Machell had been less experienced and determined to have his own way, and if McCalmont had been less willing to give him his head in matters of racing policy, the wonderful racing career of Isinglass would never have come to fruition.

Isinglass won his first race at Newmarket as a two-year-old, and then went to Royal Ascot for the New Stakes, which he won convincingly by two lengths from Fealar. The third in the New Stakes was Ravensbury, a horse who was to meet Isinglass time and time again and must have been sick to death of the sight of him by the time he finished racing. Isinglass ran only once more that season, and that was in the six furlongs Middle Park Stakes at Newmarket in October. Isinglass started at the surprisingly long odds of 10–1 owing to the heavy backing of Dame President who, however, was not concerned in the finish. Isinglass was a decisive winner, and had one and a half lengths to spare from Ravensbury, while Le Nicham was a neck away third and Raeburn was fourth in a field of fourteen. The Middle Park Stakes, of all two-year-old races, has the reputation of having a close bearing on the next year's Classic races, though with the increasing specialization of the twentieth century this connection has been with the Two Thousand Guineas rather than the longer Classic races. But never has the Middle Park Stakes been a better guide to Classic form than it was in 1892, for Isinglass, Ravensbury, Le Nicham and Raeburn were the only horses to occupy places in the Guineas, the Derby and the St. Leger the following year.

The spring of 1893 was dry, and was followed by a dry summer. The Newmarket training grounds were as hard as iron, and the conditions were nightmarish for the preparation of a horse like Isinglass, who was a big, heavy-topped bay and did not have the best of forelegs. To make matters worse, Isinglass was incorrigibly lazy and needed an immense amount of work to get him fit. Jimmy Jewitt, the former steeplechase jockey who was the trainer at the Bedford

Lodge stable managed by Machell, declared roundly that it was impossible to get Isinglass ready for the Guineas. Machell asserted that it was possible provided that his instructions were carried out. As Jewitt, handsome and always impeccably turned out, was as quick-tempered as Machell, their voices, raised in anger, could often be heard all over Newmarket Heath as they wrangled over the training of Isinglass in the early months of 1893. But it was the will of Machell that prevailed, and at his insistence Isinglass was taken out twice a day and cantered up the tan gallop on the Bury Hill time after time.

Right up to the day of the race Jewitt continued to protest that no horse could win a Guineas on such a preparation, but Machell countered with the argument that Isinglass was a stone better than any colt of his generation and that his class would see him through. Isinglass started at 5–4 on and, though making very heavy weather of it, vindicated Machell's judgment by scraping home by three-quarters of a length from Ravensbury, with Raeburn in third place. Two weeks later he gained an easier victory in the $1\frac{1}{4}$ miles Newmarket Stakes, beating Ravensbury into third place.

These performances were considered to have established Isinglass's supremacy among the three-year-old colts, and he was at 9–4 on in the Derby. However the Epsom course was bare and unresilient, and Isinglass gave another laborious display. Indeed there were moments a quarter of a mile from home when Raeburn was alongside him and apparently going the better, but then Tom Loates set about Isinglass and that lazy colt, though hating the ground, asserted his superiority to beat the luckless Ravensbury by one and a half lengths, while the weary Raeburn finished two lengths further back in third place.

Harry Barker, a versatile rider who had also finished second on Aesop in the Grand National the same year, was much criticized for being beaten on Ravensbury in the Guineas and the Derby. It was freely stated that he would have won both races if he had been as strong a finisher as Loates. George Lambton took the opposite view, and argued in his memoirs *Men and Horses I Have Known* that Loates, with his short legs, could never ride the long-striding Isinglass properly and that Isinglass would have beaten Ravensbury much more easily with the jockeys reversed. Richard Marsh put forward a similar argument in *A Trainer to Two Kings*, pointing out that Isinglass was very wide besides a very lazy horse, and that a long-legged jockey like Watts, who actually rode Raeburn in the Derby, would have suited him much better. In the circumstances Loates was excessively dependent on the whip when riding Isinglass.

There seemed to be no end to the misfortunes of Ravensbury. After the Derby he was sent over to Longchamp to run in the Grand Prix but was placed second to Ragotsky though Morny Cannon, who had replaced Barker, and all impartial observers, were convinced he had won.

Isinglass did not run again until the St. Leger, which he won by half a length from Ravensbury though with much more in hand than in either of the earlier Classic races, as he was hard held at the finish. Thus Isinglass and Ravensbury had accomplished the remarkable feat of finishing first and second in each of the three Classic races in which colts may run. Raeburn, who had been third in the Two Thousand Guineas and the Derby, was absent from the St. Leger, in which Le Nicham, having started at 53–1 in a field of five, occupied third place.

The next and last race for Isinglass as a three-year-old was the Great Lancashire Stakes at Manchester two weeks after the St. Leger. The distance of a mile was too short for Isinglass at that stage of the season and, although Loates tried to make his stamina tell by making all the running, he found the task of conceding 10 lb. to Raeburn, who was a fresh horse after missing the St. Leger, just too great and was beaten by a length. Nevertheless Isinglass still finished half a length in front of La Flèche, the brilliant filly who had won three Classic races the previous year, on weight for age and sex terms.

That autumn Machell became seriously ill while staying at the Adelphi Hotel in Liverpool and was taken to hospital. After the illness he went to live in Italy for a time for the benefit of his health, and on returning to England resided alternately in Newmarket and Hastings, where he died in 1902, the same year as Harry McCalmont. If Machell's health had broken a few months earlier the career of Isinglass would have been very different, and his towering ability might never have been revealed as a three-year-old. Nobody but Machell would have had the audacity to train the colt by cantering on the tan, and nobody but Machell would have had the confidence and the enterprise to run him in the Guineas on such an unorthodox preparation. And if Isinglass had missed the Guineas he would probably have missed the Derby too, since hard ground persisted through the summer.

The ground was hard again when Isinglass had his first outing as a four-year-old in the Princess of Wales's Stakes at the Newmarket July meeting, a race which was being run for the first time. His opponents included that year's Derby winner Ladas. Isinglass showed that he had lost none of his dislike of the going by running sluggishly, but he managed to scrape home by a head from the three-year-old Bullingdon, with Ladas in third place three lengths behind and Ravensbury unplaced. That night the weather broke and rain continued to fall almost incessantly until the Eclipse Stakes at Sandown Park two weeks later. On the morning of the race Jewitt told friends that Isinglass would really show what he could do that day, as it was the first time that he had been properly galloped in preparation for a race and the first time that he had been able to run on the yielding surface a horse with his dubious forelegs needed. Jewitt was right. For once Isinglass was able to stride out with complete freedom and, instead of hanging about and scrambling home after seeming to be beaten, he outclassed his opponents from start to finish and won in a canter from Ladas and Ravensbury. Throstle, who was to win the St. Leger two months later, and his Manchester conqueror Raeburn, were unplaced.

The result of the Eclipse Stakes, more than any other race in which he took part, confirmed the greatness of Isinglass, and justi-fied Machell's claim that he was a stone better than any other horse in England. His remaining races were in the nature of anticlimax. He completed his activities as a four-year-old by winning the Jockey Club Stakes very easily from the French horse Gouvernail, with Raeburn and Throstle, who ran off the course, unplaced; and he had only one race as a five-year-old, when he toyed with his two opponents Reminder and Kilsallaghan in the Ascot Gold Cup.

Having won eleven races and suffered only one defeat despite the persistence of unsuitable going for much of his four seasons in training, Isinglass retired in glory to the Cheveley Park Stud near Newmarket. There McCalmont built a new stallion box for him with a plaque listing his victories inset in the wall. At stud he failed to attain the same eminence as he had done on the racecourse. He did not sire any horse nearly as good as himself. On the other hand he was certainly not a failure. He was second in the list of sires of winners twice, and once headed the list of sires of dams of winners.

His progeny included the Oaks winners Cherry Lass and Glass Doll, the Two Thousand Guineas winner Louvois, and John O'Gaunt and Louviers, who both finished second in the Derby. John O'Gaunt in England and Louviers in Germany both founded powerful branches of his male line.

The limitations of Isinglass as a sire have been attributed to the poor quality of his female line. His sire Isonomy was a supremely game horse. Incredibly, he missed the Classic races of 1878 so as to land a gamble in the Cambridgeshire, but afterwards won the Ascot Gold Cup twice. He had sired another winner of the Triple Crown, Common, before Isinglass.

Isinglass was a better, more thoroughly tested racehorse than Common. He was an infinitely better sire. He stands out as one of the most brilliant products of a golden age.

Diamond Jubilee (1897)

No mare has yet produced two winners of the Triple Crown but
Perdita II, owned by the Prince of Wales, later King Edward VII,
came close to so doing. In 1896 her son Persimmon, by St. Simon,
won the Derby and the St. Leger; four years later Persimmon's full
brother Diamond Jubilee won the Triple Crown. 1900 was in fact
"annus mirabilis" on the Turf for the Prince of Wales as he also
won the Grand National with Ambush II. He is the only owner so
far to have won the Derby and the Grand National in the same year.

Perdita II, by Hampton, had been bought on the Prince's behalf
by John Porter, who was at that time his trainer, for 900 guineas.
When old Sir Dighton Probyn handed over the Prince's cheque to
Porter, he remarked with gloom and foreboding: "You'll ruin the
Prince if you go on buying those thoroughbreds." Perdita II proved
a marvellous bargain, as her offspring won twenty-six races worth
over £72,000, a lot for those days when prize money was nothing
like as high as it is now.

Because he was exceptionally good-looking and because he was
Persimmon's brother, Diamond Jubilee, foaled in the sixtieth year
of Queen Victoria's reign, was petted and fussed over in his early
days to an undesirable extent. He became in consequence a typical
spoiled child who was apt to get peevish and ill-tempered if he did
not secure his own way at once.

When he joined Richard Marsh's Newmarket stable in 1898 he
was already handsome and Marsh, whose standards were high,
always declared him to be the only perfectly formed thoroughbred,
impossible to fault, that he had ever set eyes on. This view was
endorsed by such a shrewd and experienced judge as Lord Chaplin.
As a yearling Diamond Jubilee stood 15 hands $3\frac{1}{2}$ inches and was a
bright bay with dark legs and a dark line down the middle of his

back to the root of his tail. His head was bold and intelligent and he possessed a perfect back and loins. From his youngest days he was fearless to the point of arrogance and in Marsh's words "he would walk straight at you, and over you if you did not give way".

Breaking him in proved not the simplest of tasks but in the end was successfully accomplished. He did well physically during the winter and grew into a magnificent specimen of a two-year-old. Just after the Derby he was tried by Marsh with eminently satisfactory results and it was anticipated, therefore, with no little confidence that he would follow in Persimmon's footsteps and win the Coventry Stakes at Royal Ascot.

It was unfortunate that Marsh was just telling Sir Dighton Probyn in the paddock at Ascot what a nice colt Diamond Jubilee was when Diamond Jubilee suddenly elected to demonstrate to the full the flaws in his temperament. He began by kicking an inoffensive bystander in the paddock on the hand. The man had his hands in his pockets at the time. At the start, Diamond Jubilee's conduct became worse and he was either walking around on his hind legs or twisting himself into a knot trying to eat that fine horseman, Jack Watts, who rode him. Watts, a man of singularly placid disposition who rarely displayed emotion, subsequently expressed to Marsh his opinion of Diamond Jubilee in terms that gave Marsh quite a shock. After the race, in which Diamond Jubilee finished unplaced, Mr. Arthur Coventry, the Starter, said he had never before seen a two-year-old behave quite so badly.

On returning home to Newmarket, Diamond Jubilee conducted himself with such decorum both in the stable and at exercise that Marsh was prepared to believe that the Ascot fiasco might prove to be just an isolated incident. At all events hopes ran high when Diamond Jubilee took the short walk to the Newmarket July Course to take part in the July Stakes for which he was favourite as he had also been at Ascot. Unfortunately his conduct was again deplorable. He unseated Watts and careered down the course. When caught and remounted, he simply declined to race and finished last. After this second disappointment all sorts of remedies, some drastic, were suggested to the Prince of Wales and his racing manager Lord Marcus Beresford, but Marsh pleaded for Diamond Jubilee to be given one final chance. It was obvious that for some reason Diamond Jubilee loathed Jack Watts and doubtless the dislike was mutual. In the Prince of Wales's Stakes at Goodwood—he was again favourite—

Diamond Jubilee was partnered, therefore, by Mornington Cannon. Though beaten in the end by Lord Rosebery's Epsom Lad, destined to win the Eclipse Stakes as a four-year-old, he both ran and behaved very much better than previously. In the autumn, he opened his account, again ridden by Cannon, when winning the Boscawen Stakes at Newmarket but he only scraped home by inches from a moderate animal called Paigle. Cannon was unable to ride him in the Middle Park Plate, but he went quite kindly for Watts and finished second, half a length behind Democrat who received a 3 lb. gelding allowance. The pair met again in the Dewhurst Stakes and this time Democrat, conceding a pound, won by three parts of a length. Democrat became useless for racing after his first season and ended up as Lord Kitchener's charger in India.

It was not possible to forecast any resounding triumphs for Diamond Jubilee as a three-year-old judged from what he had actually accomplished his first season, but at least he seemed to be settling down in the autumn and he was a member of a family, the representatives of which were inclined to improve with age. During the winter Marsh gave him plenty of work to prevent him from becoming obnoxiously above himself and the colt was usually ridden by a lad called Herbert Jones, whose father, Jack Jones, had once trained jumpers at Epsom for the Prince and for Lord Marcus Beresford. Young Jones took immense trouble with Diamond Jubilee and certainly seemed to get on better with him than anyone else.

On a Tuesday morning early in April 1900 Mornington Cannon came down to Newmarket to ride Diamond Jubilee round the private gallop at Egerton. The Prince of Wales was due to come and watch his colt work on the Thursday. After pulling up, Cannon dismounted and led Diamond Jubilee by the bridle rein. This was Diamond Jubilee's opportunity. In a trice he had rolled Cannon over and he would probably have killed him if help had not been close at hand. Naturally Cannon was somewhat shaken by this frightening experience.

Not long before the Two Thousand Guineas, Cannon rode Diamond Jubilee again. Marsh thought Diamond Jubilee had worked exceptionally well but Cannon apparently thought otherwise. He said the colt would not go for him and suggested that another jockey be engaged. Under the circumstances Cannon's attitude was understandable. It was not easy to find a suitable replacement at such short notice and after much deliberation it was decided to take a chance and to put up the little-known and inexperienced Herbert Jones. The experiment proved a success and Diamond Jubilee, starting at 11-4, won the Two Thousand Guineas by four lengths. It was a fine performance even if the field was not a particularly strong one.

Diamond Jubilee followed up this success by winning the ten furlong Newmarket Stakes, though only by a head from Chevening. At home he remained unpredictable. Some mornings he danced about on his hind legs; on others he stood stock still and declined to budge. It was a commonly held opinion at Newmarket that what he really needed was a good hiding, but Marsh, to his eternal credit, never lost his temper or his patience and resolutely refused to countenance any action that might conceivably have broken the spirit of a high-mettled, hot-tempered colt.

The South African war was at its height when the Derby was run. There had been some humiliating defeats chiefly due to the shaming incompetence of elderly generals, and the general public, thirsting for victories, were gripped by a "jingoistic" spirit that sometimes led them into comical situations. A rumour, entirely without foundation, reached Epsom that Lord Roberts's army had entered Pretoria, thereby inducing several thousand over-excited and overheated racegoers to bawl out "God Save the Queen" in front of the Royal Stand.

In those more free-and-easy days, participation in the parade of the Derby runners in front of the stands was not compulsory as it later became. Marsh would have preferred to send Diamond Jubilee straight down to the start but he received a message from the Prince that the Princess of Wales wanted to see Diamond Jubilee in the parade. Accordingly he told Jones to join the parade but to leave it and head for the start at the slightest hint of trouble. As it happened, Diamond Jubilee was on his best behaviour; furthermore, he gave no trouble at the starting gate, which was used for the first time in this particular race.

Chevening was the first to show in front but after half a mile he gave way to Forfarshire, who had been highly tried and was greatly fancied. Disguise II, ridden by the brilliant but ill-disciplined Tod Sloan, and Diamond Jubilee were not far behind and approaching Tattenham Corner Disguise II headed Forfarshire. In so doing he came right across Forfarshire who had to be checked. For this distinctly dangerous piece of riding, Sloan was subsequently reprimanded by the Stewards.

Half way up the straight Disguise II began to tire and was headed, first, amid a storm of cheers, by Diamond Jubilee and then by the Duke of Portland's Simon Dale. At one point Simon Dale seemed to be going just the better, but ridden with faultless judgment by Jones, Diamond Jubilee battled on with admirable resolution to win by a length and a half. Disguise II was a length away third. The victory of Diamond Jubilee, favourite at 6–4, was of course tremendously popular but the reception given to him just seemed to lack the wholly spontaneous warmth that had marked the scenes after the triumph of Persimmon.

Diamond Jubilee missed Ascot and went instead for the $1\frac{1}{2}$ mile Princess of Wales's Stakes at Newmarket, a race at that time both more valuable and more significant than it is today. He was confidently expected to win but came up against a smart filly of Colonel Hall-Walker's called Merry Gal. He had to concede her 19 lb. and never looked like being able to give the weight away, Merry Gal, subsequently the dam of White Eagle, winning by four lengths. However he picked up the winning thread again in the ten furlong Eclipse Stakes at Sandown, worth over £9,000 to the winner, nearly £4,000 more than the Derby. In this race he gave 10 lb. to Chevening, who had run him so close in the Newmarket Stakes.

In the St. Leger Diamond Jubilee was in one of his most devilish moods. It took the unfortunate Marsh twenty minutes to get a saddle on his back, by which time both horse and man were in a muck sweat. Diamond Jubilee's approach to the starting gate was conducted almost entirely on his hind legs but he was well enough away, and favourite at 7–2 on, he won by a length and a half from Elopement.

After that race Diamond Jubilee was never so good again and he seemed to have burnt himself out. In the Jockey Club Stakes that autumn he was unplaced behind Disguise II. The following year he was second to Epsom Lad in the Princess of Wales's Stakes; fourth to Epsom Lad in the Eclipse; and third to Pietermaritzburg and Epsom Lad in the Jockey Club Stakes. He was then retired to the Sandringham Stud at a fee of 300 guineas, having won over £29,000 in stakes. It was perhaps not a vintage year the season that he won his Triple Crown but at his best he was unquestionably a very good horse indeed. His career, and the glittering triumphs that accompanied it, were above all a tribute to the superb professional skill of Richard Marsh, whose handling of a difficult, unpredictable and occasionally dangerous colt was beyond all praise. Great credit, too, must be awarded to Herbert Jones for the excellent races he rode on Diamond Jubilee and above all for sheer physical courage, that quality being generously recognized by his fellow jockeys, not least by Mornington Cannon. By the end of 1900 Diamond Jubilee had in fact been beginning to get Jones down, both physically and mentally, and Marsh, realizing that Jones was utterly exhausted, wisely sent him off for a holiday at Brighton to recuperate.

At the stud Diamond Jubilee seemed determined to live up to his reputation. He was a demon to start with at Sandringham but gradually he settled down and became more amenable. In 1906 he was sold to a South American breeder for £31,500. He proved a great success in the Argentine where he died at the ripe age of twenty-six. In this country he stood seventh in the sires' list in 1907.

There are grounds for believing that at one point in Diamond Jubilee's two-year-old career his temper was so obnoxious that it was decided to castrate him. However, according to this story, when the vet arrived to carry out the operation, it was found that Diamond Jubilee was a one-sided rig and so nothing was done.

Ard Patrick (1899)

The claim of Ard Patrick to be regarded as a great horse is simply stated. Sceptre, winner of four Classic races, has been called "the greatest of all great mares". Ard Patrick beat Sceptre twice, in the Derby as a three-year-old and in the Eclipse Stakes the next year, and Sceptre beat him only once, when they finished first and third in the Two Thousand Guineas.

Ard Patrick, foaled in 1899, was a product of the rapid expansion and improvement of the Irish breeding industry in the second half of the nineteenth century. His breeder Captain John Gubbins, who was also a brilliant man to hounds and master of the Limerick Hunt for many years, was one of the leaders of this progress. As a young man Jack Gubbins inherited a fortune from an uncle and founded two studs, the home farm Bruree and Knockany, in the Golden Vale of Limerick which comprises some of the best land in Ireland. These studs he stocked with mares of the choicest pedigree and in the eighteen-nineties he also owned no fewer than six stallions of whom Kendal, who won six races in scintillating style before breaking down as a two-year-old, commanded the then tip-top fee of 200 guineas. Most of the horses he raced were home-bred and were by his own stallions.

The most inspired broodmare purchase by Gubbins was Morganette, who cost him £200 or £300 and spent her entire stud life at Knockany. Bred by Mr. J. H. Houldsworth in 1884, Morganette had been practically useless on the racecourse but had an excellent pedigree. She was by Springfield, a versatile horse who won the July Cup twice and as a four-year-old beat the Derby winner Silvio in the Champion Stakes. Springfield sired the Derby winner Sanfoin. Lady Morgan, the dam of Morganette, was a half-sister of the Oaks and St. Leger winner Marie Stuart, and was a granddaughter of the Oaks winner Miami. Thus classically bred, Morganette proved herself one of the finest broodmares ever to dwell in Ireland.

Morganette's third foal was a colt called Blairfinde, by Kendal. Trained, like most of Gubbins's horses, by Sam Darling, Blairfinde was sent over to run in the 1894 Irish Derby at the Curragh, and, despite being castigated by the local trainer Linde as "a damned coach-horse" before the race, proceeded to win by 20 lengths. Three years later Blairfinde's own brother Galtee More, named after the highest peak in the Galtee Mountains overlooking the Golden Vale, became not only the first Irish-bred colt to win the Derby at Epsom but also the winner of the English Triple Crown. The achievements of Galtee More aroused tremendous enthusiasm in his native land and, in the words of one Irishman, "the mountains were alight with whisky" in celebration of his Derby triumph. Unfortunately Galtee More "had a leg" as a four-year-old and the plan to run him in the Ascot Gold Cup had to be abandoned. He was sold to go to Russia as a stallion for 20,000 guineas and, after several successful seasons there, was re-sold to go to stud in Germany.

In 1898 Morganette was booked to go to another of the Knockany stallions, St. Florian, who had been a moderate racehorse but was very well-bred as he was by St. Simon and was a half-brother of the Oaks winner Musa. Although only seven years old, St. Florian was ailing at the beginning of the covering season and Gubbins was strongly advised to cancel the arrangement. However Gubbins insisted that the mating should take place as planned, and accordingly Morganette was covered by St. Florian, who was dead within a week. The foal that resulted from this extraordinary union was Ard Patrick.

Ard Patrick, like Galtee More, was named after a local landmark, in his case a peak in the Bruree Mountains. A big colt of athletic appearance, full of quality and handsome apart from his rather bent hocks, Ard Patrick was fortunate to be trained by Sam Darling. The Beckhampton trainer, whose son Fred was responsible for seven Derby winners, had infinite patience and gave Ard Patrick, who was very backward in his early days, all the time he needed to develop his strength. Ard Patrick did not run until September of his two-year-old season, when he made his début in the Imperial Produce Plate at Kempton Park. He ran very green, and all the persuasive powers of Danny Maher, an artist in the sympathetic handling of

Plate 1   Blink Bonny

Plate 2   Shotover

Plate 3 Iroquois

Plate 4 La Flèche

Plate 5   Isinglass

Plate 6   Diamond Jubilee

Plate 7 Ard Partick

Plate 8 Sunstar

immature animals, were required to enable him to win by a neck from Royal Lancer, who was giving him 13 lb. The two colts met again in the Clearwell Stakes at Newmarket four days later and, although the difference in the weights was reduced to 3 lb., Ard Patrick had learnt so much from the previous race that he won again. His third and last appearance as a two-year-old was in the Dewhurst Plate at Newmarket, but on that occasion he was beaten a neck by Game Chick, to whom he was conceding 2 lb. Game Chick had some distinguished victims that season, as he had beaten Sceptre in the Champagne Stakes at Doncaster.

Sam Darling was run down in health at the end of the 1901 season and left England for a long holiday in South Africa despite the fact that the Boer War was still in progress. When he arrived home at the end of February he found Ard Patrick, who was by no means a spring horse, again very backward in condition. For this reason he was not in the least disheartened by the fact that Ard Patrick was only third, beaten by two lengths and three lengths by Sceptre and Pistol, in the Two Thousand Guineas. Rather was Darling encouraged by the fact that the colt could run so prominently when palpably not at his best, while Sceptre, who had begun the season by finishing second to St. Maclou in the Lincolnshire Handicap, was as fit as she could ever be.

Ard Patrick was in action again in the May Plate at Kempton Park the following week, but failed by two lengths to concede 21 lb. to Royal Ivy. However he was improving all the time and in his third race of the season, the Newmarket Stakes over $1\frac{1}{4}$ miles, he was first past the winning post from Fowling Piece, only to be disqualified. Jenkins, the rider of Fowling Piece, objected to Ard Patrick on the grounds of bumping and boring, and also complained that Mornington Cannon, on Ard Patrick, had dangled his whip in front of Fowling Piece. The Stewards sustained the objection for bumping and boring, but exonerated Cannon on the charge of foul riding.

Ard Patrick had got unbalanced in the closing stages of the Newmarket Stakes, but he was making excellent progress throughout the month of May and Darling was well satisfied with him when he arrived at Epsom. An incident at this stage of his preparation illustrated Darling's remarkable eye for detail. When Ard Patrick came out on the Epsom Downs to work Darling noticed that he was staring at the stands, and that he continued to do so even when he did a steady canter past them. Accordingly he gave the colt several more canters until he had settled down.

Darling's hopes were raised when he saw Sceptre, who had supplemented her Two Thousand Guineas victory by winning the One Thousand Guineas, out on the course on the morning of the Derby. She was looking very light and was fretting badly, and Darling formed the opinion that Ard Patrick was sure to beat her. Later in the morning he met Gubbins who was a martyr to gout and was hobbling along with the aid of two sticks. He reminded the owner that he had written to him in the spring saying that he ought to back Ard Patrick for the Derby and that he had put £1,000 on the horse, and that Gubbins could have all or what part he liked of the bet. Gubbins replied that he had £2,000 on the horse on his own account.

"I suppose," said Darling, "that means I've got to stand what I was going for you."

"Well, I don't suppose you mind that," rejoined Gubbins. Darling stood the bet and won about £6,000.

In the Derby, Mornington Cannon was claimed to ride the Duke of Portland's Friar Tuck, and Darling gave the mount on Ard Patrick to J. H. "Skeets" Martin. One of the band of American jockeys who had invaded England since the days of Galtee More, Martin was a fine rider with beautiful hands, and was particularly good on two-year-olds and hard-pulling horses. Later in life he became an alcoholic, given to alternate fits of taciturnity and furious rages, but at the time he rode Ard Patrick his only fault as a jockey was a lack of the self-confidence that makes the difference between a good jockey and a great one. He rode a perfect race on Ard Patrick, getting him away well, keeping him in a handy position throughout and allowing him to go to the front approaching Tattenham Corner. Randall did not ride Sceptre so judiciously. He took her down to the start the reverse way with the permission of the Stewards, but did so at a walk, which cannot have helped her to become any less fretful on a cold, wet day. She was restive at the start and dwelt, losing several lengths, and Randall rode her all the way up the hill in an over-hasty attempt to make up the ground. She came round Tattenham Corner neck and neck with Ard Patrick and seemed to be going easily, but was beaten early in the straight and dropped back. Running absolutely straight, and without so much as a glance at the stands, Ard Patrick forged ahead to win very easily by three lengths from Rising Glass, with Friar Tuck the same distance away third.

Sam Darling's confidence that he would beat Sceptre that day had been fully justified, though it is only fair to add that she won the Oaks in most convincing fashion two days later and went on to win the St. Leger. The rest of the season did not work out so happily for Ard Patrick. His next race after the Derby was the Prince of Wales's Stakes at Royal Ascot. During the canter on the way to the start he faltered so badly in a soft patch of newly laid turf opposite the stands that Darling thought for a moment that he had broken a leg. Fortunately the injury was not so serious, but Ard Patrick was plainly not himself in the race in spite of the fact that he was awarded it on the disqualification of Cupbearer for boring. Afterwards he was found to have sprained a tendon and was confined to walking exercise for a long period. There was no question of training him for the St. Leger and, although he was able to run in the Jockey Club Stakes at Newmarket in the autumn, he had not recovered his form and was a poor third to Rising Glass and Templemore.

Ard Patrick shook off all traces of his leg trouble during the winter of 1902-3, and seemed to be better than ever when he resumed strenuous training in the spring. He was led in most of his work by Sweet Sounds, who may have been sweet by name but certainly was not sweet by nature, and once threw his lad and savaged him severely as they pulled up at the end of a gallop. When Darling wanted to make sure that Ard Patrick was back at his best, however, he tried him with a good handicap filly called Caravel. Ard Patrick was set to give Caravel 3 st. over a mile and beat her by a neck, a performance which gave Darling all the encouragement he needed to make the £10,000 Eclipse Stakes the colt's objective for the season.

This prize, enormous by the standards of the time, was run over 1¼ miles at Sandown Park in July and provided the surest means of comparing the merits of the leading three-year-olds and four-year-yolds. Ard Patrick had a preliminary outing in the Princess of Wales's Stakes on the Newmarket July course, and passed the test with flying colours. A much harder task awaited him in the Eclipse Stakes, since his opponents were to include not only Sceptre but Rock Sand, who had already won the Two Thousand Guineas and the Derby—he was to complete the Triple Crown series by winning the St. Leger—and was a formidable representative of the younger generation. Again showing his characteristic attention to detail, Darling sent his assistant Heard with Ard Patrick and a lead horse to Sandown several days before the race with instructions to work him over the full course so that he should get accustomed to the turns. He had known many horses to show fear of galloping into the boundary fence boards at the far end of the course if they had never raced there before. The ground was terribly hard and slippery, and Darling had him shod with flanges on the outer heels and with new large headed nails in order to give him a better grip on the turns. In view of the way the race was run, and the closeness of the finish, it may be argued that these expedients were decisive.

Sam Darling, who had been up at Newmarket, called on Gubbins on his way through London on the eve of the race and told him he thought Ard Patrick would win. He was a good deal less sanguine about the outcome after he had seen Sceptre at exercise on the course the next morning, as he thought that she had made extraordinary improvement, though he still believed that Ard Patrick should just beat her. In the parade-ring before the race Ard Patrick and Sceptre made a deep impression as magnificent thoroughbreds. George Lambton related in his book *Men and Horses I Have Known* how he went to the meeting intending to back Rock Sand, and continued: "But when I saw these three champions walking round the ring, much as I loved Rock Sand, and often as I had won money on him, I had to give him third place. A beautifully made horse and not by any means a small one, yet the other two were a pair of giants, both in performance and stature, and the old saying that a good big one will beat a good little one was borne irresistibly into my mind."

Lambton's judgment was vindicated in the race, for Ard Patrick, who came round the turns on the inside without giving an inch away, and Sceptre outpaced Rock Sand in the straight and engaged in one of the great duels of racing history. Sceptre looked to be having the better of it with two furlongs still to run, but Otto Madden, who was adept at saving a final reserve of his mount's energy for the finish and always knew exactly where the winning post was, put Ard Patrick ahead in the last hundred yards to beat Sceptre by a neck. The crowds were practically struck dumb by the defeat of their idol Sceptre, and Ard Patrick was denied the ovation which his superb performance merited.

Ard Patrick had his last outing in the Eclipse Stakes, for his old leg trouble reasserted itself after the race. Negotiations had been in progress between Count Lehndorff, the Director of the Prussian Government Studs, and William Allison, bloodstock agent, racing journalist, commercial breeder and interpreter of the breeding theories of the egregious Bruce Lowe, for some months concerning the sale of Ard Patrick, and after the Princess of Wales's Stakes Lehndorff agreed to a price of 20,000 guineas, granting Gubbins the right to run the horse in the rest of his weight-for-age engagements that year. Ard Patrick was released at once after the Eclipse Stakes, and spent his stud life at the Government stud at Altefeld, where he died in 1923 at the age of twenty-four. He was leading sire in Germany four times, and sired the German Derby winner Ariel. His influence permeates the pedigrees of modern German thoroughbreds.

The verdict of most Turf historians has been that Sceptre was better than Ard Patrick when she was at her best. Sam Darling did not agree with this judgment. He discounted the Derby form, declaring that Sceptre was much below par on that occasion, but believed that the result of the Eclipse Stakes was a true reflection of their merits. Asked to express an opinion which of the two great half-brothers Galtee More and Ard Patrick was the better, he wrote: "I have never been very emphatic which was the better. Galtee More had a thickening of the tendon under the knee, and this at different times caused me no little anxiety, and in the end was the cause of my not training him as a four-year-old for the Gold Cup at Ascot. The benefit of the doubt would probably be given to Ard Patrick." However the critic may twist and turn in his efforts to be fair to Ard Patrick, Sceptre and Galtee More, the summary beating that he handed out to Rock Sand in the Eclipse Stakes established the claim of Ard Patrick to a place in the gallery of great racehorses.

Sunstar (1908)

Mr. J. B. Joel, an exceptionally shrewd man of humble origin who had accumulated a vast fortune in South Africa, owned two remarkable Derby winners, Sunstar and Humorist. Sunstar won on three legs. Humorist, at the time of his Epsom triumph, was, unknown to anyone, suffering from a tubercular lung condition. A fortnight after the Derby he was dead.

Sunstar had a most improbable pedigree for a Derby winner. His sire Sundridge, by Amphion, had gone in his wind and at one time competed in selling races. He was a good, tough horse though, and became a very good sprinter. He was in training for five seasons and won sixteen short-distance races worth £6,716. He retired to the stud at the nominal fee of nine guineas but lived to become not only champion sire, but the leading sire of broodmares as well. Besides Sunstar, he sired Jest, winner of the One Thousand Guineas and the Oaks and dam of Humorist; Sun Worship, dam of the St. Leger and Gold Cup winner Solario; and the brothers Sun Briar and Sunreigh who both exercised considerable influence on bloodstock breeding in the United States.

Doris, Sunstar's dam, was by Loved One out of Lauretta, by Petrarch. She, too, competed in sellers but in her case no advancement was ever made to a loftier status. Little more than a pony, she had originally belonged to Mr. Joel's brother, Mr. "Solly" Joel. The latter thought little of Doris and one day observed to his brother: "Oh, I don't think she's much good. You can have her if you like." The offer was accepted and this tiny selling plater produced not only Sunstar, but the Oaks winner Princess Dorrie. Altogether she bred ten winners of thirty-two races worth over £38,000.

Mr. Joel's trainer in Sunstar's time was Charles Morton whose stable was at Wantage. A trainer of the old school rather than of the old school tie, Morton had come up the hard way to the top of his profession. A great stableman, cautious by nature, neat and dapper in appearance, he believed in personal supervision down to the smallest detail. He never left home unless it was imperative for him to do so. Seldom was he under the impression that his day's work was done and after dinner he would go and ascertain if this horse or that had eaten up in a satisfactory manner. What he did not know about horses' legs simply was not worth the bother of finding out. He was loyal to his employers, no matter what he thought of them as individuals, and he knew how to keep his mouth shut. Two luxuries only he permitted himself; a glass of champagne in the evening and the best cigars that money could buy.

Sunstar arrived at Morton's stable in the autumn of 1909. Every year he received a batch of yearlings from Mr. Joel's Hertfordshire stud varying in numbers from half a dozen to twenty. A few days later Mr. Joel would ring him up and ask him which he liked best. Morton thought Sunstar a nice stamp of colt, nothing to rave about, but sure to win races of one sort or another.

As a two-year-old Sunstar did not convey the impression that he was ever likely to prove top class. The first race he won was the International Stakes at Kempton when he beat some fairly useful performers. The very next race on the card, the Bedfont Plate, worth £107 to the winner, was won by Prince Palatine, destined to become the best stayer in the country and to be bought by Mr. Joel for the then enormous price of £40,000. Sunstar subsequently won the Exeter Stakes at Newmarket, but his best performance was in the Hopeful Stakes at Newmarket in the autumn when he dead-heated with Borrow, a fast colt that subsequently won the Middle Park Stakes. In the Champagne Stakes, though, Sunstar had been well beaten by Pietri, while in an earlier race he had been beaten by Mr. "Solly" Joel's St. Nat. Certainly neither Mr. Joel nor Morton viewed him as a prospective winner of the Derby.

It was only when Sunstar was in serious work again the following March that Morton realized that Sunstar, apart from having grown considerably, had unquestionably improved out of all knowledge. Morton had some pretty good horses in his stable at the time and Sunstar appeared to be pulling over them all. In Morton's words: "In a full racing gallop he could lose everything we had, and I could then see that, all going well, we had a potential Derby winner."

On Good Friday morning Mr. Joel came down to Wantage with a party of friends to see his horse tried. Sunstar, ridden by a stable lad, was galloped against that famous old handicapper Dean Swift, Spanish Prince, The Story, Lycaon and several others. The trial took place on the Faringdon Road gallop which is judged a severe one, being against the collar the whole way without any suspicion of a dip to give the participants a breather. After a furlong Sunstar was out in front and he eventually won the gallop pulling up. This seemed almost too good to be true so it was deemed advisable to test on the racecourse at the earliest opportunity some of the horses that had finished behind him. The Story was sent to Epsom and won the Prince of Wales's Stakes carrying no less than 10 st. 4 lb. Better still, Spanish Prince won that highly competitive handicap, the Victoria Cup at Hurst Park, in a hack canter.

George Stern was engaged to ride Sunstar in the Two Thousand Guineas. He was the leading jockey in France and like many members of the French racing community of that period, he had been born in France of English parents. He was a fine rider and a particularly strong finisher. In all circumstances he knew how to look after himself, and any uncouth tactics in a race were liable to inspire some very painful reprisals. He had never been on Sunstar's back before he cantered down to the post for the Two Thousand Guineas. Sunstar, starting at 5–1, won that race by a very comfortable two lengths from Lord Derby's Stedfast with Mr. Joel's second string, Lycaon, third.

A fortnight later Sunstar won the ten furlong Newmarket Stakes. Some of the critics were unimpressed, but Stern reassured Morton by saying that Sunstar had in fact run lazily and had won with a great deal in hand. Everything seemed nicely set for the Derby.

It was an exceptionally dry spring in 1911 and the gallops at Wantage became extremely firm. In fact their condition caused no little concern to Morton as Sunstar was a red-hot favourite for the Derby and had been backed to win a fortune by Mr. Joel and his friends. Eight days before the Epsom meeting began, Sunstar did a ten-furlong gallop and finished so lame that he could hardly put his foot to the ground.

When Sunstar pulled up in this sorry conditions, he was some distance away from the other horses. Morton at once got hold of Sunstar's lad and told him at all costs to keep his mouth shut, promising him a good present if he kept quiet, nothing, or worse than nothing, if he talked. He then rang up Mr. Joel and explained the position.

Morton, cautious as ever, made no rash promises and expressed no extravagant hopes. He did emphasize, though, that Sunstar was so fit that if by some remote chance the lameness could be got rid of —Sunstar had strained a suspensory ligament—the favourite might still be able to run. Bearing in mind the weight of public money on his horse, and doubtless not totally unmindful of his own substantial wagers as well, Mr. Joel decreed that no effort must be spared to get Sunstar to the post. Morton agreed to do this but he added: "You must realize that this will be his last race; he will never run again."

Skilfully Morton dispersed the lameness, but of course the news of the mishap gradually leaked out. Extraordinary rumours began to circulate and it was said that Sunstar had been "got at" by bookmakers who simply could not afford to let him win. Another story told of a plot to put George Stern over the rails on the descent to Tattenham Corner. Morton, who, apart from his other worries, had fallen heavily and injured a shoulder so badly that he was unable to saddle Sunstar himself at Epsom, was hardly in the mood for hearty laughs, but knowing Stern and his methods as he did, this particular rumour drew from him a wan and transient smile.

Despite the mishap and the rumours, Sunstar started favourite at 13–8. The bookmakers had started to lay him when whispers of his injury began to circulate but Mr. Joel had bravely retaliated by backing him more heavily than ever. Pietri, who had beaten Sunstar the previous year in the Champagne Stakes, was second favourite at 7–1 while Lord Derby's pair, King William and Stedfast, were popular each way choices.

It was a close, sultry afternoon and there was a large and rather unruly crowd round the starting gate. Stedfast got thoroughly worked up and as the tapes rose he whipped round and lost nearly a hundred yards. But for this, it is arguable that Stedfast would have won.

Sunstar settled down well and at half-way he was going so easily that it seemed just a question of keeping him on his legs in order for him to win. His backers had one nasty moment below the distance when he faltered, but Stern gave him a single tap with the whip and he immediately rallied to win by two lengths from

Stedfast, who had made up an immense amount of ground in the straight, with Royal Tender four lengths away third.

There can be little doubt that Sunstar's leg "went" again at the point where he faltered. He was dead lame when he pulled up and could barely walk to the unsaddling enclosure. A horse of great courage, he had won the Derby on three legs and a "swinger". Admittedly he had luck on his side in that Stedfast lost so much ground at the start. Stedfast, a big, slashing chestnut, was a really good horse. He won all his next eight races including the St. James's Palace Stakes and the Jockey Club Stakes. He did not compete in the St. Leger, won by Prince Palatine. Altogether he won twenty races and over £26,000 in stakes.

The Derby was not only a triumph for Sunstar but also for the skill and dedication of Morton who, between the accident and the race, hardly left Sunstar's side, treating his leg and never knowing from one minute to the next whether the horse was going to break down for good. It is an interesting commentary on the discipline and conditions existing in stables in those days that not until after the Derby were the extent and gravity of Sunstar's injury made fully known to the public. A similar situation would be quite inconceivable today. Within minutes of the mishap, someone in the stable would be informing a bookmaker, while another would be selling the story to a newspaper. The telephones of the owner and the trainer would begin to ring and before long the stable would be invaded by commando teams of duffle-coated, bearded TV cameramen, while brash interviewers would be at work with thrusting microphones and naïve questions.

Sunstar never ran again. After the Derby, Mr. Joel had him at home for a bit and the horse appeared to become sound again. Accordingly he was sent back to Wantage but after his very first canter he pulled up lame and that was that. Whether Sunstar could have gained the Triple Crown by beating such a fine stayer as Prince Palatine is a matter of opinion. Morton, of course, had no doubts on that score. All that can be said is that in the St. Leger Prince Palatine beat Mr. Joel's Lycaon by six lengths. In the pre-Derby trial at Wantage, Sunstar had beaten Lycaon, pulling up, by thirty lengths.

Sunstar proved a highly successful stallion. He lived until he was eighteen and altogether his stock won 440 races worth over £229,000. Among his best winners were Buchan, second in the Derby and later champion sire; Craig-an-Eran, winner of the Two Thousand Guineas and second in the Derby; and Galloper Light, winner of the Grand Prix de Paris. In addition he was leading sire of brood-mares in 1928 and 1930. At one stage of his stud career there was a rumpus over the number of mares Mr. Joel permitted him to cover. Sunstar, in fact, was an exceptionally virile stallion and there are no grounds for thinking that the prolific use made of him resulted in poor quality stock. He is said to have sired more foals than any other stallion this century.

Fifinella (1913)

Obviously it takes an exceptional filly to win both the Derby and the Oaks. Only four have succeeded in doing so since those races were founded, the last one to achieve the feat being Fifinella in 1916. Fifinella's triumphs were in fact gained, because of World War I, at Newmarket but that can hardly be held to detract from the merit of her victories. She was undoubtedly a great filly, but one of peculiar and not entirely likeable temperament.

Fifinella was owned and bred by Mr. (later Sir) Edward Hulton, a leading newspaper proprietor. Delicate and studious as a boy, Hulton was trained for the priesthood but the death of his elder brother forced him to enter the newspaper world in order to assist his father. To begin with, his interest in sport was minimal, but close association with various sporting publications gradually induced a taste in that direction. Coursing was his first love and he twice won the Waterloo Cup but in the end it was racing that provided him with both an absorbing hobby and a relaxation. He was unlike the majority of rich men who take up racing in that he possessed an expert knowledge of the sport before he launched out into ownership. When he died at the early age of fifty-three, his horses were all sold and realized 288,380 guineas.

Fifinella was a chestnut by Polymelus out of Silver Fowl, by Wildfowler. Polymelus, a good middle-distance horse by Cyllene, landed a tremendous gamble in the Cambridgeshire for Mr. S. B. Joel, and though his stamina was suspect, he finished second in the 1905 St. Leger. As a sire he was an outstanding success. He was five times champion and in addition to Fifinella, he sired two Derby winners in Pommern and Humorist. He has exerted immense influence on bloodstock breeding throughout the world, but this influence is derived not from his Classic winners, but through the handicapper Phalaris. Maid Marian, the dam of Polymelus, was a half-sister to two great fillies, La Flèche and Memoir.

Silver Fowl's sire Wildfowler had won the 1896 St. Leger but proved an unsuccessful stallion and in his old age was sold for £10. Silver Fowl herself was bred in Ireland by Mr. D. Shanahan for whom she won three races there, including the National Produce Stakes. Shanahan then sold her for £1,500 to Hulton, who was just at the start of his racing career. She entered the stable of Richard Wootton, who trained for Hulton up to the war, but she lost her form completely and so was sent to the stud as a four-year-old. Before she could be covered, she got loose and injured herself severely on some wire. Hulton ordered her immediate destruction. Wootton ignored the order and in due course she made a complete recovery.

Silver Fowl expressed her gratitude for this fortunate reprieve in practical terms, breeding eleven winners of over £28,000. These included, besides Fifinella, Silver Tag who won the Cambridgeshire and bred Shrove, dam of Shred, a good winner in France; Silvern, winner of the Coronation Cup; and Soubriquet, second in both the One Thousand Guineas and the Oaks, the grandam of the Two Thousand Guineas winner Pasch and the great grandam of the Derby winner Pinza.

Fifinella was sent to Richard Dawson whose stable was then at Newmarket. Originally he had trained at Whatcombe in Berkshire, but he went to Newmarket in 1915 to train for Hulton. The association terminated somewhat abruptly in 1916 when Dawson declined to go on training the Hulton horses for fifty shillings a week and returned to Whatcombe. An Irishman with a drooping moustache and pince-nez who, as far as appearances went, was hardly a typical member of his profession, he had originally concentrated on jumpers many of whom were ridden by Mr. "Atty" Persse, and he had won the Grand National with a horse he had bought at the Dublin Show called Drogheda. Later he turned his attention exclusively to the flat and before 1914 he had won some good handicaps with horses owned by Lord Carnarvon. For a time after the war he trained with great success for the Aga Khan but there was a row between the two in 1931 and the Aga took all his horses away. Dawson and his brother owned the great sire Blandford, whom they had bought for only 720 guineas. Dawson trained two Derby winners by Blandford, Trigo and Blenheim.

As a yearling, Fifinella was not in the least attractive, being mean and weakly in appearance. In fact at one stage it was thought that her lungs were affected. During the winter, though, she put on weight and became much stronger. Unfortunately her manners did not improve with her physique. She was catty, peevish and unpredictable. Despite her ability, Dawson never felt very much affection for her. Nor did others whose duties brought them into close contact with her. She was well-galloped as a two-year-old and her first race, the Fulbourne Stakes at Newmarket, she won in splendid style by five lengths. The next time she ran, though, a very fast filly of Mr. Jack Joel's called Telephone Girl gave her 10 lb. and beat her by a head. However she finished the season on a more satisfactory note by defeating three rivals in the six furlong Cheveley Park Stakes.

In all her two-year-old races Fifinella was ridden by Steve Donoghue. With his beautiful hands and his sympathy with horses not least with difficult ones, he was the ideal partner for such a temperamental performer and it was a pity he was not available to ride her the following season. He had the patience to humour her when she was in her most exasperating moods.

As a three-year-old, Fifinella soon showed Dawson that when she felt disposed to co-operate she was a filly of outstanding ability. In April she was tried with a useful colt, Salandra, to whom she conceded 10 lb. She beat him with ease. When Salandra proceeded to win the Wood Ditton Stakes at Newmarket, hopes ran high of Fifinella winning the One Thousand Guineas. As it happened, Fifinella was in one of her least charming moods on One Thousand Guineas day and was thoroughly perverse and annoying. Donoghue would have been patient and understanding and could no doubt have jollied her along. However her rider was the formidable Joe Childs. Of Childs's ability there was never any question and he was one of the most accomplished and strongest jockeys of his day. His best friend, though, could hardly have claimed that Childs possessed the sweetest of tempers. He did not relish opposition either from human beings or from horses. When Fifinella played up at the start, he hit her good and hard. Because of this, she sulked for the entire race and flatly refused to exert herself. She was literally only cantering when beaten less than a length by Lord Derby's Canyon, subsequently the dam of the Two Thousand Guineas winner Colorado.

The field for the Derby looked like being somewhat undistinguished in character so it was decided to permit Fifinella to take her chance against the colts. On the morning of the race she could hardly have been in a worse temper. She never remained still for two seconds together, and declined to be dressed over to permit her lad to complete plaiting her mane. She looked a dreadful sight when she arrived at the racecourse. Again partnered by Childs, she was rather slowly away. Soon after the start she received a bump and at once demonstrated her resentment by dropping her bit. She took no further interest until close home when she suddenly decided to race in earnest. She then accelerated, darted through an extremely narrow gap and won by a neck from Kwang-Su, a half-brother to Bayardo and Lemberg, with Nassovian, a half-brother to Craganour, a head away third. Although the margins at the finish were narrow, she literally won in a canter and if she had raced properly throughout she would very likely have won by half a dozen lengths. Her starting price was 11–2.

As she had taken very little out of herself, it was decided to run her in the Oaks two days later. This time her behaviour was faultless. There was a beautiful sheen on her coat and her mane was neatly plaited. In the race she never put a foot wrong and gave Childs a perfect ride, winning as she pleased by five lengths from Salamandra, subsequently the dam of the St. Leger winner Salmon Trout. She did not run in the September Stakes, the war-substitute St. Leger. This was just as well as she would have clashed with the mighty Hurry On, unquestionably the best of his age and described by Fred Darling as "the best horse I have ever trained, the best I am ever likely to train". In the autumn Fifinella ran once, finishing third of three behind Phalaris at Newmarket, after which she was retired to the stud. Dawson expressed no regret at seeing her go. Whereas her half-sister Silver Tag had the kindest of dispositions, Fifinella's usual greeting was to bite and kick.

Fifinella was twelve years of age when her owner died. Together with her foal by Tetratema, she was sold to Lord Woolavington for 12,000 guineas. She was not a great success at the stud, not least because her offspring were inclined to inherit some of their mother's less amiable characteristics. She did, however, produce eight winners, one of which, Fifine, by Sunstar, bred seven winners including Portofino who won over £5,000 before being exported to Australia. The best of Fifinella's children, though, was Press Gang, by Hurry On. He won over £10,000 in stakes, including the Middle Park and Princess of Wales's Stakes. He was never, though, considered entirely reliable. He was sent to the stud in France but ended his days in Russia.

Gainsborough (1915)

Volodyovski, known to bookmakers as "Bottle of Whisky", became in 1901 the first Derby winner to have been bred by a woman, Lady Meux. In 1918 Gainsborough became the first Derby winner to be owned by a woman, Lady James Douglas, who also bred him. Gainsborough's Derby triumph was achieved at Newmarket during World War I and the first Epsom Derby winner to carry a woman's colours came in 1937 when Midday Sun, owned in partnership by Mrs. G. B. Miller and her mother, Mrs. Talbot, was the victor. Of those three horses, by far the best was Gainsborough.

Lady James Douglas, who was eighty-seven years old when she died in 1941, was born in France, the daughter of Mr. F. Hennessy, a member of the famous Anglo-French family of brandy distillers. She married firstly another member of the Hennessy family, Mr. R. Hennessy of Bagnolet, Cognac, and on his death she married in 1888 Lord James Douglas, fourth son of the seventh Marquis of Queensberry. Lord James Douglas died in 1891. The best-known photograph of Lady James Douglas is the one of her taken side by side with Gainsborough. She is seen as a short, erect and stoutly-built figure attired in a coat and skirt of severe cut, spats, a bow tie and a hat more practical than alluring. The photograph conveys a strong impression of a woman of independent and determined character.

In 1910 Lady James Douglas bought the Harwood property a few miles from Newbury and sought the advice of the former Kingsclere trainer, old John Porter, on the establishment of a stud. One of her very first purchases was Sir William Bass's Oaks winner Rosedrop, who was out of a mare called Rosaline, by Trenton. Rosaline had once belonged to Mr. Jack Joel, and Mr. Joel, usually so shrewd, held such a low opinion of her that he presented her to the Fresh

Air Fund to be sold for £25. Mated with St. Frusquin, she produced Rosedrop.

In 1914 Rosedrop was covered by Bayardo, winner of the St. Leger, Eclipse Stakes and Ascot Gold Cup and one of the outstanding English horses of this century. The produce of this mating was a bay colt foal, named Gainsborough, born on January 24th, 1915. It was Lady James Douglas's practice to sell the majority of her yearlings and Gainsborough was sent off to the Newmarket Sales with a reserve on him of 2,000 guineas. This was a stiff reserve bearing in mind the war situation and the reduced value of bloodstock at that time. Gainsborough, luckily for his owner, failed to reach that figure and an offer of 1,800 guineas was declined. Accordingly he joined Colledge Leader's stable at Newmarket. Soon afterwards Leader joined the forces and Gainsborough was transferred to the care of the famous Alec Taylor of Manton.

In Taylor's stable was a Bayardo colt named Gay Crusader, a year older than Gainsborough. Taylor could never really make his mind up whether Bayardo or Gay Crusader was the best horse he ever trained. He did, however, confide one day to Mr. Sidney Galtrey, at that time racing correspondent of the *Daily Telegraph*, that Gay Crusader might have proved superior to his sire had he been able to train him as a four-year-old. "Because," Taylor said, "he was equally brilliant whether at five furlongs or two miles; in fact I really don't know how good he was. It was just a disaster that I was not able to train him as a four-year-old and prove it to the world."

Gay Crusader won a war-time Triple Crown. At the stud his services to begin with were in great demand and soon after the war his owner, Mr. Cox, turned down an offer of £100,000 from Mr. Jack Joel. Unfortunately, though, Gay Crusader proved a very disappointing sire. Many of his offspring were unreliable and he himself became very tricky and ill-tempered as he grew older.

Gainsborough, a bay, was far more typical of Bayardo than the lighter-framed Gay Crusader ever was. He was extremely powerful and muscular, with good bone, a short strong back and excellent limbs. One critic described him as "the blood hunter type plus quality". As a two-year-old he was rather too thick-set and appeared heavy-shouldered in consequence, but he fined down the following season and was then an exceptionally handsome horse of his particular type. In temperament he was placid, sensible and kind, both in and out of the stable. His action was always flawless.

Gainsborough's record in 1917 was really nothing out of the ordinary. He made his first racecourse appearance in a minor event at Newmarket in July and finished fourth. Next time out he was third at Newmarket, again in a race of scant significance. He finished the season, though, with quite an impressive win in the Autumn Stakes, run over the six furlong Bretby Course at Newmarket.

Even if Gainsborough had failed to set the Thames on fire, he had shown considerable promise and clearly carried scope for improvement. Some big offers were made for him, including a number from the United States. They were all, however, turned down and eventually his owner found it necessary to issue a statement declaring firmly that he was not for sale. It would have been a tragedy for the British bloodstock industry if in fact he had been sold for export.

The following year the Two Thousand Guineas was Gainsborough's first major objective. Before that, however, Alec Taylor decided to sharpen him up by running him in the five furlong Severals Stakes at the Newmarket Craven Meeting. In that race he was unplaced behind Mr. S. B. Joel's good sprinter Sicyon. That outing brought him on nicely and on April 24th he was tried at home against four other three-year-olds. Ridden by Steve Donoghue, he won by a comfortable half length from Blink, subsequently second in the Derby, with Prince Chimay third. Prince Chimay was a very useful horse that belonged to Mr. W. M. Cazalet, father of the well-known National Hunt trainer Peter Cazalet. In this trial Blink was ridden by Jack Colling, later a highly successful trainer.

Gainsborough looked fit to run for his life on Two Thousand Guineas day, and ridden by that fine jockey, the beetle-browed and sometimes irascible Joe Childs, he duly won by a length and a half from Somme Kiss with Blink six lengths away third. His starting price in a field of thirteen was 4–1. Thus Lady James Douglas became the first woman to win a Classic race with a horse carrying her own colours and she was warmly applauded as she stood by Gainsborough in the unsaddling enclosure. Joe Childs was serving in the 4th Hussars at this period following some rather unhappy experiences in the Royal Flying Corps. The 4th Hussars, a broad-minded regiment, gave him plenty of leave to ride in races and in return he passed on his riding fees to regimental funds.

Gainsborough continued to please Alec Taylor, who did not deem it necessary to subject him to a trial before the Derby which took place on June 4th and because of war-time restrictions was run at

Newmarket. The war was far from being won at this stage of the year and racing, which took place on a greatly reduced scale, was naturally at a somewhat low ebb. The field for the Derby was certainly not a strong one and Gainsborough, Childs up, was a hot favourite at 13–8 on in a field of thirteen. Half a mile from home he moved smoothly into the lead and although his stable companion Blink, ridden by Jack Colling, very nearly drew level at the distance, he responded immediately as soon as Childs flourished his whip and won readily by a length and a half. Third, two lengths behind Blink, was Treclare, owned by Sir William Tatem, who the following year, as Lord Glanely, won the Derby with Grand Parade. Two days after Gainsborough's victory, the Manton stable won the Oaks with My Dear, by Beppo out of Silesia, a half-sister to Bayardo.

Before the St. Leger, Gainsborough demonstrated his stamina by winning the Newmarket Gold Cup run over 2 miles and 24 yards, this being the war-substitute race for the Ascot Gold Cup. In the September Stakes, the substitute St. Leger run at Newmarket, he had a simple task as only four rivals opposed him and two of these, My Dear and Prince Chimay, came from his own stable. The others were Ferry, winner of the One Thousand Guineas, and Zinovia, who had been second favourite in the Derby and who won the Cambridgeshire later that season with 8 st. 1 lb. Gainsborough won in a hack canter by three lengths from My Dear with Prince Chimay four lengths away third. Thus the first three were all trained by Alec Taylor. Gainsborough's starting price, a not ungenerous one in the circumstances, was 11–4 on.

There were three Triple Crown winners during the war years— Pommern, Gay Crusader and Gainsborough. Their status as such, and their achievements, have sometimes been subject to sharp devaluation on the grounds that competition was far less intense than usual owing to war-time restrictions on racing. Furthermore it is said that since all the war-time Classic races were run at Newmarket, war-time Classic contenders did not have to cope with the differing conditions existing at Epsom and Doncaster. The fact remains, though, that the war-time Triple Crown winners proved themselves beyond argument the best of their respective generations and they would in all probability have exercised a similar superiority under peace-time conditions.

Gainsborough's final race, the 1¾ mile Jockey Club Stakes at Newmarket, was sensational, and as far as Gainsborough himself was concerned, disastrous, since he was beaten a length by his stable companion Prince Chimay, whom he had defeated with the greatest possible ease in the St. Leger. Various explanations were advanced for this truly astonishing result but the least improbable one is that Childs was outsmarted by the crafty Otto Madden on Prince Chimay. Prince Chimay, by Chaucer, was exported to France and among his offspring there was Vatout, sire of the 1938 Derby winner Bois Roussel.

On this depressingly low note—Gainsborough had started at 11–2 on—his racing career drew to an end. He had won five races worth £14,080. Fine racehorse as he undoubtedly was, he earned even greater fame as one of the most successful and influential stallions ever to stand in this country. He was champion sire in 1932 and 1933, second in 1931, third in 1930 and 1935, and fourth in 1925, 1926 and 1927. His colts were noticeably better that his fillies, and when he died at the ripe age of thirty, his colts had earned eighty-three per cent of the stake money, totalling £340,144, won by his stock.

His most notable winner was, of course, Hyperion who won the Derby and St. Leger and was champion sire on six occasions. Oddly enough, Hyperion's fillies were, if anything, a shade better than his colts, the best of them being the brilliant and temperamental Sun Chariot. In this country Hyperion's son Aureole has twice been champion sire. In America Alibhai, Khaled and Heliopolis all did extremely well at the stud, while in New Zealand, Australia, the Argentine and South Africa the Hyperion male line has been worthily represented by Ruthless, Helio, Selim Hassan and Deimos respectively.

Gainsborough also sired Orwell (Two Thousand Guineas), Singapore (St. Leger) and Solario (St. Leger and Ascot Gold Cup). Orwell was a stud failure but Singapore sired the St. Leger winner Chulmleigh as well as Indian Call, the dam of Ballymoss, winner of the St. Leger and the Prix de l'Arc de Triomphe. Solario was champion sire once; he was second twice and third twice. Among his big winners were Midday Sun and Straight Deal, who both won the Derby, and Exhibitionnist, winner of the One Thousand Guineas and the Oaks.

Gainsborough's most successful filly was Gainsborough Lass who won over £7,000 in stakes. He was leading sire of broodmares in 1931, his daughter Una Cameron having bred Cameronian, winner that year of the Two Thousand Guineas and the Derby. His daughter Imagery bred two Irish Derby winners in Museum and Phideas, while another daughter, Mah Mahal, produced Mahmoud who won the 1936 Derby in record time and became a highly successful sire in America.

In 1940 Lady James Douglas, being in failing health, decided to dispose of all her mares and the Harwood Stud was sold to Mr. Herbert Blagrave. A condition of the sale was that Gainsborough was to stay at the stud for as long as he lived. In 1940, aged twenty-five, he covered eight mares and got them all in foal. In 1941, the year of his owner's death, he covered the twenty-three-year-old mare Tilly and successfully got her in foal. He was scheduled to cover sixteen other mares but he was beginning to fail and the bookings had to be cancelled. He died in 1945.

In 1970 Gainsborough's name appeared in the pedigree of the winners of the Two Thousand Guineas, the One Thousand Guineas, the Derby, the Oaks, the St. Leger, the Irish Two Thousand Guineas, the Irish One Thousand Guineas, the Irish Derby, the Irish Oaks, the French Two Thousand Guineas, the French Derby, the Grand Prix, the Prix de l'Arc de Triomphe, the German Derby, the German Oaks, the Italian Derby and the Italian Oaks.

Gainsborough is also great-grandsire of the outstanding jumping sire Vulgan, whose son Gay Trip won the 1970 Grand National.

Contrary to a common belief, Gainsborough was not named after the great artist. Not knowing what to call her colt, Lady James Douglas picked up a railway guide and starting with the letter A, turned over page after page until she came to Gainsborough, the town in Lincolnshire. She liked the sound of that name and selected it.

Ksar (1918)

Ksar was more than a great racehorse in his own right. He was a portent and a token of the renaissance of French racing and breeding after the disruption of the First World War—a war in which racing was prohibited by the Government and the testing of bloodstock was confined to a few "Épreuves de Sélection" without prize money and without spectators.

This abeyance caused a sharp decline in the quality and quantity of French bloodstock. In England racing was permitted, albeit on a reduced scale, throughout the war years, and adequate testing of bloodstock continued without interruption. The result was that the standards of English thoroughbreds were much better maintained and English horses enjoyed a clear superiority when French racing was resumed and international competition became feasible after the war. In 1919 the English horse Galloper Light won the Grand Prix de Paris, then the most important race in France, and the following year the English horse Comrade won the Grand Prix and then the first running of the Prix de l'Arc de Triomphe, the race instituted as the climax of the Longchamp autumn season and destined to become, nearly half a century later, the most valuable race in the world.

Inevitably the morale of French breeders and the whole French racing community sank to a low ebb in the face of these reverses. And it was into this atmosphere fraught with despondency that Ksar stepped in 1921 and 1922 and proved himself the first genuine crack international racehorse bred in France since the war. His achievements effectively restored the morale of French breeders and gained him the status of a national hero, much as the victories of that French horse of steel Gladiateur in the English Triple Crown had earned him the title of "The Avenger of Waterloo" nearly sixty years earlier.

Ksar was bred by Evremond de Saint-Alary at his stud Saint-Pair-Du-Mont near Lisieux in the heart of the rich Normandy stud farming region. Saint-Alary had come into racing in 1891, and the very next year had the good fortune to buy as a yearling Omnium II, who won him the French Derby and became an influential stallion although he died after only four stud seasons. Omnium played a vital part in the breeding of the two best horses to carry Saint-Alary's yellow and maroon striped colours up to the outbreak of the First World War, namely Kizil Kourgan and Bruleur. He was the sire of Kizil Kourgan, who was one of the best fillies ever to grace the French Turf and won the Grand Prix, in addition to the French One Thousand Guineas and the French Oaks, in 1902; he was the maternal grandsire of Bruleur, who won the Grand Prix in addition to the French St. Leger in 1913. And it was a mating of the seven-year-old Bruleur, with the eighteen-year-old Kizil Kourgan which was responsible for the birth in 1918 of Ksar.

Thus Ksar was the offspring of parents each of whom had won France's greatest race. The Classic purity of his pedigree was enhanced by the fact that his grandam Kasbah had won the French Oaks and traced her descent in the direct female line from Pocahontas, one of the most distinguished broodmares of the nineteenth century and the dam of the "Emperor of Stallions" Stockwell. The other salient aspect of his pedigree was that he was inbred to Omnium II in the second and third generations, a degree of inbreeding which is by no means common in the thoroughbred.

Ksar was submitted with the Saint-Pair-Du-Mont contingent of yearlings at the Deauville Sales in August 1919. It was Saint-Alary's practice to waste as little time and effort as possible on the preparation of yearlings for sale, and the youthful Ksar was presented at Deauville after nothing more than the most perfunctory grooming. His scruffy condition was accentuated by his awkward gait, his large plebeian feet, and his generally unfurnished appearance. Nevertheless the reputation of his breeder for producing animals of the highest class and his superb pedigree transcended these disadvantages, and the bidding reached 151,000 francs (about £6,000) before he was knocked down to Edmond Blanc. This price exceeded by 51,000 francs the previous record, paid for Mont D'Or at Deauville seven years earlier, for a yearling at public auction in France.

After the fall of the hammer Blanc's racing manager Wulfram

Canaple ventured to suggest that the colt was a bit plain. "I agree," replied Blanc, "but he is plain in the same way as Omnium II. That is a kind of plainness that does not displease me at all." Blanc discerned the effects of inbreeding in Ksar, and inbreeding in the thoroughbred was something towards which experience predisposed him. In 1900 he had bought Flying Fox, the Triple Crown winner of the previous year, when that horse came up for sale at Kingsclere as a result of the death of his owner the Duke of Westminster. The price, 37,500 guineas, was considered ridiculously high at the time, and remained the record for a horse at auction in Great Britain until the St. Leger winner and successful stallion Solario fetched 47,000 guineas at the Newmarket July Sales in 1932. But Blanc was justified when Flying Fox sired Ajax, winner of the French Derby and the Grand Prix, in his first stud season and founded one of the world's most powerful Classic dynasties. Flying Fox was inbred in precisely the same degree as Ksar, since his sire Orme was out of a mare by Galopin and his dam Vampire was by Galopin. Thus Galopin occupied the same places in the pedigree of Flying Fox as Omnium II occupied in the pedigree of Ksar, and Galopin, like Omnium II, was a top class racehorse and sire, winning the Derby and getting the brilliant St. Simon.

The purchases of Flying Fox and Ksar demonstrated Blanc's willingness and ability to pay top prices for the choicest bloodstock. He had inherited a fortune from his father, who had held the lucrative concession for operating the casino at Monte Carlo. This source of Blanc's wealth was considered not quite respectable in the higher social circles of the French Turf, and Edmond Blanc was never elected to the committee of the Société d'Encouragement, the ruling body of French racing. Nevertheless he had, for most of the last quarter of the nineteenth and most of the first quarter of the twentieth century, the most powerful stable in France. He won the French Derby six times and the Grand Prix seven times. On the other hand he was unable to fulfil his ambition to win the Derby at Epsom, in which his horses Vinicius and Jardy (by Flying Fox) finished second in 1903 and 1905 respectively; nor did he live to see the major triumphs of Ksar, as he died when that horse was a two-year-old. Ksar was running in the name of Blanc's widow when he established himself as the first great French racehorse of the post First World War period.

Ksar was a singularly docile horse and showed, from the moment

3*

he arrived at the training centre of La Fouilleuse adjoining Saint-Cloud racecourse, that he had inherited none of the vicious temper of his sire Bruleur. He had a wonderful appetite and, throughout his career, his one idea on reaching his box after work or a race was to get his head into his manger without delay. In his early days, when he was broken and began to be taught the rudiments of his craft, he was extraordinarily quick to learn. At the end of November 1919 Blanc's trainer Walton gave his yearlings a sharp piece of work over three furlongs to find out which of them could really go; and it was Ksar who won the gallop by two lengths despite taking the whole proceedings so calmly that he lost a little ground at the start. Like every horse worthy of the epithet "great", Ksar had absolutely first rate speed and, when he made his racecourse début in the Prix de Sablonville over the straight five furlongs at Longchamp on September 19th, 1920, he proved an impressive winner.

Ksar had been plain as a yearling. His appearance as a three-year-old was still unprepossessing. His physical immaturity was obvious. He had not muscled up properly and his action was far from fluent in his slower paces, though his shortcomings were partly redeemed by his elegant head and concave, Arab-like profile. But if critics cavilled at his looks, they were soon silenced by his performances. He began his campaign by winning the Prix Hocquart and the Prix Lupin, the two most important French Classic trials run over $1\frac{1}{2}$ miles and 1 mile $2\frac{1}{2}$ furlongs respectively at Longchamp. As a result he started a hot favourite at 11–10 for the French Derby run over $1\frac{1}{2}$ miles at Chantilly on June 12th, and had no trouble in justifying the confidence of the public. Ridden with perfect judgment by the English jockey Frank Bullock, he took the lead soon after turning into the straight, brushed aside the challenge of George Stern on the game little grey colt Grazing and raced ahead to beat Grazing by one and a half lengths.

Ksar had only French-trained rivals at Chantilly, but his victory had been so impressive that there were few doubts about his ability to beat the English horses in the Grand Prix, run over the extra three furlongs at Longchamp two weeks later. The English contingent consisted of Lemonora and Beauregard, but Beauregard, who had finished no nearer than ninth in the Derby, was merely a forlorn hope. English hopes were centred in Lemonora, who had proved his Classic credentials by finishing second to Craig-an-Eran in the Two Thousand Guineas and third to Humorist and Craig-an-Eran in the Derby. Nevertheless Lemonora had finished more than eight lengths behind the winner at Epsom, and French race-goers would not hear of him being good enough to pose a real threat to their champion in the Grand Prix. Ksar started a red-hot favourite at 6–5, while Lemonora was next in the betting at nearly 6½–1.

The result was a dreadful let-down for French pride. Ksar, ridden by George Stern, made no show at all, and Lemonora was the winner from the French horses Fléchois, Harpocrate and Tacite. The spectators made no attempt to hide their dismay, and the winner and placed horses returned to the unsaddling enclosure in a silence that could almost be felt. The total eclipse of Ksar seemed inexplicable. Recriminations were heaped on the hapless Stern, but the favourite had run such a lack-lustre race that the jockey's tactics could not fairly be held responsible. It is far more likely that Ksar had not fully recovered from his exertions in the French Derby, or simply had an off day. What is certain is that he did not show his true form in the Grand Prix. In the French Derby Harpocrate finished fourth, about two lengths behind him, and Harpocrate finished about a length behind Lemonora in the Grand Prix. This line of form suggests that Ksar ought to have beaten Lemonora, and it is confirmed by the subsequent results of the French St. Leger, in which he beat the Grand Prix runner-up Fléchois and Harpocrate, and the Prix de l'Arc de Triomphe, in which he again accounted for Fléchois.

The lesson of the Grand Prix, that French horses still faced a very powerful challenge from their cross-Channel rivals, was rubbed in when the English five-year-old Pomme-de-Terre won the Prix du President de la Republique—the race that afterwards became the Grand Prix de Saint-Cloud—over 1 mile 4½ furlongs a week later. Sourbier, the winner of the French Derby the previous year, was only third, and his defeat seemed all the more significant since Pomme-de-Terre was not even placed in any of the three races in which he ran in England that season. Indeed Pomme-de-Terre had never been anything more than a good handicapper, and had won the Manchester Cup, the Great Yorkshire Handicap and the Manchester November Handicap in 1920.

The euphoria induced by Ksar's victory in the French Derby evaporated after the Grand Prix and the Prix du President. Ksar, so the evidence suggested, had been found wanting when opposed to a good English horse, and the pretensions of so-called French Classic horses had been ruthlessly exposed by an English handicapper at Saint-Cloud. Happily for French pride the big summer races of 1921 represented the darkest hour before the dawn. With the benefit of a rest of nearly three months, Ksar gained his victory over Fléchois in the French St. Leger by three lengths in brilliant style. So impressive was this performance that Ksar's eclipse in the Grand Prix was instantly forgiven and forgotten, and he was made an 11–10 favourite for the Prix de l'Arc de Triomphe three weeks later. Four English horses came over for the "Arc", for which the first prize equivalent to more than £13,000 made it a powerful attraction. They were Pomme-de-Terre; Square Measure, who had been second to Pomme-de-Terre in the Manchester Cup and had won the Royal Hunt Cup and the Liverpool Autumn Cup in 1920; Blue Dun, who had been fourth to Comrade in the Grand Prix the previous year and was to win the Liverpool Autumn Cup later the same season; and Torelore, who had won the Jockey Club Stakes and run a dead-heat with Pomme-de-Terre in a match for the Lowther Stakes over 1¾ miles at Newmarket the previous autumn. They composed a strong team, if not quite a Classic team. They had no chance with Ksar. The filly Blue Dun set off from the start at a terrific pace and soon opened up a long lead, but she could not keep up the gallop the whole way and was joined by Fléchois, Square Measure, Odol and Cid Campeador at the last turn. Stern rode a waiting race on Ksar, but he gave the chestnut colt his head as soon as they had entered the straight. Ksar accelerated in a style that satisfied the most fervent hopes of his admirers, collared the leaders with little trouble and raced clear in the closing stages to beat Fléchois by two lengths, with Square Measure one and a half lengths away third. Blue Dun finished sixth, and Torelore and Pomme-de-Terre were way back in the ruck.

Ksar's victory was the morale-booster that the French racing community had been longing for. He had won so easily that nobody could question his status of top class horse by international standards, and Fléchois confirmed this judgment when he beat Square Measure, who ran badly, again in the Prix du Conseil Municipal on the same course a week later.

The four-year-old campaign of Ksar did much more than endorse the reputation he had earned by his "Arc" victory the previous October. It extended the range of his talents and enabled him to show a toughness and a versatility with which otherwise he would not have been credited. His spring campaign brought victories in the Prix des Sablons (afterwards the Prix Ganay) over 1 mile 2½ furlongs and the Prix du Cadran (the French race corresponding to the Ascot Gold Cup) over 2½ miles at Longchamp. In the summer he had a lapse when Kircubbin, who had won the Irish St. Leger the previous year but had been imported into France after that success, beat him in the Prix du President. However Ksar's defeat on that occasion was attributed to the fact that the race was run on his own training ground, Saint-Cloud, and, through over-familiarity, he declined to exert himself. He was his real self again in his preparatory race for the "Arc", the Prix du Prince d'Orange, and in the "Arc" itself.

Thanks to Ksar's splendid deeds, not a single English horse was thought worthy of challenging him in his second Prix de l'Arc de Triomphe, a state of affairs which was a strange contrast with his first. On the other hand the French 1921 Classic generation was strongly represented by the French Derby winner Ramus and the Grand Prix winner Kefalin. But it was Ksar's old rival and contemporary Fléchois who put up the strongest resistance, though Ksar's winning margin of two and a half lengths hardly expressed the measure of his superiority.

Ksar's racing career ended on a note of anticlimax when he was beaten by the gallant Fléchois in a pointless slogging match for the Prix Gladiateur, then run over 4 miles. It was an indignity to which he should never have been submitted. After it he retired to the Blanc stud, the Haras de Jardy, where those famous stallions Flying Fox and Ajax had held court. If Ksar symbolized by his racing performances the renaissance of French breeding after the First World War, he also made a vital contribution to the further progress of the French thoroughbred by his influence as a stallion. This phlegmatic chestnut horse sired the French Derby winners Tourbillon and Thor, the French Oaks winner Ukrania and the Two Thousand Guineas winner Le Ksar. It was Tourbillon who proved the principal channel through which the influence of Ksar passed to later generations. Indeed it is not too much to say that Tourbillon and his son Djebel were, by their excellence as stallions, the chief architects of the decade of French supremacy that followed the Second World War.

The Americans were putting out feelers to buy Ksar even while he was in training. It was not until 1935, when he was seventeen years old, that the Blanc family agreed to sell him and he was transferred to the Montana Hall Stud in Virginia. There he died of an internal haemorrhage two years later. He had been exported too late to make an impact on American breeding and too late to be badly missed in his native country. It is in France that Ksar will always be remembered as one of the most epoch-making racehorses and stallions of all time.

Easter Hero (1920)

Between the wars the two greatest steeplechasers beyond a doubt were Easter Hero and Golden Miller. Golden Miller remains to this day the only horse to have brought off the Gold Cup-Grand National double but Easter Hero went very close indeed to doing it, too, and his achievement in finishing second in the 1929 Grand National carrying 12 st. 7 lb. in heavy going against sixty-five opponents represents one of the most gallant failures in steeplechasing history. It is arguable that for sheer brilliance and panache, no chaser, not even the mighty Arkle, has surpassed, or even equalled, Easter Hero.

Foaled in 1920, Easter Hero was bred by Mr. Larry King in Co. Meath and was a chestnut, in due course gelded, by My Prince out of Easter Week, by Outbreak. Easter Week, who only ran once herself, was a member of the half-bred Arab Maid family. Arab Maid herself is reputed to have cleared thirty feet when competing in a steeplechase at Athlone.

My Prince was the most famous sire of jumpers of his time. He had quite a good record on the flat and ran in the Derby. In the autumn of 1914, his owner, Lord St. Davids, decided to sell all his bloodstock. The market at the time was anything but buoyant and My Prince failed to reach even his modest reserve of 100 guineas. However, before he left the yard he was bought "on spec" for that amount by the British Bloodstock Agency and six weeks later he was re-sold for £200 to the Irish Board of Agriculture.

My Prince sired three Grand National Winners in Gregalach, Reynoldstown and Royal Mail. They were all good winners of that race as Gregalach won with 11 st. 4 lb. and was subsequently second with 12 st.; Reynoldstown won with 11 st. 4 lb. and again with 12 st. 2 lb.; Royal Mail won with 11 st. 13 lb. My Prince also sired two outstanding Cheltenham Gold Cup winners in Easter Hero and Prince Regent, both of whom were placed in the Grand National carrying 12 st. 7 lb. and 12 st. 5 lb. respectively. When he sired Prince Regent, My Prince was in his twenty-fifth year.

Mr. King used to train his own horses and ride them himself sometimes, too. Like most Irish farmers of that era, he found that money was not plentiful at times and it could never be said that the stable was run on luxurious lines.

No attempt was made to hurry Easter Hero. His first racecourse appearance was in a 1½ mile flat race for amateur riders at the Curragh in the autumn of 1924. Ridden by Mr. Joe Osborne, he did his level best to bolt on the way to the start and in fact expended most of his strength and energy before the contest had even begun. Not surprisingly he finished unplaced. Osborne's confidence in his mount had hardly been augmented when King observed as he gave him a leg up: "Mind yourself, now. He hasn't had a saddle on for three weeks."

After Easter Hero had been unplaced in a flat race at Baldoyle on January 1st, King sold him cheaply to an English owner, a Mr. Bartholomew. In this ownership Easter Hero, still trained by King, ran eight times. He made several journeys to England where he won the Ellesmere Chase (£118) at Manchester and was second in a novices' chase at Sandown. His jumping, though, was impetuous and erratic and he had falls at Manchester, Hurst Park and Cheltenham.

By the summer of 1926 Mr. Bartholomew had had enough of Easter Hero and offered him for sale at £400. It so happened that an accomplished amateur rider of that period, Mr. Stratford Dennis, was on the look-out for a suitable young chaser. He nearly bought Easter Hero on his appearance alone but thought it as well to ride him first and accordingly took the mount on him in a two mile chase at Limerick in July. Dennis was a strong horseman and a fit one too, but he had no chance against Easter Hero. The pair made two flat-out circuits of the track before Dennis steered Easter Hero into a haystack standing on the edge of the course. Even so, Easter Hero came under starter's orders but he had very little left in him by then and he had to be pulled up after jumping the first four fences quite beautifully. Dennis decided not to buy him and was not entirely displeased when at Mallow soon afterwards he saw Easter Hero make off with one of the leading English professionals, Eric Foster.

Also interested in Easter Hero was Mr. Frank Barbour of

Trimblestown, Co. Meath, a rich and slightly eccentric bachelor. A fine horseman who went exceptionally well to hounds, he was a wonderful judge of a young horse likely to make a steeplechaser. One of his first major successes had been to win the Cheltenham Gold Cup with Koko. At Trimblestown there were excellent gallops and every variety of fence for schooling purposes. Barbour schooled his horses there with the utmost care but once he sent them to his trainer in England, they were never allowed to jump except in a race.

To ensure that the deal was swiftly and irrevocably completed, for King was reputed to be not the easiest of men to tie down, Barbour motored down to buy Easter Hero with a considerable sum of money in cash and a horse-box. Five hundred pounds were duly handed over and Easter Hero was then driven off at once in the horse-box before any second thoughts could arise.

At the time of this sale Easter Hero was six years old. He was not a typical steeplechaser of those times to look at, being a bloodlike chestnut that would not have looked out of place in the paddock at Royal Ascot. He certainly did not seem to be the ideal type to shoulder big weights in chases run over three miles or more. He possessed, however, tremendous vitality combined with a bold outlook and a most imposing presence. Above all, he had that particular quality that can only be described as panache. In the stable he was placid and easy to deal with and he always ate up well after a race. At exercise, though, if the pace exceeded a steady canter, he took a most formidable hold. In a race he loathed restraint and was inclined to jump crooked if not permitted to stride along in front.

At Trimblestown Easter Hero was well and truly schooled by Barbour's jockey, Paddy Powell senior, and his jumping greatly improved in accuracy without forfeiting its essential boldness. Powell had actually first ridden out on Easter Hero at Delamere Forest, Cheshire, where Bickley, Barbour's English trainer, had his stable. No one there could hold Easter Hero at all. They had him in a running rein but Powell had that changed to a twisted snaffle and a cross nose-band with excellent result. Powell used to take Easter Hero out every day to pick grass and thereby got to know him well. To this day he can still remember Easter Hero's zest for racing and how, after landing over a fence, Easter Hero would give a kick and a squeal from sheer exuberance and delight.

Easter Hero's form now began to improve. Up till the end of October 1926 he had only won three races worth the meagre total of £289. His first major victory came at the Liverpool Autumn Meeting in the 2¼ mile Molyneux Chase, a handicap worth £415 to the winner. Ridden by Powell and with only 10 st. to carry, Easter Hero jumped brilliantly and won with ease. Despite his light weight, his performance attracted considerable attention and the critics judged him a potentially brilliant horse, though one with marked stamina limitations.

In December, carrying 11 st. 6 lb. and ridden by the brave but somewhat unpolished Eric Foster, he won the Gamecock Chase at Kempton, while at Manchester, ridden by Powell, he shouldered 12 st. 7 lb. successfully in the 2 mile Waterloo Chase. A failure in the 3 mile Metropolitan Chase at Baldoyle merely confirmed the view that he did not stay.

The following season, that of 1927–28, Easter Hero was soon in action, his first outing being the Galway Plate at Galway, a 2½ mile chase run at the end of July. Favourite at even money, he ran a fine race under 12 st. 3 lb. but in a tremendous finish he was beaten a short head by Tony Lad. In the meantime Mr. Barbour, not the easiest of men to work for, had changed his trainer in England and when Easter Hero left Ireland in the autumn, he joined Pardy's stable at Bishops Canning in Wiltshire.

At the Liverpool Autumn Meeting Easter Hero again showed how easily he could cope with those big Aintree fences and with 12 st. on his back he won the 2½ mile Becher Chase in masterful style, the critics as usual admiring his quality, deploring his lack of conventional power and substance, and doubting his ability to stay. He followed up this success by winning the 2½ mile Middlesex Chase at Kempton with 12 st. 7 lb.

Rather to the general surprise, Easter Hero was entered for the Grand National and the handicapper, taking no chances, gave him the steadier of 12 st. 5 lb. Few indeed expected him to run with that stiff burden.

In January and February Easter Hero rested and in March Mr. Barbour decided that the time had come to put Easter Hero's stamina to the test. Accordingly, carrying 12 st. 7 lb. and ridden by Powell, Easter Hero took the field in the 3½ mile Coventry Chase at Kempton. There was a big field and a strong one, too, but Easter Hero delighted his admirers by making all the running and winning without being fully extended. This admirable performance placed Easter Hero's capabilities in a new light and most racing correspondents felt obliged to make a swift re-appraisal of his Grand National prospects.

During the National Hunt Meeting at Cheltenham that took place soon after Kempton, it became known that Captain Percy Whitaker, a former amateur rider then training at St. Giles in Dorset, had bought Easter Hero on behalf of the Belgian financier, Captain Alfred Loewenstein, and that the price paid was £7,000 with a contingency of £3,000 if Easter Hero was successful in the Grand National. It was also stated that Easter Hero would not change stables till after the Grand National, in which he would be ridden by Powell, and that he would not run in the National Hunt Handicap at Cheltenham as Mr. Barbour had planned.

It rained heavily the day and the night before the National and the going became very soft. This was thought unlikely to suit Easter Hero who started at 100–8. According to one racing correspondent, Sprig (12 st. 7 lb.), Brights Boy (12 st. 7 lb.) and the French mare Maguelonne (10 st. 13 lb.) stood out in the parade. He added for good measure that Easter Hero compared unfavourably with those three and had been bought for a ridiculous sum.

As usual Easter Hero took a strong hold and soon pulled his way to the front. He was first over Becher's and was a clear leader as the field approached the Canal Turn. The Canal Turn fence was then a big open ditch and formed a particularly formidable obstacle in view of the sharp turn to the left on landing. Powell steered Easter Hero to take the fence at the most advantageous angle but unfortunately Easter Hero slipped on the soft ground taking off. He landed slap on top of the fence, baulking the horses that came immediately behind him, while they in turn ran down the take-off side hampering others. In a trice twenty horses had been put out of the race and as the original cause of the trouble, Easter Hero gained a certain notoriety that took him some little time to live down. The ditch at the Canal Turn fence was subsequently filled in.

It only remains to add that the race was won by the one horse to complete the 4½ mile course without a fall—the 100–1 outsider Tipperary Tim, ridden by Mr. Bill Dutton, at that time a Cheshire solicitor. Tubed, parrot-mouthed and extremely slow, Tipperary Tim had been on offer for £200 up to the day of the race.

There was no rest for Easter Hero during the summer as Captain

Loewenstein decided to send him to France with the target of winning the Grand Steeplechase de Paris at Auteuil. In France Easter Hero boarded at Willy Pratt's stable and so did his new jockey, that powerful and artistic rider F. B. Rees. One June 9th Easter Hero was unplaced in the Prix Saint Sauveur at Auteuil but shaped well enough to start favourite for the Grand Steeplechase five days later. It was a very hot day and unfortunately Rees was not at his best. The course seemed to confuse him and he parted company with Easter Hero at the water. This was a regrettable fiasco, but Easter Hero's trip to France was not entirely without profit as ridden by the French jockey Biarotte, he shortly afterwards won the valuable Prix des Drags.

Later that summer Captain Loewenstein disappeared from his aircraft during the course of a flight from London to Brussels. It was presumed he had fallen out, but no trace of his body was ever discovered. Six months later his horses were put up for sale. Easter Hero and Maguelonne were bought for £11,000 the pair by Mr. J. H. Whitney, a young American then only twenty-four years of age and not long down from Oxford. "Why a man with a horse like that," observed Mr. Whitney many years later, "should step out of an aeroplane confounds me." Easter Hero was sent to Letcombe Regis in Berkshire to be trained by Jack Anthony, one of three Welsh brothers who played a leading part in National Hunt racing in the first half of the century. A fourth brother entered the Army and became a Major-General. Owen Anthony trained a Grand National winner and three Gold Cup winners; Ivor Anthony two Grand National winners and two Gold Cup winners; Jack Anthony rode three Grand National winners and trained two Gold Cup winners but he never succeeded in training a winner of the National.

Mr. Whitney and Jack Anthony decided that the target for Easter Hero in the 1928–29 season would be the Gold Cup-Grand National double. To avoid any risk of over-racing such a high-mettled horse, Easter Hero did not race over fences before Christmas. He had a series of races over hurdles though, and partnered by that superb hurdle-race rider George Duller, he won with ease on each occasion.

After Christmas the weather turned bitterly cold and for weeks on end no racing was possible. The big Cheltenham meeting had to be postponed and when the Gold Cup took place on March 12th, Easter Hero had not jumped a fence in public that season. Favourite at 7–4 in a field of twelve, he gave a most brilliant performance. In front from the start, he set a fierce gallop and such was the speed and accuracy of his jumping that he increased his lead at every fence. By halfway he was twenty lengths clear. At that point Rees decided to give him a breather and permitted his rivals to narrow the gap. Some spectators thought that Easter Hero had run himself out, but Brights Boy and Grakle were only in close touch on sufferance. As soon as Rees wanted, Easter Hero went clear again and he passed the post twenty lengths ahead of the weary Lloydie. He was no more distressed himself than if he had taken part in an exercise canter. His display had thrilled and delighted the huge crowd by its boldness and panache, and it was this race that really laid the foundation of the fame he was to earn as one of the greatest of steeplechasers.

Unfortunately Rees had contracted to ride Lloydie in the Grand National so the services of Jack Moloney were secured for Easter Hero. Though never in the same superlative class of Rees when Rees was at his best, Moloney was a very good rider, tough, courageous and with beautiful hands. Horses went well for him and he excelled at Aintree. Before he was knocked down by a car and fatally injured in 1969, he had undergone many changes of fortune. At one stage, not many years before his death, he was back at the point where he started, "doing his two". However, he never let adverse circumstances depress him for long. "Times are a bit hard," he admitted, soon after Mr. Whitney had been appointed United States Ambassador to this country. "Look at poor Mr. Whitney. Even he's had to get a job now."

It rained very hard the day before the National and the going became heavy, a serious disadvantage for Easter Hero with his burden of 12 st. 7 lb. Another horse reckoned to be ill-suited to the ground was Gregalach (11 st. 4 lb.) and at one point it seemed likely he would be taken out of the race but in the end it was decided to let him take his chance. He was the least fancied of Tom Leader's fleet of runners and was ridden by the then little-known Bob Everett, an Australian by birth who had served as a midshipman in the Royal Navy. It was Everett's first ride over fences for several weeks. He did not stay in racing long and probably his heart was always in flying. He was awarded the DSO and killed in action in 1941 when serving with the Fleet Air Arm.

The rain stopped on the morning of the Grand National and the weather was perfect. In those days the crowd at Aintree used to be enormous and it was estimated that 300,000 people were present. There was a record field of sixty-six and because of this and the fear of wholesale disaster at the first few fences, there was more than the usual atmosphere of tension as Easter Hero headed the parade in front of the stands. Like Arkle in later years, he bore himself superbly and there was more than a hint of pride in the way he carried his head. By comparison, some of his massive opponents looked coarse and cumbersome.

The course proved amply wide enough for the runners to start in a single line and the competitors were off without any appreciable delay. A great sigh of relief went up when it was seen that there was not a single faller at the first, and in fact, there was only one at the second, Ardeen. There was serious trouble soon afterwards, though, when Ardeen ran down a fence and put ten horses out of the race including Lloydie.

Moloney's orders from Anthony had been to make no attempt to restrain Easter Hero, but to permit him to stride along in front notwithstanding his big weight and the heavy going. Coming to Becher's, therefore, Easter Hero, favourite at 9–1, was in the lead followed by the six-year-old Richmond II and Sandy Hook, one of Tom Leader's runners ridden by a not particularly fashionable jockey called Fish. Easter Hero was measuring the big fences with flawless accuracy and thereby conserving his strength. At the water jump, the halfway mark, he was travelling very easily and leading by several lengths from Richmond II, Sandy Hook, Beech Marten, Grakle and Gregalach.

Beech Marten was down at Becher's and at the Canal Turn second time round Easter Hero still led from Richmond II and Sandy Hook, these three being some way ahead of the next group that included Gregalach. At Valentine's Easter Hero made his first and only mistake. It was not a serious one, but he sprawled on landing and inevitably took something out of himself. Moloney was always emphatic that Easter Hero was never going quite so smoothly afterwards. It may have been at this stage that Easter Hero suffered a misfortune the precise effect of which it is impossible to estimate. He spread a plate that stuck out sideways twisted into the form of the letter S. Luckily he was not cut but this must have been a handicap in the closing stages of such a tough and exacting race.

At the very next fence Richmond II made a far worse blunder and brought down the luckless Sandy Hook. Richmond II himself survived through a brilliant recovery by lionhearted Billy Stott, but his chance of winning had gone.

As Easter Hero led coming on to the racecourse, it really looked as if he was going to win and a great cheer went up. His weight, though, and the going were beginning to tell and for a few strides he faltered, only to rally with superb courage and battle on. Suddenly, however, it became apparent that the 100–1 outsider Gregalach was gaining on him and closing the once long gap with every stride. By the last fence but one Easter Hero had given all he had and could find no more. Gregalach headed him and from then on the issue was never in doubt, Gregalach staying on stoutly to win by six lengths from the very weary Easter Hero with Richmond II ten lengths away third. Only nine of the sixty-six runners completed the course without mishap. The finish, with almost everyone present longing for Easter Hero to win was something of an anti-climax, but the bookmakers gave the gallant winner a cheer. They at least had had a highly profitable week as two days earlier Elton, trained by Harvey Leader, had won the Lincoln at 100–1.

Thus Easter Hero failed, but what a glorious failure it was. Not built to carry big weights, he had shouldered 12 st. 7 lb. in heavy ground, made every yard of the running till headed at the last fence but one, and had defeated sixty-four of his sixty-five opponents. Moreover he had been handicapped by a spread plate. Never since has a horse been placed in the Grand National carrying 12 st. 7 lb. A famous racing journalist, the late Mr. Sidney Galtrey of the *Daily Telegraph*, summed up the feelings of most followers of racing when he described Easter Hero as "the most brilliant horse I have ever seen at Aintree, or indeed, at any other course".

Nor must it be overlooked that Gregalach, who was receiving 17 lb., though a 100–1 outsider was in fact an extremely good horse. In 1931, carrying 12 st., he was only just beaten in the Grand National by another good horse, Grakle, to whom he was giving 7 lb. In 1934, when in his thirteenth year, he was seventh in the National to Golden Miller carrying 12 st. 7 lb. and conceding Golden Miller 5 lb. Nor was he a mere Aintree specialist. He was in fact a chaser with first class speed and won good two mile races at Kempton and Newbury under big weights.

In the summer Easter Hero made a second attempt to win the Grand Steeplechase de Paris but again the venture proved a fiasco. A hot favourite, he was almost certainly "got at". He never took hold of his bit and could only crawl over his fences. He had not gone far when Moloney felt compelled to pull him up. He came out in lumps afterwards and was a sick horse for several days.

The following season the Gold Cup-Grand National double was again Easter Hero's objective. Once more his preparation was a light one and his only outings before Cheltenham were in minor events over fences at Wolverhampton and Leicester, both of which he won. In the Gold Cup he was faced by three opponents, one being Grakle. The most formidable of the three, though, was Gib, a tall, rangey seven-year-old trained by Percy Woodland and ridden by Rees. He had some excellent form to his credit and had won the Troytown Chase at Lingfield, then a race of no little significance, carrying 12 st. 9 lb. Among the horses he beat in that event was Gregalach, who was receiving 6 lb.

Easter Hero started off with impetuous zest. He dashed at the first fence, hit it hard, and did precisely the same thing at the second. This second mistake steadied him up and Cullinan, who was riding for Anthony that season, was able to obtain a measure of control. For the rest of the race Easter Hero's jumping was perfect.

Gib, though, was running a great race and at the last fence but one he took off almost level with the favourite. There was this big difference, however; Gib was being hard ridden by Rees, while Cullinan had not moved on Easter Hero. Gib hit the fence low down and could not recover so Easter Hero was able to cruise home on his own to win his second Gold Cup, again by a margin of twenty lengths. Gib was never of any account again afterwards. Unfortunately Easter Hero injured a tendon and could not run in the Grand National in which he would again have had to carry 12 st. 7 lb. Cullinan therefore had a lucky chance ride on Shaun Goilin, who just won in a desperate finish with Mellerays Belle and Mr. Whitney's Sir Lindsay. Sir Lindsay could well have been an unlucky loser as his rider D. Williams lost both irons at the final fence. Cullinan, who did not remain at the top of the tree for long and who died in tragic circumstances some years later, remains the only jockey to have ridden the winners of the Champion Hurdle, the Gold Cup and the Grand National the same season.

The season of 1930–31 was destined to be Easter Hero's last. The usual campaign was mapped out for him and his first appearance was at Wolverhampton on Boxing Day when he was given a walkover. Soon afterwards he won the Wigston Chase, value £83, at

Leicester. Then came a sterner test in the 2½ mile Mole Chase at
Sandown. Carrying 12 st. 7 lb., he had to give 7 lb. to Blaris, a
really good horse that had won the Champion Hurdle. Blaris, who
started at 11–8, was tremendously fancied, but Easter Hero,
favourite at 5–4 on, made mincemeat of him and won as he pleased
by eight lengths.

Easter Hero's next race was sensational. Starting at 6–1 on in the
Buckhurst Chase at Lingfield, he went under by a head to Major
Colin Davy's old chaser Desert Chief. Admittedly Desert Chief was
receiving 23 lb., but the result seemed to indicate that at last the
years were beginning to take their toll of Easter Hero who was now
eleven years of age.

There was no Gold Cup this year because of the weather. The
public soon forgave Easter Hero his little lapse and made him
favourite once more for the National though the task of carrying
12 st. 7 lb. was formidable indeed for a horse in his twelfth year.
Ridden by Rees, Easter Hero did not pull quite as hard as usual but
at halfway he was going really well and his backers were entitled
to feel optimistic. At Becher's second time round he took off just
behind the leader, Solanum. Solanum fell and brought down
Easter Hero, Aspirant and Theras with him. Drintyre was kicked
on the knee and had to be pulled up soon afterwards, while D.
Williams on Ballasport had a leather wrenched from his saddle. It
was a typical Grand National shemozzle. The finish was fought
out by Easter Hero's old rivals Gregalach and Grakle, Grakle
winning a great race by a length and a half.

As Easter Hero seemed none the worse for his exertions the
decision was taken to run him the following day in the Champion
Chase. This took place over a distance just short of three miles and
the runners all carried 12 st. Coming to the racecourse Easter Hero,
favourite at 9–4, looked sure to win but in fact he was beginning to
tire. He made a mistake at the last fence but one and a worse one at
the last, at which he was headed by Coup de Chapeau ridden by
Gerry Wilson. Easter Hero, though, refused to give in. He rallied his
final reserves of strength, and fighting back with wonderful courage,
he forced a dead-heat in the very last stride. No horse could have
run a gamer race.

Mr. Whitney wisely and kindly decided to retire Easter Hero
forthwith, having no desire to see a great and gallant racehorse slip
downhill. Soon afterwards Easter Hero left for America where he

lived for a further sixteen years. Let Mr. Whitney have the final word: "I brought him back to Upperville, Virginia, and hunted him with the Piedmont and Middleburg hounds—even though he was not really up to my weight. He jumped our timber fences superbly but I was done if somebody came up alongside during a run. Once as I flew by the Master, top hat bouncing on my back, I could only apologize and say, 'Maybe you can stop him—I can't.' Jack Anthony was the ideal trainer for him and loved him as did I. The only flaw I can find in that great horse is that I was awfully young to own him."

Epinard (1920)

French racing writers of the nineteen-twenties dubbed Epinard
"*Le Cheval Volant*", the flying horse. If their English colleagues did
not echo that plaudit precisely they, and the English racing public,
were practically unanimous in hailing Epinard as the greatest miler
in the world after he had failed by only a neck to concede 18 lb. to
Verdict in the Cambridgeshire in 1923. He was carrying 9 st. 2 lb., a
bigger weight than any three-year-old had carried to victory in the
famous handicap over the straight nine furlongs at Newmarket, and,
in view of the quality of the opposition, his must be regarded as one
of the finest performances ever given in a handicap of any kind.

Like so many brilliant horses, Epinard was a bit of a freak. His
breeding certainly was not calculated to produce a champion. His
fourth dam, Eye Sweet, had been bought in England for 510 guineas
in 1892 and exported to the United States, but the family had
achieved little of note. His grandam, White Thorn, was sent to
France by Mr. August Belmont, a man who numbered among his
many honours on the American Turf the chairmanship of the New
York Jockey Club and left an enduring mark on the evolution of the
thoroughbred by breeding the mighty Man o' War. In 1913, White
Thorn, who had been covered by the Triple Crown winner Rock
Sand before she left Belmont's stud in Kentucky, bred the filly
Epine Blanche, who was denied the opportunity to run by the pro-
hibition of all racing in France during the First World War. It is
doubtful whether she would have distinguished herself on the
racecourse since, by all accounts, she was a miserable specimen of
the breed. Nor was her early stud record auspicious in any way.
Sent to stud when she was three, she was barren the first season,
produced a dead foal the second, and was barren again the third.

Epine Blanche had changed hands before she was barren the

87

second time. When the United States entered the war Belmont sold most of his bloodstock in order to concentrate on his duties as chief purchaser of mules for the army—it was for this reason that Man o' War was sold as a yearling—and in 1918 the wealthy young scent manufacturer Pierre Wertheimer bought Epine Blanche for 8,400 francs at the dispersal sale of Belmont's bloodstock in France. Some time before the sale Belmont had offered her to a French breeder for 1,000 francs, but the offer was refused on the grounds that she was in such poor condition. The following year when she was sent to be covered by Badajoz, the stallion's owner, M. Lazard, was urged by his stud groom to forbid the mating because she was unworthy of the horse, but Lazard preferred to swallow his pride, or rather that of Badajoz, and accept the 5,000 francs stud fee. It was a happy decision, as the issue of the alliance was Epinard.

Badajoz was a tough and versatile racehorse. In three seasons in training he won seventeen races over distances from six and a half to fifteen furlongs of which the most important were the Prix Boiard in France, the Grosser Preis von Baden in Germany and the Premio Omnium in Italy. Thus he was a performer of note on the international circuit, but he was a long way from a top class horse, and he was sinking quietly into oblivion when Epinard came on the scene and gave him a lasting place in the annals of the Turf.

Epine Blanche was a mare of unprepossessing appearance. Her celebrated son, a chestnut with a white blaze, was considerably better looking, though he did not completely fill the eye as a thoroughbred of the highest class. His neck was short and thick and, although he had a good front and powerful shoulders, he fell away somewhat behind the saddle and had hind legs that were far from perfect. In general he gave the observer the impression of being rather lacking in quality. But whatever reservation might be made about his looks, no praise could be too high for his performances as a two-year-old in 1922 when he was not only superior to, but absolutely outclassed, all the other two-year-olds in France.

Fortunately the name Epinard sounds less commonplace than it does in English translation. There was nothing commonplace about his performance on his first appearance in the Prix Yacowlef one of the big Deauville two-year-old races, on August 11th, for he won in scintillating fashion by five lengths. Less than a week later he was in action again to win the Prix de la Touques on the same course and in similar style, but on his third appearance within nine days, in the

"Juvenile Classic" Prix Morny, he got left at the start and suffered his only defeat of the season. It was surely asking a lot of the young horse, however brilliant, to begin his career with three races in such a short time, but his lapse in the Prix Morny was forgiven when he reappeared after a six weeks' rest and toyed with his opponents, who included such leaders of his age group as Cerfeuil and Niceas, in the six and a half furlong Criterium de Maisons Laffitte. On October 7th he won the five furlong Prix des Coteaux at Longchamp by six lengths, and nine days later made every yard of the running in the principal French two-year-old race, the Grand Criterium over the Longchamp mile, to beat Niceas by three lengths, with Cerfeuil straggling in third a further five lengths back. After an interval of exactly a week he was back at Longchamp to get his revenge over Mackenzie, the winner of the Prix Morny, in the seven furlong Prix de la Forêt. Although his winning margin of a length was modest by his own standards, it was decisive.

In his first season Epinard had proved himself, in the engaging phrase of French racing journalism, "*un véritable* crack". Except in the Prix Morny, he had been tremendously fast from the starting gate and had been in command of the situation throughout every race. He was able to produce instant acceleration and leave his rivals standing at the beginning, in the middle or at the end of a race. No two-year-old to compare with him in virtuosity had ever appeared on the French Turf. With no Classic engagements to preoccupy him, he was able to move remorselessly towards a confrontation with the fastest horses of Great Britain during his second season. Before the end of June 1922, he had won four races in France, the last of them the valuable Prix d'Ispahan over nine and a quarter furlongs at Longchamp on Grand Prix day. After that victory Wertheimer and his American trainer Eugene Leigh, who had trained in England some years earlier and was thoroughly conversant with the details of the English racing calendar, set their sights on the Stewards Cup, the richest sprint handicap of the year and run over six furlongs at Goodwood on July 31st.

In those far-off days the idea that horses without English form should be debarred from handicaps was not so much as a gleam in a Turf legislator's eye, and many years were to pass before the rule that foreign horses must qualify for entry in handicaps by running at least three times in weight-for-age races was written into the statute book. So Epinard was entered for the Stewards Cup and was allotted 8 st. 6 lb. by the handicapper. This was 6 lb. more than any three-year-old had carried to victory in the race, and the first reaction of English students of the form book was that it was more than enough. Wertheimer and Leigh thought otherwise. Money for Epinard began to flow across the Channel in an ever rising stream. The first part of the commission was placed at 100–8 when the ante-post market opened, but so heavy and persistent was the support for him that he finally went to the post a red-hot favourite at 7–2, with Jarvie, Silver Grass and Precious the joint second favourites at 10–1.

The Stewards Cup is usually one of the most competitive races of the year, and often as many as ten horses are still in it with a winning chance a furlong from home. This was not the case in 1923. The first furlong of the straight six furlongs course at Goodwood is invisible from the stands. When the field came into sight over the brow of the hill Epinard was cantering in front with Linby, and from half-way he drew ahead of the field in effortless fashion to win on the bit by two lengths from Jarvie, a fellow three-year-old to whom he was conceding a stone.

Wertheimer and Leigh decided that Epinard would run in the Cambridgeshire provided that he was not set to carry more than 9 st. 5 lb. When the weights were published and Epinard was given 9 st. 2 lb. the confidence of his owner and trainer was unlimited. Just how good they believed the colt to be is indicated by the fact that the biggest weight that any three-year-old had carried success-fully in the Cambridgeshire was 9 st., and the horse to do so, Foxhall in 1881, had won the Grand Prix and was a performer of the highest international class. Epinard, accompanied by his trainer, returned to England in the middle of September and, after several weeks at Goodwood, was taken to Newmarket about ten days before the Cambridgeshire, which was run on October 31st at the Newmarket Houghton meeting.

Epinard needed a tremendous amount of work to get him com-pletely fit, and the preparation that Leigh gave him for the Cam-bridgeshire would have killed many horses. It did kill, for all useful racing purposes, two of his galloping companions, Chibouk and Select, but unfortunately two others, Pantagruel and Français II, a four-year-old who won a good class selling race at Kempton Park in September with ease, were more than adequate trial tackle. Two days before the race Leigh gave Epinard a top pace gallop over the full

Cambridgeshire distance. Pantagruel lagged behind from the start, but Français II would not allow himself to be shaken off and was no more than half a length behind Epinard at the finish. As the horses pulled up a friend suggested to Leigh that it had not been a particularly impressive performance by Epinard. "Perhaps not," rejoined the saturnine and inscrutable trainer without troubling to remove the inevitable cigar from his mouth, "but he was giving Français 36 lb."

Indeed Leigh, who gave Epinard a solo work-out over the course on the eve of the race, was utterly confident of the outcome. Epinard had been quoted at 15–1 in the early stages of the ante-post market, but those odds were not available for long as money, much of it representing inspired support, piled on him. In the end he started at 3–1, with Dumas, who had won his previous four races, next in demand at 7–1, Pharos at 100–12 and Verdict, Stratford and Epinard's old rival Jarvie at 100–7.

Epinard did not win the Cambridgeshire, but probably a large majority of the 20,000 crowd that saw the race thought that he should have done. The wide open spaces of Newmarket Heath are, metaphorically speaking, full of pitfalls for inexperienced riders, who are apt to have the gravest difficulty in adjusting their judgement of pace and distance to the requirements of this unique course. If a Brownie Carslake or a Doug Smith, jockeys who have excelled at Newmarket, had been available Epinard would no doubt have won easily. Probably any competent English jockey who had ridden the course frequently would have won on him. But the hapless American jockey Everett Haynes, who had been Epinard's regular partner and had not made a mistake up to that time, seemed to get quite lost on that broad, undulating and dead straight ribbon of turf with its bewildering absence of landmarks. As was his wont, Epinard jumped off in front, but then Haynes allowed him to drift about as aimlessly as a rudderless boat and, in the course of the race, he came right across from the far side where he started to finish on the stands side. He set and maintained a terrific gallop, and it was only in the final uphill furlong that he began to tire and slacken pace a little. It was then that Verdict was able to get to grips with him, and in the last few strides she collared him and went ahead to win by a neck. The consistent Dumas was a length away third and Pharos occupied fourth place.

Verdict was given a warm reception when she returned to the

winner's enclosure, for she had battled out the finish with determination and her owner Lord Coventry was the doyen of the Turf. But Epinard was awarded a louder and more enthusiastic ovation on his return, because onlookers were not slow to realize that they had witnessed from him a performance as great in its courage as in its quality.

Michael Beary, who rode Verdict, afterwards expressed amazement that Epinard had been able to keep up the gallop as long as he did. Although he knew him to be a great horse, he had not thought it possible for a three-year-old so weighted to go so fast for so long. "It was the last twenty yards that beat Epinard," he said.

The magnitude of Epinard's achievement in getting so close to victory is disclosed by an analysis of the strength of the opposition. Verdict, though technically "half-bred"—her great granddaughter Lavant was admitted to the *General Stud Book* nearly half a century later after breeding the champion sprinters Lucasland and So Blessed —was a top class filly and, the following June, beat her contemporary Parth, who had been third in the Derby and won the Prix de l'Arc de Triomphe, in the Coronation Cup. Epinard was trying to give her 15 lb. more than the sex allowance, and he gave 9 lb. and a beating of more than a length to Pharos, who had separated Papyrus and Parth at the finish of the Derby four months earlier.

Perhaps Pharos was not at his best when he ran in the Cambridgeshire. The possibility must be accepted, but it is surely significant that his trainer George Lambton, in the monograph he wrote about Pharos's dam Scapa Flow and her offspring, merely reported his running in the Cambridgeshire without comment. If there had been an excuse for his defeat, presumably he would have stated it. The form lines through Verdict and Pharos suggest that Epinard was considerably better than the top Classic colts of his age, and there is no cogent reason for disputing their validity.

A plan for Epinard to accompany Papyrus on the ill-fated journey to the United States which culminated in the disastrous match of the Derby winner with Zev at Belmont Park in October had been mooted but fortunately discarded. However Wertheimer, foreseeing that Epinard's opportunities as a four-year-old would be limited in Europe, toured the United States during the winter of 1923–4 and signed an agreement to run him in three special weight-for-age races during the following autumn. These were to be over six furlongs at Belmont Park, New York, over a mile at the other New

York track, Aqueduct, and over 1¼ miles at Latonia, Kentucky, against all comers.

Before crossing the Atlantic, Epinard had some business to finish in Europe. The original plan was to run him in the Lincolnshire Handicap in March, but this was abandoned for the ostensible reason that he had some foot trouble and had done insufficient work. The injury may have been diplomatic, because the handicapper allotted him 10 st. and set him to concede 23 lb. to the previous year's French Two Thousand Guineas winner Sir Gallahad III, a seemingly impossible task. In the absence of Epinard, Sir Gallahad III won in a canter. That the handicapper had been far too lenient with Sir Gallahad III at Lincoln was demonstrated with dramatic force at St. Cloud on May 19th, when he and Epinard met in a match over six and a half furlongs. The weights carried were Epinard 9 st. 5 lb., Sir Gallahad III 8 st. 7 lb.—a difference of 12 lb.—but Sir Gallahad III still prevailed by a head after a thrilling duel.

The result of the St. Cloud match again emphasized the superiority of Epinard to the Classic form of 1923, but his visit to the United States ended in anticlimax. He was accorded VIP treatment from the moment he landed on American soil, and he went down to the start of the first of his series of races at Belmont to the accompaniment of a band playing the Marseillaise. But in the event he was beaten by half a length by Wise Counsellor, and it was the same story at Aqueduct, where his storming late run failed to overtake Ladkin by a head, and at Latonia, where the gelding Sarazen beat him by one and half lengths in the then exceptionally fast time of 2 minutes 0·8 seconds. His racing career terminated at Laurel on October 18th when he split a hoof and finished lame in fifth place.

In his races in the United States, Epinard was not the horse he had been in France earlier in the year, in France and England as a three-year-old and in France as a two-year-old. The proof of his deterioration is that he had lost his former dash. Whereas in the past he had outpaced his rivals from the start, in his American races he himself was outpaced in the first few furlongs of his races. "Is Epinard as good as he was last year?" Haynes was asked at Aqueduct.

"I couldn't say that. He isn't as quick and sharp as he was," answered the jockey.

One of the ironies of Turf history is that Sir Gallahad III, who could be adjudged 10 or 11 lb. inferior to Epinard on their running in the St. Cloud match, became one of the sires of the century in the

United States; but Epinard failed to have a comparable influence on the progress of the breed. His relative failure as a stallion was due, in part at least, to the fact that he was shuttled to and fro between France and the United States and was not given a chance to settle down. He sired some high class progeny, including the Two Thousand Guineas winner Rodosto, but his achievements at stud in no way equalled his excellence on the racecourse. "Brilliant" and "excellent" were adjectives that had to be applied to his racing ability. While he was racing in America one critic remarked: "France has produced some great racehorses lately—Massine, Filibert de Savoie, Capucin . . ."

"And Epinard," Pierre Wertheimer added with a smile.

Brown Jack (1924)

Brown Jack, whose life span covered the years 1924 to 1948, vies with Arkle for the title of the most popular horse ever to have raced in the British Isles. The most popular horses are bound to be geldings, because only geldings remain in training long enough for their characters and performances to gain a firm hold on the affections of the public. With racehorses, familiarity does not breed contempt, but precisely the opposite. And although geldings cannot influence future generations of thoroughbreds, the best of them have done as much to furbish the image of racing as any entire horse or mare by their courage, intelligence and records of high and sustained achievement. Brown Jack and Arkle, geldings both, earned renown far outside the bounds of the ordinary racing public, while within those bounds they transcended all sordid and mercenary considerations so that their triumphs and tribulations were followed with deep emotion by backers who had never risked a penny piece on them. Such horses raise the status of racing as a sport, and give the lie direct to those who, like Admiral Rous in a cynical moment, dismiss it simply as "a gambling speculation".

If this assessment of the roles of Brown Jack and Arkle puts a strain on credibility, the evidence of a clergyman who visited Wroughton, the Wiltshire village where Brown Jack was trained, at the height of that horse's career may be cited in support of it. He made Brown Jack the subject of his sermon, saying that he brought sunshine into many people's lives and that he was an example to all men for his courage, his kindliness and the way he always gave of his best.

Brown Jack's record of six victories in the Queen Alexandra Stakes, the longest flat race in Great Britain run over $2\frac{3}{4}$ miles at Royal Ascot, together with his victory in the Champion Hurdle in his only season over jumps, proved him not merely a great stayer but also a horse of exceptional versatility. He was ineligible to run in the Ascot Gold Cup because that supreme test of stamina, like the Classic races and the championship races over other distances, are properly confined to the entire colts and fillies on whom the future of the breed must depend. Nevertheless he undoubtedly had the ability to win the Gold Cup, probably more than once, as on two occasions he gave weight and a beating to the Gold Cup winner of the same year. Nevertheless, as has been the case with many other great horses, Brown Jack's life began inauspiciously and, but for the skill and judgment of those most closely concerned with his development, he might not have made any sort of name for himself.

Not that Brown Jack had plebeian origins by thoroughbred standards. Bred by Mr. George Webb of Corolanty, the Master of the Ormond Hounds, he was by Jackdaw, a good stayer who had gained what might be regarded as a prophetic victory in the Queen Alexandra Stakes, then called the Alexandra Plate, in 1912. Jackdaw was to make his name principally as a sire of jumpers, and got the two Grand National winners Grakle and Kellsboro' Jack. Querquidella, the dam of Brown Jack, was by Kroonstad, an exceptionally tough horse who ran in ninety-one races during seven seasons and won twenty-two of them. Querquidella's female line may not have seemed very distinguished at the time Brown Jack was foaled in April 1924, but its solid, indeed classic, merit was revealed at a later date when Wattle Bough, a full sister of Querquidella, became the fifth dam of Cavan, the winner of the Belmont Stakes in 1958, and Indiana, the winner of the St. Leger six years later. Moreover Brown Jill, a sister of Brown Jack, was the grandam of the 1962 Grand National winner Kilmore. Brown Jack was inbred to St. Simon, the greatest racehorse and sire of all time, in the fourth generation, and had a third cross of St. Simon's sire Galopin, a Derby winner of the highest standing, close up in his pedigree. No, Brown Jack was well enough bred for most purposes from chasing at Aintree to competing in Classic long distance races. But he did not find favour with some reputed judges of bloodstock in his early days. When George Webb put him in the yearling class at Birr Show he was placed last of the four entries, and when Webb submitted him at the Dublin Sales in August of the same year he failed to attract a single bid.

As Webb was leaving the Sales paddock in disconsolate mood, he ran into Marcus Thompson of Kilmore House, Golden, in County Tipperary. On hearing what had happened, Thompson went to see Brown Jack, liked him and bought him for £110. What appealed to him was that Brown Jack was an excellent mover and, being slightly over at the knee, was likely to stand up to plenty of galloping. Thompson took him home, had him gelded, and turned him out.

A year later Charlie Rogers, the well-known Irish trainer, ran out of petrol near Kilmore House when on his way to Limerick Junction races and, on seeking help from Marcus Thompson, caught sight of Brown Jack grazing with a donkey in a paddock in front of the house, and took a great liking to him. His first offer was refused, but when he telephoned the next day and increased his bid to £275 it was accepted. For the next six months Rogers turned Brown Jack out in County Meath, where he was a paddock companion of Arctic Star, another notable stayer in the making and a rival of Brown Jack in several important races.

Rogers put Brown Jack into training early in 1927, when he was officially just three years old. Brown Jack was fat, idle, and seemingly half asleep most of the time, but his first visit to a racecourse to run in a six furlong race at Navan on May 23rd woke him up a good deal and he ran much better when he made his second appearance in a race over five furlongs at Phoenix Park a month later. Rogers was so encouraged by the Phoenix Park running that he wrote immediately to Aubrey Hastings, the Wroughton trainer, asking him to come over and see the gelding, as he was sure he would buy him.

Aubrey Hastings, who had trained and ridden Ascetic's Silver to win the 1906 Grand National and trained three other Grand National winners, had a keen eye for potential jumping material. At that time he was looking out for a young horse for Colonel Sir Harold Wernher, the Joint Master of the Fernie Hounds, who was particularly anxious to win the newly instituted Champion Hurdle at Cheltenham. Accordingly he lost no time in responding to Rogers's invitation, liked Brown Jack and bought him on behalf of Sir Harold for £750, with a £50 contingency if he won a race. No sooner had he arrived at Wroughton, however, than Brown Jack caught a chill and became seriously ill. Fortunately he never went off his feed, and a diet of warm beer, eggs and whisky, combined with a powerful constitution, eventually pulled him round. As soon as he was in regular work again Hastings began to school him, and Brown Jack at once revealed himself as a natural jumper. Such was his talent that he never made the semblance of a mistake either in practice or in any of his races, and his legs remained absolutely unmarked to the end of his life.

Brown Jack had his first outing in England in the Southampton Hurdle for three-year-olds at Bournemouth, a meeting long since defunct, on September 16th, 1927. He was inexperienced and not completely fit, and the race was mainly educative. In the circumstances he showed promise in finishing third, but he was allowed to start with "the others" at 100–6 in his next race at Wolverhampton ten days later. However he had learnt his lesson so well that he won comfortably, and he proceeded to win four more races at Wincanton, Cardiff, Nottingham and Liverpool before the middle of November. By then he was acknowledged as one of the leading young hurdlers, but a recurrence of his illness kept him out of action for the next three months. He was not back at his best when he reappeared at Newbury in February, but he struck form again with a head victory at Leicester before the end of the month and earned the right to have a tilt at the Champion Hurdle when he separated the high class older hurdlers Peace River and Zeno in the Lingfield Hurdle Cup on March 9th. He was considered unlucky at Lingfield, as he and the stable jockey L. B. (Bilby) Rees were caught unawares by a whirlwind finish by Peace River after seeming to have victory in their grasp.

At Cheltenham Blaris, who had won the inaugural Champion Hurdle the previous year, was favourite. But it was Peace River, not Blaris, who proved the main danger. Saved for another late challenge, Peace River loomed up in threatening fashion after the last hurdle, but this time Brown Jack and Rees were ready for him, and Brown Jack ran on up the hill to beat him decisively by one and a half lengths.

Aubrey Hastings already had an inkling that Brown Jack could do well on the flat. He asked Steve Donoghue, who was present at Cheltenham, to watch him carefully, and after the race Donoghue told him: "He will win races, and I will ride him." The die was cast. Brown Jack was never to run over hurdles again. Long before the end of the 1928 season Brown Jack had established himself as a more than useful stayer on the flat and, although blandishments in the form of forecasts that he could win a series of Champion Hurdles and even the Grand National were dangled in front of him, Sir Harold was not to be moved from his determination that Brown Jack should not be risked at the perilous jumping game.

The first important objective of Brown Jack on the flat was the Ascot Stakes, and after three preliminary outings which brought him victories in minor races at Windsor and Kempton Park, he duly won the big $2\frac{1}{2}$ mile handicap at Royal Ascot. Ridden by Steve Donoghue, he started joint favourite with his old paddock companion Arctic Star, who had joined Tabor's Epsom stable, but had far the better of the exchanges, as he won easily by three lengths, whereas Arctic Star was unplaced. It was a different story when they met again in the Cesarewitch four months later, when Arctic Star was the winner and Brown Jack, who started a clear favourite, finished down the field. Experience was to show that Brown Jack, although he did finish third in the Cesarewitch a year later, was not at his best on the long straight stretches of Newmarket Heath, but much prefered courses with plenty of turns like Ascot, Chester and Epsom.

It would be wearisome for the reader to describe in detail each campaign and every race as the career of Brown Jack unfolded. It will suffice to give an account of the salient aspects of his activities on and off the racecourse in order to convey an impression of his greatness. Except when the jockey was injured, as he was more than once, Brown Jack was always ridden by Donoghue, and such complete mutual confidence existed between horse and rider that they were known as "the old firm". Brown Jack never lost the indolence of his youth. He could not be made to work properly in home gallops. Gordon Richards once remarked after riding him in a gallop and driving him hard all the way: "You would not want to ride this fellow after a night out." Yet the sight and sounds of a racecourse shook him out of his lethargy immediately, so there was no alternative but to let him do most of his training in public. There was a regular routine of two or three races at the beginning of each season, mostly over distances short of his best, when he was limbering up and no one expected him to shine. He would set off at a great pace and run out of breath long before the finish, whereupon he would give a half glance backwards at Donoghue as if to say "that's enough for today", and Donoghue would allow him to canter in. Once he was fit Brown Jack would fight to the last gasp if necessary unless the ground was firm and hurt his rather thin-soled feet, and then nothing would induce him to try at all. But for all his battling spirit, he was not prepared to exert himself more than was required to ensure victory. When he knew he had the race won he would prick his ears, slacken pace, and dance a curious little two-step shuffle of triumph as he passed the post.

Like many intelligent great horses, Brown Jack owed a lot of his success to his ability to conserve all his energy for the business of racing. When he was not racing he liked to divide his time between eating and sleeping. Indeed those who saw him in his box at Wroughton in the afternoon, dozing with his broad behind resting on the edge of the manger, found it hard to believe that he was the same horse they had seen shaking at the knees and sweating in nervous anticipation in the paddock before his races. Donoghue used to say that he drew himself up and stood inches taller as he was mounted in the parade-ring.

The least successful season for Brown Jack was 1929, when he won only two small races apart from his first victory in the Queen Alexandra Stakes. The stumbling block was another fine stayer, Old Orkney, who beat Brown Jack by a short head when receiving 10 lb. in the Ascot Stakes and again beat him by a short head, but at level weights, in the Goodwood Cup. Brown Jack did finish four lengths in front of Old Orkney in the Prince Edward Handicap at Manchester in September of the same season, but this was only a partial revenge as Brown Jack himself was beaten by the lightly weighted Medarlin. Brown Jack had to wait until the Queen Alexandra Stakes the next year to assert his superiority in unmistakable fashion, and he then beat Old Orkney by one and a half lengths at level weights. Nevertheless the Goodwood Cup of 1929, in which those two great stayers fought stride for stride over the last three furlongs, was one of the most magnificent long distance races of all time.

The season of 1930 and 1931 saw Brown Jack attain the peak of his form. It had been evident for some time that he could do himself justice only in a really strong run race, and in the first of these two seasons his effectiveness was increased by the recruitment of Mailed Fist to be a regular member of his racing team in the role of pacemaker. Mailed Fist could go a tremendous gallop for one and half miles, but had lost the will to win races on his own account. Setting the pace for Brown Jack provided him with a new and valuable function. Once his job was done he used to drop right out and finish tailed off, but was always sure of a special cheer of his own from Brown Jack's legion of admirers for having played his part nobly.

In 1931 Brown Jack added to his habitual victory in the Queen Alexandra Stakes successes in the two biggest weight-for-age long distance races for which geldings are eligible, the Goodwood Cup and the Doncaster Cup. Coming to hand unusually early in 1931, he gave one of the best performances of his career by giving 6 lb. and a length beating to Trimdon, who was to win the Ascot Gold Cup that year and the next, in the Chester Cup on May 6th. In the Queen Alexandra Stakes he gave 5 lb. and a beating to his older rival Arctic Star, and carried 9 st. 5 lb. to a glorious two lengths victory in the Ebor Handicap, always one of the hardest long distance handicaps to win.

It would probably be incorrect to say that Brown Jack was showing any signs of deterioration during his last three seasons. The truth is that the handicappers were exacting a heavy toll for his resounding victories of 1931, and that races like the Goodwood and Doncaster Cups were contested by considerably higher class fields than they were when Brown Jack won them. His form, if analysed with care, was just about as good as it had ever been, and some of his efforts, when the handicappers gave him half a chance, were positively scintillating. His whole career contained few, if any, better performances than his in the Rosebery Memorial Handicap over $2\frac{1}{4}$ miles at the Epsom Summer Meeting in 1933, when he gave 2 st. and a length beating to the King's four-year-old Foxearth.

So Brown Jack, his honours thick upon him, came at last to his sixth Queen Alexandra Stakes on June 22nd, 1934. He was ten, and with their ages in double figures the vast majority of flat racehorses enter a period of steep decline. The opposition, too, was stronger than it had been for years past, containing as it did stayers of quality like Nitsichin, Harinero, Loosetrife, and Solatium. For all concerned, and that phrase embraces the huge crowd practically to a man, the occasion was fraught with almost unbearable tension. For his trainer Ivor Anthony, who had taken over the Wroughton stable on the death of Hastings in 1929, the strain was such that he could not bring himself to watch the race, but sat it out on a seat in the paddock. By the time the bell was rung to announce that the runners were entering the straight Brown Jack and Solatium had sorted themselves out from the others and had the race to themselves. Solatium hung on grimly, and there were agonizing moments when defeat for Brown Jack in the race he had made peculiarly his own seemed imminent. But the old hero was not to be denied his final triumph. Gradually he wore down his persistent rival, and in the last furlong forged ahead to win by the decisive margin of two lengths.

5*

The scene that followed has had few parallels in British racing. Hats were flung in the air in every enclosure, and the ovation was deafening. Thousands converged on the unsaddling enclosure as fast as their legs would carry them. Brown Jack, with his flawless sense of occasion, halted at the entrance to the winner's circle, and defied all Donoghue's inducements to move on until he judged that all his admirers able to do so had arrived. Then he walked quietly forward to round after round of cheers. Many of the onlookers, not normally given to displays of sentimentality, were overcome by emotion and wept unashamedly.

Brown Jack had run his last race. Sir Harold Wernher decided that he had done enough, and sent him into retirement at his home, Thorpe Lubenham Hall, Market Harborough. There Brown Jack remained in the perfect health and spirits that had lasted since the illness of his early months in England until finally he caught a chill and had to be put down in 1948.

Brown Jack, with his bold, intelligent head and eye, his perfect front and shoulders, his powerful but shapely quarters and his limbs that had never known a day's unsoundness, filled the eye of most observers as an ideal staying thoroughbred. He ran in sixty-five races and won twenty-five of them, with a total value of £23,150. He won races at seven consecutive Royal Ascot meetings, and the races which fell to him included, in addition to the Queen Alexandra Stakes, such important tests of stamina as the Ascot Stakes, the Goodwood Cup, the Doncaster Cup, the Chester Cup, the Ebor Handicap, the Rosebery Memorial Handicap and the Champion Hurdle. This is a record which, for sure, will stand for ever and sustain the imperishable Brown Jack legend, while at Ascot he is commemorated by a bronze statuette outside the weighing room and a race named after him over the same distance as the Queen Alexandra Stakes at the July meeting.

Fairway (1925)

Fairway had many of the characteristics and qualifications of an ideal racehorse. He had the speed and precocity to win over five furlongs in the best company as a two-year-old, the middle distance ability to prove himself the best Classic colt of his age as a three-year-old, and the constitution to keep his form and the stamina to win over distances up to 2¼ miles as a four-year-old. Bred by the seventeenth Earl of Derby, and so a product of the greatest British stud of the first half of the twentieth century, Fairway had a record that invites comparison with another of Lord Derby's famous horses, the five-years-younger Hyperion. Nor would the comparison be wholly unfavourable to Fairway for, although Hyperion won the Derby and Fairway failed at Epsom, Fairway did the better as a four-year-old and showed more stamina.

Frank Butters, who trained many of the best horses in England during the second quarter of the twentieth century—he did not however have charge of Hyperion—placed Fairway second only to the Triple Crown winner Bahram of the horses that passed through his hands, considering him superior to such exceptionally gifted performers as Colorado, Toboggan, Felicitation and the record-breaking Derby winner Mahmoud.

Fairway, foaled in 1925, was bred in the high noon period of the fortunes of the Stanley House Stud, when Lord Derby had a top class horse or two to carry his colours practically every season and had won his first Derby with Sansovino the previous year. He was by Phalaris out of Scapa Flow, whose dam Anchora had been recruited to the broodmare strength of Stanley House in 1912 as a result of one of those inspired purchases that can alter the whole course of a stud's history. Walter Alston, who was then the stud manager, had studied Anchora's pedigree and decided that she would make a perfect mate for Lord Derby's stallion Chaucer, with the result that she was purchased for 1,300 guineas from George Edwardes, of musical comedy fame. She was in some respects an unlikely mare for a leading stud owner to buy, as she had been hard raced during a period of six seasons and had run fifty times to gain eight successes. Lord Derby's trainer George Lambton described her as "just a good second class stayer, game, sound and with a grand constitution". He attributed her good qualities to the influences of her sire Love Wisely, whom Alec Taylor had considered the toughest horse he ever trained. Her arduous racing career certainly did not detract from her breeding value and, through various daughters, she was the ancestress of such class horses as the Coronation Cup winner Plassy and the Eclipse Stakes winner Miracle. Of more immediate concern was her daughter Scapa Flow, foaled in 1914 as a result of her initial mating with Chaucer. Scapa Flow was small and, though quite shapely, rather insignificant in her looks, which held no suggestion that she was to become one of the great broodmares of all time. Nor was her racing form much more encouraging, at least until late in her three-year-old season. As a two-year-old she ran twice inconspicuously, and as a three-year-old she ran in two selling races, in both of which she was second. Although this indicated that she was held in low esteem, some inkling that one day she might aspire to higher things must have been dawning, because a friendly claim was arranged in order to retain her after she was second at Stockton. In the autumn she began to make rapid improvement and to show increasing stamina, winning races over $1\frac{1}{2}$ miles at Brighton, Stockton and Newmarket. Lambton commented that she would probably have developed into as good a staying mare as Anchora if she had been kept in training longer, as Anchora showed little worthwhile form until she was four.

Scapa Flow bred eight winners altogether and five of them were by Lord Derby's own stallion Phalaris. Three of her Phalaris offspring reached Classic standard. These were Pharos, who was second in the Derby, and Fair Isle, who won the One Thousand Guineas, in addition to Fairway, and collectively they formed one of the strongest foundations for the belief that Phalaris "nicked" with Chaucer mares. On the other hand the physical differences between the three best offspring of Scapa Flow were as marked as their resemblance in racing ability. Pharos, foaled in 1920, was a stocky, round-barrelled, short-legged colt. Fair Isle, foaled in 1927, was tiny, but had exceptional length for her size. Fairway was lanky and light of frame, and Lambton and others expressed the opinion that he took after his grandsire Polymelus more than Phalaris. He also inherited the amazingly long stride and fluent action of Polymelus, but in his tendency to sweat freely before his races he was akin to Phalaris and to several other good progeny of that sire.

Lambton had been replaced by Frank Butters as Lord Derby's trainer when Fairway was a yearling, but continued as racing manager and so was intimately concerned with the racing career of Scapa Flow's most distinguished son. Although he was still leggy and light-framed when he went into training, neither Lambton nor Butters was in any doubt that he was a colt of the very first class from the moment he began active work. In his monograph on Scapa Flow and her offspring Lambton wrote of Fairway: "He had beautiful shoulders and the best set of legs and feet that I have ever seen on a racehorse—hard ground or soft ground came alike to him —and, added to other qualities, the bloodlike intelligent head of the high class thoroughbred." He was also high-couraged, nervous and fretful when put into fast work, and Butters, who had the reputation of being severe on his horses, decided to let him learn his business on the racecourse and not to try him at home. Consequently he was neither fully wound up nor much fancied when he ran for the first time in the Eglinton Stakes at York on May 17th, 1927, and it was the observations of the Newmarket touts that caused him to start favourite at 100–30. In the event he got away badly and ran green, and his final position of sixth, running on, was considered perfectly satisfactory. The outing had taught him all he needed to know, and when he next ran in the Coventry Stakes at Royal Ascot a month later he won in a canter by three lengths after starting at 7–1. His was a performance as impressive as that of Hyperion in another Ascot two-year-old race, the New Stakes, five years later.

Fairway had a more searching test when he ran in the July Stakes over the 5 furlongs and 140 yards of the New Two-Year-Old course on the Newmarket July course a fortnight later. His opponents included the very speedy colt, Hakim, the winner of the New Stakes. There was a long delay at the start, and when at last they were despatched Fairway lost lengths. At half-way his case looked hopeless but, patiently and sympathetically ridden by Tommy Weston, he produced an irresistible burst of speed in the last furlong and got up to beat Hakim by a head.

Although the verdict was so narrow, Weston had contrived not to give him a hard race. Nevertheless Fairway was still unfurnished and Butters decided to give him plenty of time to develop. Accordingly Fairway did not race again until the Champagne Stakes at Doncaster in September, when he started at 9–4 on and beat Nance by two lengths. Many critics were unimpressed, arguing that the opposition had not amounted to much and that he could have pulled out little extra if he had needed to. This opinion was not shared by Weston. The truth was that Fairway was acquiring a mature attitude towards racing and, like many great horses, was unprepared to exert himself more than was required to ensure victory.

The intention had been to run Fairway once more as a two-year-old in the Middle Park Stakes, but coughing and slight lameness intervened after Doncaster and he was retired for the season instead. He was given equal top weight of 9 st. with The Hermit II and Buland in the Free Handicap, from which Hakim, who had been destroyed after breaking a leg in a gallop at Whatcombe in August, was excluded. Fairway was turned out for a spell at the Stanley House Stud and then, thoroughly freshened up, went back into training to embark on his preparation for the 1928 Classic races. He thrived in the early spring, and hopes were high that he would win the Two Thousand Guineas until an abscess broke out in his mouth only forty-eight hours before the race, leaving Butters no option but to withdraw him. Pharamond, who had deputized successfully for Fairway in the Middle Park Stakes, again represented Lord Derby, and the prominent running which brought him fourth place behind Flamingo conveyed the strong impression that Fairway, who was vastly his superior at home, would have won if he had been fit.

Fortunately the abscess soon cleared up and Fairway was able to to turn out for, and win easily, the Newmarket Stakes over the straight 1¼ miles Across the Flat two weeks later. Instantly he became a hot favourite for the Derby, for which he actually started at 3–1, and the only doubt that remained in most people's minds was whether he would stay the distance at Epsom. Phalaris himself had been a non-stayer, and Pharos had just failed to stay when he was second to Papyrus five years earlier. Frank Butters did not have an easy job to get the light-fleshed colt, who was troubled briefly by a further outbreak of boils, fighting fit for the Derby, but this dedicated trainer contrived to do so, and all was well until the runners left the Epsom paddock to parade in front of the stands. Then a total lack of adequate crowd control became apparent, and Fairway was mobbed by thousands of admirers, who did not scruple to pull handfuls of hairs from his tail in their frenzied search for souvenirs. The process was repeated after the preliminary canter, when the runners had passed through the paddock and were walking across the Downs to the start. Fairway and Weston had to fight their way through the throng, and by the time they finally reached the start Fairway was a nervous wreck. "He looked as though he had been dragged through a pond," said Butters afterwards.

Fairway had melted away, and he was a beaten horse before he had taken a single stride. He finished thirteenth in the field of nineteen for a race which had another sensational element provided by the break-neck gallop set by Flamingo and Sunny Trace, who exhausted themselves and allowed the outsider Felstead, ridden with sober judgment by Harry Wragg, to come through in the last two furlongs and win comfortably.

After the race Fairway was labelled "soft" and "non-stayer" by the people who did not understand the severity of the ordeal through which he passed. Practically alone, Lord Derby, Butters, Lambton and Weston still believed in the horse. Lambton, who was combining journalism with his managerial post, wrote that ninety-nine horses out of a hundred would have failed in similar circumstances. Happily Fairway made an astonishingly rapid recovery. He did not run at Royal Ascot, but Butters sent him to the meeting to show him that a racecourse was not necessarily bedlam. The cure worked and, apart from a moment's hesitation as he left the paddock, Fairway was calm when he turned out against such celebrities as the St. James's Palace Stakes winner Royal Minstrel and the previous year's St. Leger winner Book Law in the Eclipse Stakes on July 20th. The parade in front of the stands did not upset him and in the race he out-classed his rivals, taking the lead half-way up the straight and draw-ing right away to beat Royal Minstrel by the overwhelming margin of eight lengths. The result was an exception to Fairway's rule to do no more than was essential to win, and the probable reason was that Weston, on edge since the Epsom fiasco, set him alight in uncharac-teristic fashion. At least the result demonstrated just how brilliant a colt Fairway was at that stage of his career.

His reputation restored, Fairway went through his preparation for the St. Leger without a single setback. Felstead became a victim of splints and was scratched, and on the day Fairway was favourite at

7-4, with Flamingo, Cyclonic and the French colt Palais Royal II his most serious opponents. Thanks to Lodore, the race was run at a fast pace and Weston was content to keep Fairway well back in the early stages. Once Fairway began his forward move in the straight there was no doubt about the result, and he went on to win decisively from Palais Royal II and Cyclonic, with Flamingo in fourth place. By that time Fairway was a self-confident, top class colt, and he concluded his activities for the season by beating the good five-year-old mare Foliation cleverly by a neck in the Champion Stakes.

Fairway reached his peak as a four-year-old. He had matured physically and lost his leggy, light-framed look, so that he presented to the observer a perfect picture of a thoroughbred in his prime. He won five of his six races that season, gaining his victories in the Rous Memorial Stakes at Royal Ascot and the Burwell, the Princess of Wales's, the Champion Stakes, and the Jockey Club Cup, all at Newmarket. His only defeat was suffered, inexplicably, at the hands of Royal Minstrel, in the Eclipse Stakes. Royal Minstrel, so easily beaten in the race the previous year, obtained his revenge with such devastating thoroughness that he won by four lengths, and Fairway clearly was not himself that day.

Lord Derby believed in submitting his horses on the racecourse test in no half-hearted fashion. After Fairway had beaten Palais Royal II, who had been third two heads behind Double Life and Vatout in the Cambridgeshire twenty-four hours earlier, in a muddling race for the $2\frac{1}{4}$ mile Jockey Club Cup, he said that he would like the horse to be trained for the Ascot Gold Cup the following year. Accordingly Fairway, before going into winter quarters, was given a really searching gallop to find out whether he had reasonable prospects of staying the distance at Ascot. The gallop was over $2\frac{1}{2}$ miles at Newmarket, finishing at the old Cambridgeshire winning post, and was the hardest imaginable, since the last five furlongs were uphill and there was only one turn in the whole distance. His principal companion was Bosworth, who had been beaten by a short head by Trigo in the St. Leger, but to make sure of a true pace two good handicappers were put in for the first mile, and two others then jumped in to take it up. Weston was instructed to lie up the whole way instead of using his habitual waiting tactics and, after a great race, Fairway beat Bosworth by half a length.

Fairway had answered the question affirmatively. He did not leave an oat that evening, and came out of his box the next morning

Plate 9 Fifinella
Plate 10 Gainsborough

Plate 11 Ksar

Plate 12   Easter Hero

Plate 13   Epinard

Plate 14 Brown Jack

Plate 15 Fairway

as fresh as paint. But he was not to have the chance to show what he could do in the rôle of out-and-out stayer in the Gold Cup, because he developed tendon trouble the next spring and had to be taken out of training. Bosworth ran in and won the Gold Cup in his place.

Fairway began his stud career at Lord Derby's Woodland Stud in 1931. His covering fee was 400 guineas. He proved one of the great sires of the century, transmitting his wonderful quality and action to so many of his progeny that he was leading sire of winners four times, and was second in the list of sires of winners on three other occasions. His sons Blue Peter and Watling Street won the Derby, but his non-Derby winning sons, Fair Trial and Honeyway, were more successful in perpetuating his male dynasty.

Nearly a quarter of a century after the death of Fairway in 1948, it is still an open question whether Fairway or his elder brother Pharos has exerted a more positive influence on the progress of the breed. What is beyond doubt is that Fairway was the better race-horse, and that he had it in him to win the Triple Crown if a minor ailment and the unbridled enthusiasm of the Epsom crowd had not intervened.

Cameronian (1928)

That Cameronian won the Two Thousand Guineas and the Derby for Mr. J. A. Dewar in 1931 was in some measure due to Mr. Edgar Wallace, the well-known author and journalist, who happened to be a keen but markedly unsuccessful patron of the Turf. Mr. Wallace's racing ventures must have cost him a great deal of money.

Over the years, the problem of nominations rendered void by the death of an owner had been a source of worry to the Jockey Club. Backed by the highest legal opinion, the Jockey Club had based its rules on the assumption that fees and forfeits incurred by horses entered for races under Jockey Club Rules could not be recovered under process of law, because if they were contracts, they were contracts by way of gambling and wagering and accordingly not subject to legal sanction. If a living owner failed to pay his forfeit liabilities, his name appeared in the forfeit list in the "Racing Calendar". It was felt that this deterrent could not be applied with decency to a dead man or to his executors, so accordingly the Void Nomination Rule came into existence. This rule stipulated that when an owner died, all entries for his horses ceased to exist.

Obviously the rule possessed serious disadvantages and in 1927 Mr. Wallace agreed to be sued in the High Court for the recovery of £4 due in respect of a horse of his entered at Newmarket. Unfortunately the verdict in the Chancery Court was in favour of Mr. Wallace, who, while the case was pending, was unable to run any of his horses, since if he had happened to win a race, he would have had a credit balance at the office of the Jockey Club and the £4 in dispute would at once have been appropriated. The case then went to the Court of Appeal where the Master of the Rolls and Lord Justices Lawrence and Russell found for the Jockey Club. The judgment made it possible for the rule to be changed in 1929 just in time for Cameronian, whose owner-breeder, Lord Dewar, died in 1930 leaving the colt to his nephew, Mr. John Dewar.

Cameronian was a bay colt by Lord Derby's great sire Pharos, out of Una Cameron, by the Triple Crown winner Gainsborough out of Cherimoya, by Cherry Tree. Bred in England, Cherry Tree never ran in this country and was sent to America where he competed without success. He was brought back to the land of his birth and stood at Ecchinswell, a village near Newbury, at a fee of 18 guineas.

Cherimoya, ridden by Fred Winter senior, won the Oaks in 1911, that being the only race in which she ever ran. Lord Dewar bought her for 2,300 guineas in 1915 after her owner, Mr. Broderick Cloete, had been drowned when the *Lusitania* was torpedoed by a German submarine. Cherimoya bred three winners, one of which, The Cheerful Abbot, won ten races and dead-heated in another. A daughter of Cherimoya, Sunny Moya, won two minor events and bred the Royal Hunt Cup winner The Macnab, later a stallion in France, and Sunny Trace, favourite for the Two Thousand Guineas in 1928. Una Cameron ran eight times without winning. Besides Cameronian, she bred the useful Lovat Scout who was later exported to South America.

Cameronian was sent to Beckhampton to be trained by the great Fred Darling, martinet and perfectionist. Like a good many other famous Beckhampton horses, Cameronian was given his first experience of racing at neighbouring Salisbury, the event chosen for him being the five furlong Salisbury Stakes on May 29th, 1930. Ridden by Fred Fox, he did not appear to be greatly fancied and started at 8–1, but won with a lot in hand from sixteen rivals. This was an encouraging start if nothing more, but Cameronian did not race again that season. That was due not to any undue solicitude on the part of Darling, but to the fact that Cameronian's joints caused a certain degree of concern. Naturally he was seldom mentioned when the Derby came up for discussion once the flat-racing season was over.

During the winter months, however, Cameronian did exceptionally well in a physical sense and in the spring he began to be both talked about and written up as a possible contender for the Classics. Thoughts went back to another Beckhampton colt, Captain Cuttle, who had had a single race as a two-year-old in 1921 and had won the Derby the following season. Great interest was therefore taken in

Cameronian when he turned out for the 1 mile Craven Stakes at
Newmarket on April 16th. On the whole, the paddock critics were
favourably impressed. They saw a medium-sized colt, a good hard
bay in colour, compact, beautifully proportioned and full of the
quality so often found in the descendants of Phalaris. He had
plenty of depth, his shoulders were excellent and he possessed
exceptional strength in his thighs and quarters. One or two of the
more demanding critics complained that his joints were perhaps not
all that they might have been and that when he was standing, he had
his forelegs too far under him. In general, though, he was not an
easy horse to fault. In certain respects he was very like the Phalaris
colt Manna, whom Darling had trained to win the Two Thousand
Guineas and the Derby, but he was far more even-tempered.

As a matter of fact Cameronian was still backward at this stage.
Favourite at 11–4 and riden by Fox, he could do no more than finish
third, beaten a length and a head, behind Philae, trained by Lord
George Dundas, and Truculent, both of whom were receiving 8 lb.
Among the "also ran" was Lord Rosebery's Sandwich, a half-
brother by the Derby winner Sansovino to Manna. Thus the Craven
Stakes field contained the future winners of the Two Thousand
Guineas, the Derby and the St. Leger.

Darling was not greatly disappointed by Cameronian's inability to
win and reckoned he would be very much fitter by Epsom. In any
case he had another candidate for the Guineas in Lord Ellesmere's
Lemnarchus, by Friar Marcus. Lemnarchus had perhaps given a
false idea of the stamina he possessed by winning a slow-run race for
the Nonsuch Stakes at Epsom, while in a rough gallop with
Cameronian at Beckhampton he showed such admirable speed that
Fox elected to ride him in the Newmarket Classic, the services of
Joe Childs being secured for Cameronian.

It was a damp, misty day for the Two Thousand and the going was
on the soft side. This did not suit the two best-backed horses,
Portlaw and Lemnarchus, who both turned out to be non-stayers.
There was a lot of money for Goyescas, a Gainsborough colt that
Basil Jarvis trained at Newmarket for M. M. Boussac, while
Cameronian was a fairly popular each way chance at 100–8. There
were twenty-four runners.

The start was a good one except that Goyescas lost ground. He was
caught at an unpropitious moment when Captain Allison pulled the
lever and lost three or four lengths in consequence. "That's finished

it; he has no chance now," observed M. Boussac gloomily after the field had covered a furlong.

Coming to the Bushes, two furlongs from home, Portlaw just led from Lemnarchus. Almost immediately Portlaw was done with and Lemnarchus did not last much longer. This left Cameronian, going very easily, in front from Orpen and Link Boy, both members of Joe Lawson's stable at Manton. In the Dip Cameronian looked sure to win and the Manton pair appeared equally certain to be placed, when all of a sudden along came Goyescas with a tremendous late run. He passed horse after horse and looked really dangerous for a few seconds but his brave effort petered out in the final hundred yards and Cameronian won in decisive fashion by two lengths; Orpen was third, three lengths behind Goyescas. The Craven Stakes winner Philae, now meeting Cameronian on even terms, finished something like fifteen lengths behind him.

Two days later the Beckhampton stable completed a fine double when Lord Ellesmere's Four Course, by Tetratema, won the One Thousand Guineas by a head from Lady Marjorie, who would surely have won had she not swerved at a critical stage of the race.

Darling decided there was no need to give Cameronian another outing before Epsom so the colt's ability to stay a mile and a half had to be taken on trust. On breeding he was no cast-iron certainty to last out a mile and a half; his sire Pharos, though second to Papyrus in the Derby, was essentially a ten furlong horse while despite Cherimoya, Cameronian's tail-female line was hardly that of a top-class stayer. However stable confidence in him was greatly increased after a mile and a half trial at Beckhampton on May 31st. Cameronian, ridden by W. Sherry, for many years associated with Beckhampton, carried 8 st. 9 lb. and won easily from the four-year-old Parenthesis (9 st. 3 lb.). Parenthesis had been second in the St. Leger and was to win the Coronation Cup the day after Cameronian won the Derby. Third with 7 st. 12 lb. was a useful staying handicapper called Brother-in-Law, winner of the 1 mile 5 furlong June Rose Handicap at Sandown, and fourth another handicapper, Rallye II (7 st. 1 lb.). Fifth and last was Four Course (8 st. 3 lb.) ridden by Fox.

It was a perfect June day for the Derby. The course was in good order and the going rather on the firm side. Cameronian was a warm favourite at 7–2. Next in the betting came Sandwich who had made a particularly good impression by his victory in the Chester Vase. Orpen was well backed at 9–1 but Goyescas had drifted in the

market to 100–6 following a failure in the Newmarket Stakes behind
the American-bred Sir Andrew, who figured at 25–1. Both Pomme
d'Api and Doctor Dolittle were popular each way choices.

The start was a good one and Cameronian was one of the quickest
away but Fox soon steadied him down and settled him in the middle
of the field. Sandwich, drawn number 2, got shut off in the early
stages and though he was better placed passing the mile and a quarter starting gate, he found more trouble during the descent to
Tattenham Corner. Doctor Dolittle, too, had something of a rough
passage.

At Tattenham Corner the outsider Gallini led from Armagnac,
Zanoff and Cameronian, while behind them came Pomme d'Api,
Goyescas and Estate Duty. Orpen was eighth and Sandwich some
way behind Orpen. Gallini led for a furlong into the straight at
which point he lost his off-fore plate and dropped back beaten. His
place at the head of the field was taken by Cameronian who swept to
the front on a tight rein amid cheers from all over the course. The
race, though, was by no means over as Orpen put in a resolute challenge and reduced the favourite's advantage to a head. Many of those
present expected Orpen to prove the stouter stayer of the two, but
Fox gave Cameronian a single tap with the whip and Cameronian at
once increased his lead to a length.

Just when it seemed that Cameronian had the prize at his mercy,
along came Sandwich with a fine late run on the rails. He passed at
least half a dozen horses and was clearly travelling far faster than the
two leaders but the winning post came just too soon for him. The
verdict of the judge was that Cameronian had won by three parts of a
length from Orpen with Sandwich the same distance away third.
Goyescas was fourth. "It is possible," said Sandwich's rider, Harry
Wragg, afterwards, "that I was an unlucky loser." Some of Sandwich's backers considered that comment a notable understatement.
It certainly seemed that Lord Rosebery's colt had been hampered
more than once, had been switched from one position to another,
and had only obtained a clear run when the race was as good as over.
Sir Jack Jarvis, who trained Sandwich, always reckoned that the
unluckiest Derby losers he ever saw were Sandwich in 1931 and the
French colt Shantung in 1959.

Cameronian's victory was of course a very popular one as the public had won a lot of money through his success. It is typical of racing
that Mr. Dewar should win the "Blue Riband" so early in his racing

career with a horse inherited from his uncle who had tried for so long to win a Classic without success. Three years previously Mr. Edgar Wallace had visited Lord Dewar's stud and had been shown Cameronian, then a foal. "He will win the Derby but I may not live to see it," remarked Lord Dewar. This was a rather curious statement to make as Cameronian's entry for the Derby would have become void under the rule then existing if Lord Dewar had died.

Cameronian was none the worse for his exertions in the Derby so it was decided to run him in the 1 mile St. James's Palace Stakes at Ascot on June 16th. Starting at 15–8 on, he gave a delightfully smooth performance, winning by three lengths from Trinidad, to whom he was conceding 7 lb., with the speedy Portlaw four lengths away third. This particular Royal Ascot meeting was memorable for the successes gained by horses that had run in the Derby. They were as follows, in the order in which the races were run: Queen Anne Stakes—Coldstream; Gold Vase—Pomme d'Api; Prince of Wales's Stakes—Sir Andrew; St. James's Palace Stakes—Cameronian; King Edward VII Stakes—Sandwich; Waterford Stakes—Abbot's Worthy; Cork and Orrery Stakes—Grindleton; Ribblesdale Stakes —Doctor Dolittle; and Hardwicke Stakes—Orpen. Fred Darling won five races at the meeting. At Epsom, besides winning the Derby and the Coronation Cup, he had very nearly won the Oaks as well, as Four Course, who stayed remarkably well for a daughter of Tetratema, was only caught close home by Brulette who beat her by a length.

Cameronian had stayed the Derby distance without difficulty and he now looked all set to win the Triple Crown, a distinction that had not been earned in peacetime since the triumphs of Rock Sand in 1903. The St. Leger, though, was to prove not merely a disaster for Cameronian, but a race that left in its wake suspicion, speculation and ugly rumour.

Having pleased in his preparation, it was hardly surprising that Cameronian started an odds-on favourite. Now normally he was an exceptionally placid individual but on this damp, chilly autumn afternoon he was in a condition of extreme excitement. Before the start he lashed out at Orpen, and as soon as the tapes went up he fought for his head as if he was demented. Not surprisingly, he had exhausted his strength long before the race was over. He was in fact stone cold before the final bend and finished an ignominious last.

The race was won decisively by Sandwich from Orpen and Sir Andrew.

Now if the favourite for a Classic event performed in similar fashion today, the stewards would immediately order a routine dope test to be taken. In 1931, however, stewards were less security-conscious and dope-conscious than their counterparts in modern times. Incredible as it may now seem, the Doncaster Stewards sat tight and did nothing. Of course it may be that stewards of that era were very reluctant to order dope tests, because the rules on doping that then existed were both stringent and potentially unjust, allowing little or no freedom for manœuvre on the part of the Stewards of the Jockey Club. If a horse was found to have been doped, it did not matter for disciplinary purposes whether the horse had been doped to improve its chance of success or to stop it from winning; the trainer concerned forfeited his licence. It would be easy to imagine the repercussions in the nineteen-thirties if a leading trainer, whose patrons included members of the Jockey Club, had become involved in a case in which a horse of his was found to have been doped.

More extraordinary even that the neglect of an obvious duty on the part of the Doncaster Stewards, was the cool attitude adopted by Darling. He calmly refuted any suggestion that the horse had been "got at" and contented himself with the observation that "there are many causes for a horse suddenly going wrong in this way and I put no sinister construction on the occurrence". Possibly there was a simple medical explanation for the fiasco, but none was ever given. Mr. J. B. Robertson, a veterinary surgeon of lofty reputation, offered the theory that the trouble was caused by a sudden diffusion of bacterial poison throughout the bloodstream. If that was indeed the case, the attack took place at a singularly unpropitious moment.

It must be emphasized that no proof exists that Cameronian was doped, but the situation would have been a great deal more satisfactory if some effort had been made to find out if he had been. At all events, he certainly had not been given one of those depressants that make the horse seem half-dead on the way to the start; if anything had been given to Cameronian, it had the result of hotting him up to such an extent that his chance was destroyed.

After the St. Leger, Cameronian's temperature was two degrees above normal. Full recovery was an extremely slow process and for nearly a year he ran a slight but persistent temperature. As a four-year-old he was nothing like right when he was third to Salmon Leap

and Goyescas in the Coronation Cup; and again when third to Rose
En Soleil and Hill Cat in the Ribblesdale Stakes at Ascot. He was
then rested and was almost back to his best when he reappeared in
the autumn. In the 1¾ mile Jockey Club Stakes at Newmarket he ran
most courageously to finish third, beaten a length and a head, behind
the St. Leger winner Firdaussi and a useful stayer called Gainslaw
who won the Gold Vase the following year. He was giving 12 lb. to
Firdaussi and 29 lb. to Gainslaw. A fortnight later he showed all his
old brilliance in winning the ten furlong Champion Stakes at Newmarket by four lengths from the Derby runner-up Dastur, to whom
he was giving 7 lb. The way he accelerated down the hill into the Dip
was a delight to see.

After the Champion Stakes, Cameronian was retired to the stud.
At his best he was undoubtedly a great horse and it is difficult not to
believe that he really ought to have won the Triple Crown. As a four-
year-old he only found his true form in the autumn and then ran
two races well worthy of a horse that had won the Two Thousand
Guineas and the Derby the season before.

At the stud, Cameronian failed to come up to expectations. The
best horse he sired was Scottish Union, who carried off the 1938
St. Leger and was second in the Derby to Bois Roussel. Cameronian
also sired Snowberry, the dam of the St. Leger winner and successful
sire Chamossaire. After eight seasons in England, Cameronian was
exported to South America but he did not do well there. He died in
1955.

Brantôme (1931)

The course of racing history in this century would have been very different if Blandford had actually died of the injuries he received as a yearling when some carthorses broke into his paddock at the National Stud, then at Tully, Co. Kildare. For a time his condition was critical and his recovery was so slow that at one point Sir Henry Greer, Director of the National Stud, offered him to the vet, who was attending the colt, as a gift. The offer was declined.

Blandford eventually recovered, but he could not go up to the Newmarket July Sales with the rest of the National Stud yearlings and instead was offered at the December Sales when he was bought by the Whatcombe trainer Richard Dawson, acting on behalf of himself and his brother Sam, for 730 guineas.

Blandford was a brown horse by the St. Leger winner Swynford out of Blanche, by White Eagle out of Black Cherry, by Bendigo. Blanche, one of the National Stud's original mares, never won herself but she was a half-sister to Cherry Lass, winner of the One Thousand Guineas and the Oaks. Besides Blandford, Blanche produced five winners and these included the Cesarewitch winner Seminole and Nun's Veil, a Friar Marcus mare that won three races and was grandam of the brilliant and temperamental Sun Chariot, winner of the One Thousand Guineas, Oaks and the St. Leger; and fourth dam of the Derby winner Santa Claus. Black Cherry could only win a £100 selling race but was an outstanding broodmare, her offspring winning forty-one races worth £28,383. She was a half-sister to Bay Ronald, sire of the mighty Bayardo.

Blandford was never an easy subject for Richard Dawson to train as he was a heavy-topped colt with indifferent joints. In fact he only ran four times, winning three races worth £3,839 and being narrowly beaten in the fourth. Dawson tried him very highly as a three-

year-old and declared him good enough to have won the Derby had
he been entered. After Blandford had won the 1½ mile Princess of
Wales's Stakes at Newmarket in 1922, he injured a tendon and this
terminated his racing career.

At the stud he proved during a career of no great length, since he
died suddenly at the age of sixteen, one of the greatest sires of this
century. Twice champion sire, he got four Derby winners—Trigo
(1929), Blenheim (1930), Windsor Lad (1934) and Bahram (1935).
In 1935, the year of his death, he was champion sire both in England
and France.

Opinions vary as to whether Bahram or Windsor Lad, the latter of
whom raced as a four-year-old whereas Bahram did not, was the
better racehorse; it is conceivable that both were inferior to
Brantôme, a son of Blandford who was one of the most brilliant
horses to race in France between the wars.

Foaled in 1931, Brantôme was bred and owned by Baron Edouard
de Rothschild and was a bright bay with four white feet, rather small
but beautifully made and full of vitality and courage. His dam
Vitamine was by the English-bred Two Thousand Guineas winner
Clarissimus out of Viridiflora, by Sans Souci II. Clarissimus, by the
Goodwood and Doncaster Cups winner Radium, was exported to
France after three seasons at the stud in England. He sired a lot of
winners there and his daughters did particularly well as broodmares.
Donatello II, sire of Alycidon and Crepello, and the unbeaten Pharis
were both out of mares by Clarissimus. Brantôme's dam Vitamine
also produced the Grand Prix de Paris winner Crudité, a daughter of
La Farina.

Trained by Frank Carter, Brantôme at two years of age was the
unbeaten winner of four races worth 394,055 francs. He showed that
combination of brilliant speed and unwavering stamina that was one
of his outstanding characteristics. His first appearance was in the
five furlong Prix de Martinvast at Longchamp on June 15th and this
he won without apparent difficulty. He then progressed to more
ambitious targets and carried off the French Two-Year-Old Triple
Crown by winning successively the Prix Robert Papin at Maisons
Laffitte in July, the Prix Morny at Deauville in August, and finally
the 1 mile Grand Criterium at Longchamp in October. In the Grand
Criterium he displayed stamina that justified belief in him proving a
top-class performer the following season over a mile and a half or
more.

As a three-year-old Brantôme maintained his unbeaten record yet in a sense his record was disappointing in so far as his victories did not include either the Prix du Jockey Club or the Grand Prix. He had started off in great style by winning the French Two Thousand Guineas, thereby proving he had retained his speed, and then the ten furlong Prix Lupin at Longchamp. Soon afterwards, though, he developed a cough that persisted to such an extent that he had to miss all his summer engagements. It was not until the autumn that he returned to the scene and he then delighted his admirers by showing that his stamina was on the same high level as his speed, winning the Prix Royal Oak, the French equivalent of the St. Leger, and the Prix de l'Arc de Triomphe. The Grand Prix that year was won by Admiral Drake whom Brantôme invariably beat wherever they met.

Both Brantôme and another great son of Blandford, Windsor Lad, winner of the Derby and the St. Leger, were entered for the 1935 Ascot Gold Cup run over $2\frac{1}{2}$ miles and English racegoers looked forward keenly to a battle royal between two outstanding horses of totally different type. As a four-year-old Windsor Lad was a magnificent specimen of the thoroughbred and looked powerful enough to carry a fifteen-stone man to hounds across Leicestershire. Brantôme, though in fact rather larger than he looked, was cast in a far less massive mould, and was somewhat light of bone below the knee. He hardly deserved, though, the description of "a mere polo pony" that one well-known critic bestowed on him when he appeared in the paddock at Ascot.

Unfortunately this much hoped-for duel never took place since Mr. M. H. Benson, the bookmaker who had acquired Windsor Lad after Windsor Lad's singularly unlucky defeat in the Eclipse Stakes, an event in which Smirke rode one of his rare bad races, elected to "chicken out", to use an inelegant modern expression. Deciding that prudence was the better part of valour, Mr. Benson declared that "My duty now is to see that Windsor Lad is not beaten before he retires to the stud." Mr. Benson's action, strongly criticized in racing circles, was, however, given the full support of Mr. Bob Lyle, racing correspondent of *The Times*. "Hardly a winner of that great and severe race has made a successful sire," pontificated Mr. Lyle, whose readability was not invariably equalled by his accuracy. In this case his enthusiasm for Mr. Benson's cause conveniently enabled him to forget Touchstone, Doncaster, St. Simon, Isonomy, Isinglass, Love

Wisely, Persimmon, Cyllene, William the Third, Bayardo and Solario.

Brantôme captured the imagination of the French racing world in the same way that Pharis did in 1939 and his early races in 1935 increased the esteem in which he was held. On May 1st he won the Prix Edgar Gillois run over 2 miles and 3 furlongs at Le Tremblay and eleven days later he triumphed in the $2\frac{1}{2}$ mile Prix du Cadran at Longchamp, the French equivalent of the Gold Cup. The field was a strong one and included the Grand Prix winner Admiral Drake as well as Cadmus, winner of the Prix du Conseil Municipal. Brantôme could hardly have won with greater ease and the delight of his thousands of admirers was augmented when it became known that he had established a new record for the race of 4 minutes 23·2/5ths seconds.

Brantôme's performance in the Prix du Cadran was all the more remarkable in that he had displayed such brilliant speed as a two-year-old, while at three years of age he had won a Classic race over a mile. His talent over extreme distances gives rise to speculation on what Windsor Lad and Bahram might have accomplished had their cautious owners permitted them to compete in the leading Cup races.

Evidently Brantôme was a horse that required plenty of racing to keep him up to the mark as Carter decided to start him in the Prix Dangu, run over $2\frac{1}{2}$ miles at Chantilly, only eleven days before the Gold Cup took place. While being led from his stable to the course, Brantôme broke loose from his lad and galloped away down the road. He successfully dodged the cars but he cast three plates and cut himself before he was recaptured. For four days he did no work at all and had to be given an anti-tetanus injection, the full effects of which are not always foreseeable. When he did begin to work again, he was clearly not himself and serious thought was given to abandoning the Ascot project. However on the Friday before the Ascot meeting began, he worked better and it was decided to let him take his chance. It was a bold and sporting decision, but clearly a risky one.

The weather at Ascot was damp and chilly, the going dead. Brantôme, favourite for the Cup at 13–8 on, sweated before the race on the flanks and between the thighs, but this was one of his normal characteristics when he ran and caused no concern to his owner and his trainer. Bouillon settled him down nicely and approaching the final bend he was nicely placed with Alcazar and Denver II behind the leader Tiberius. Once in the straight, spectators confidently anticipated a swift forward move by the favourite. Instead they saw Bouillon go for his whip and Brantôme unable to make the slightest response. Tiberius ran on strongly to win by eight lengths from Alcazar, with Denver II third. Brantôme finished a weary fifth. Baron de Rothschild accepted his bitter disappointment like a sportsman. "I suppose I should not have sent him over," he said, "but I knew that such a wide interest was taken in him and the Gold Cup that I wanted to keep faith with the English public."

In the early years of the century members of the English racing world were shattered to learn that their heroine Pretty Polly, unbeaten in fifteen races, had been defeated at Longchamp in the Prix du Conseil Municipal. Similarly, Frenchmen were incredulous when given news of Brantôme's defeat, and some, on being told that he had finished out of the leading three, insisted on ringing up London for confirmation. In England some unthinking critics declared that Brantôme had simply failed to stay, a rather futile judgment on a horse that had won the Prix de Cadran as he pleased in record time. The truth was that Brantôme's escapade, the stoppage in his work and the injection, combined to make him run stones below his true form. Confirmation for this is surely found in the fact that he finished behind Denver II, a French horse that was not in his class at all.

Probably Brantôme was never quite the same after Ascot. He did not run again till the autumn when he won the 1½ mile Prix de Prince d'Orange at Longchamp. His final appearance was in the Prix de l'Arc de Triomphe and in this he was only fourth to the three-year-old Samos, though he did once again finish in front of Admiral Drake. In extenuation of this defeat, it must be added that he was never the most placid of individuals and on this occasion he was thoroughly upset by the presence in the paddock before the race of a mare in use.

The stud career of Brantôme, who had won twelve races worth 2,048,302 francs, was sadly interrupted by the war, as after the fall of France in 1940 he was seized and taken to Germany. He was recovered after the war but it cannot be said that he proved a prolific sire of winners. However he sired two Grand Prix winners in Pensbury and Vieux Manoir. He was also the sire of Aurore Boreale, the dam of the Eclipse Stakes and Coronation Cup winner Tropique.

Aurore Boreale had been foaled in 1941 and won two races in Germany under the name of Vorderrisserin. Another daughter of Brantôme, Auld Alliance, bred by Lord Rosebery, was out of Iona, a half-sister by Hyperion to the Derby and Gold Cup winner Ocean Swell. She bred Tomy Lee, a son of Tudor Minstrel that won the 1959 Kentucky Derby. In 1971 Hamsin, winner of the Prix du Cadran, Rock Roi, winner of the Goodwood Cup and Doncaster Cup, and Hickleton, winner of the Queen Alexandra Stakes at Ascot, were all male line descendants of Brantôme.

Bahram (1932)

Winners of the Triple Crown, that insubstantial and purely honorary award for victory in the Two Thousand Guineas, the Derby and the St. Leger, have been few and far between in the twentieth century. Indeed they number only three in peacetime—Rock Sand in 1903, Bahram in 1935 and Nijinsky in 1970. At this rate of progression there will not be another before the turn of the century and, if we accept this as accomplished fact, then Bahram stands alone among twentieth-century Triple Crown winners as the one who went through his racing career undefeated.

Nevertheless, in spite of his distinction of Triple Crown victor and in spite of his unbeaten record, Bahram remains a horse who calls for a real effort of will by the critic not to underrate him. Few of his performances were spectacular or deeply impressive, and it is only too easy to point out that the horses he beat, at least in the Derby and the St. Leger, were undistinguished by Classic standards. He lacked glamour. It is necessary to remind oneself over and over again that his trainer Frank Butters, who had such brilliant horses as Fairway, Colorado and Mahmoud through his hands, considered Bahram the best horse he ever trained.

It was his indolence, the indolence that springs from complete self-confidence, that made Bahram so deceptive. Freddy Fox, who had the mount in most of his races, described him as the laziest horse he ever rode. And Butters wrote to his friend, the racing journalist Eric Rickman: "He would do just sufficient to win his races and was even less inclined to exert his real merit in his work at home. If it had been my custom to keep a trial book, nothing I could have noted in it would have shown the true Bahram, because no gallop ever tested him entirely."

Bahram was the second Derby winner owned by the Aga Khan

but the first he had bred, as Blenheim, who carried his colours to victory in the premier Classic race in 1930, had been bought as a yearling. The Aga Khan had been a lavish purchaser of bloodstock for ten years before Bahram was foaled, and it is one of the stranger ironies of thoroughbred history that Friar's Daughter, the dam of Bahram, was the acquisition that had cost him least. The yearling that he bought in 1922 included the "Flying Filly" Mumtaz Mahal, who cost 9,100 guineas, Diophon, who cost 4,000 guineas, and Salmon Trout, who cost 3,000 guineas. Friar's Daughter, way down at the bottom of the list, cost the paltry sum of 250 guineas at the Doncaster September Sales.

Mumtaz Mahal, Diophon, who won the Two Thousand Guineas, and Salmon Trout, who won the St. Leger, all became top-class racehorses. This could not be said of Friar's Daughter, who came out more than 2 st. behind Mumtaz Mahal when they were tried at home and gained her only success in a £168 two-year-old race over five furlongs at Alexandra Park. Friar's Daughter did not run after her first season, but she developed into a priceless broodmare. Of her thirteen foals no fewer than eleven won races in one part of the world or another. Apart from Bahram, the best of her offspring was the luckless Dastur, who finished second in each of the Triple Crown races but won the Irish Derby, the King Edward VII Stakes, the Sussex Stakes and the Coronation Cup by way of consolation.

The purchase of Friar's Daughter, who was actually knocked down to the Aga Khan's then trainer Dick Dawson, was an act of inspired judgment. She was lucky to have survived to reach the sale-ring as a yearling. Bred by Colonel F. Lort-Phillips in Pembroke-shire, a remote region of west Wales not normally associated with the breeding of high-class thoroughbreds, Friar's Daughter was by Friar Marcus, who had won the Middle Park Plate for King George V, out of Garron Lass, whose half-sister Plucky Liège afterwards produced the Derby winner Bois Roussel. Lort-Phillips sent her to the Newmarket December Sales as a foal, and there she was bought by Mrs. E. M. Plummer, of the Mowbray Stud, for 145 guineas. As soon as Mrs. Plummer got her home the filly developed a cold, went off her feed and then contracted pneumonia, and it was only Mrs. Plummer's devoted day and night nursing that saved her life.

That Friar's Daughter was reasonably well-bred was evident to the most casual student of her pedigree. Closer scrutiny revealed that she had the best of credentials as a prospective broodmare, for

5

St. Simon, arguably the greatest racehorse and sire of all time, appeared three times in the first four generations of her pedigree. This degree of concentration of a potent and beneficial influence is rare in the thoroughbred, and provides a ready explanation of the manner in which Friar's Daughter transcended her racing achievements when she went to stud. Bahram was the result of a mating with Blandford, the leading Classic stallion of the day and sire of the Derby winners Trigo, Blenheim and Windsor Lad.

Like his dam, Bahram was a delicate foal, and his lungs were affected by pneumonia when he was at the Aga Khan's Sheshoon Stud at the Curragh as a foal. Colonel Peacocke, who was the Aga Khan's stud manager and also a qualified vet, found him an excellent patient and he had fully recovered, and grown into a handsome colt, by the time he went into training as a yearling. He joined the Fitzroy House stable at Newmarket of Frank Butters, who had taken over the Aga Khan's horses after a violent disagreement between the Aga Khan and Dick Dawson in 1931. No sooner had he arrived at Newmarket, however, than a hitch occurred over naming him. At first the name of Bahman was submitted to the registry office, but this was refused by Weatherbys because there was already a horse called Barman and the name proposed was certain to cause confusion. So "Bahram" was substituted, and this name, with its romantic associations with "that great hunter" of Fitzgerald's *Rubaiyat*, was infinitely more suitable for one of the horses of the century.

Butters gave Bahram, whose exceptional long-term possibilities he had been quick to recognize, plenty of time to settle down, and delayed his first outing until the National Breeders Produce Stakes, then one of the most important and valuable two-year-old races in the Calendar, over five furlongs at Sandown Park on July 21st. Although Bahram's promise was obvious, he was not considered to be sufficiently tuned up to win at the first attempt, and the stable's hopes were centred on the Aga Khan's other runner, Theft, who had won the Windsor Castle Stakes at Royal Ascot. Theft, ridden by Gordon Richards, had to give Bahram 9 lb., but was heavily backed at 5–2, whereas Bahram was a forlorn outsider at 20–1. The favourite, at 13–8, was Duke John, who like Bahram was making his début, but was reported to have been showing wonderful speed with Dawson's string at Whatcombe. In the race Duke John ran very green and was soon out of the reckoning, and after half-way the Aga

Khan's pair drew away from the rest. Spectators were expecting the proven speed and experience of Theft to tell in the closing stages, but on the contrary it was Bahram who got the upper hand and beat his stable companion by a neck. Dick Perryman rode Bahram very gently, and the final impression was that he had more in hand than the judge's verdict suggested.

Bahram was saddled again for the Rous Memorial Stakes over six furlongs at Goodwood two weeks later, and this time there was no question of backers ignoring him. He started at 5–4 on, and won by a neck from the Racla colt, to whom he was conceding a stone. Next time out, in the Gimcrack Stakes at York at the end of August, he showed for the first time the reluctance to do more than was strictly necessary to win that was to become characteristic of him, and he made quite heavy weather of the task of beating Consequential by a length. The Boscawen Stakes at Newmarket on October 3rd, for which he had only two opponents and started at 10–1 on, presented him with no problems at all, but in his final race of the season, the Middle Park Stakes at Newmarket two weeks later, his laziness was again apparent and Freddy Fox had to rouse him in the Dip before he went away to beat Godolphin by two lengths, with Consequential three lengths away third.

Bahram's first campaign had brought him five victories and £11,758 in stakes. Moreover it resulted in him being placed top of the two-year-old Free Handicap with 9 st. 7 lb., 1 lb. more than each of his two stable companions Theft and Hairan. He had made excellent physical progress since his first race, and this progress continued through the winter so that he emerged as a three-year-old of tremendous power and quality. In his early days a rather weak and sparse tail had detracted from his looks, but this filled out during the winter so that he was a bay thoroughbred of flawless appearance when he ran in the 1935 Classic races. Nor was he a difficult horse to train, as he never put on much superfluous flesh and did not require any specially vigorous work to prepare him for the big occasions. Like many other great horses, he had marked idiosyncrasies. Apart from his indolence, he had a very good opinion of himself and revelled in the adulation of the racecourse crowds. He liked to show off, whenever he found the opportunity, by leaning against a wall and crossing his forelegs.

Butters had intended to give Bahram a race in the Craven Stakes at Newmarket two weeks before the Two Thousand Guineas, but on the Saturday before the Craven meeting the colt was off his feed and had a slight temperature, so the plan was scrapped. Theft, on the other hand, won the Greenham Plate at Newbury from Robin Goodfellow. Bahram was not the only notable competitor for the Guineas that year who had no preliminary outing. Another was Lord Derby's Bobsleigh, who had created a very favourable impression by his easy victory in the Richmond Stakes at Goodwood the previous year. Bobsleigh was superbly bred by Gainsborough (winner of a wartime Triple Crown in substitute races at Newmarket) out of the Oaks winner Toboggan, though his pedigree was suggestive of excellence over middle distances rather than a mile. Nevertheless Bobsleigh was made favourite for the Guineas at 7–4, with Bahram next in demand at 7–2 and Theft at 11–2. In the race Bobsleigh dwelt a little at the start and was always struggling, and in the last two furlongs the Aga Khan's pair had matters to themselves just as they had done in the National Breeders Produce Stakes the previous July. This time, however, Bahram's superiority was more decisive, and he was in command from the Dip all the way through the last furlong of rising ground to the winning post, which he passed one and a half lengths in front of Theft, with Sea Bequest two lengths away third, and Bobsleigh two lengths further behind in fourth place.

Bahram had won with the authority of an absolutely top-class colt. He was not to run again before the Derby, but when Bobsleigh reappeared in the Newmarket Stakes a fortnight after the Guineas and won running away it looked as if Bahram was going to have a real fight on his hands at Epsom. Unfortunately Bobsleigh went lame soon afterwards and had to be scratched, and the consequent poverty of the opposition to Bahram was exposed by the fact that the Aga Khan's Hairan, who had been trounced by Bobsleigh in the Newmarket Stakes, was made second favourite at 5–1. The Aga Khan was also represented in the Derby by Theft, who was by the short-running Tetratema and so had only faint hopes of staying one and a half miles. Bahram was a firm favourite, as he was fully entitled to be, at 5–4.

Derby day dawned wet and cheerless. The weather improved after mid-morning and the sun was shining by time of the race, when the course had absorbed the rain so well that the going was fast. As the race unfolded it became apparent that misfortune was a bigger threat to Bahram than any of his opponents. He was drawn number 3 near the inside of the field of sixteen, and at the notorious elbow two furlongs after the start he was in danger of being shut in. Fox, growing alarmed at the turn events were taking, called to Harry Wragg, who was just in front of him on Theft, to let him up. Knowing that Fox was on his own mount's more fancied stable companion, Wragg promptly pulled out and allowed Bahram to come through. It was all plain sailing after that. Bahram moved forward relentlessly in the straight, mastered Field Trial a quarter of a mile from home and forged ahead to beat Robin Goodfellow with complete authority by two lengths. Field Trial was third and Theft, who stayed surprisingly well in view of his breeding, was fourth.

The manœuvre which had let Bahram out of the pocket was only too obvious to the watchers on the stands, and after the race the Stewards summoned Harry Wragg before them and asked for an explanation. Wragg readily admitted what he had done, and the Stewards then drew his attention to Rule 139, which stated: "Every horse which runs in a race shall be run on his merits, whether his owner runs another horse in the race or not." They cautioned Wragg, and added the warning that any similar offence in future would be severely dealt with.

Bahram was in action again in the St. James's Palace Stakes over the Old Mile at Royal Ascot. He was in his most lackadaisical mood and, although he never looked like getting beaten, he did not exactly shine as he scrambled home by half a length from the second-class Portfolio. It was hardly the kind of performance expected of a dual Classic winner and an 8–1 on chance.

The second half of the summer of 1935 was dry and hot, and with it came a coughing epidemic. Bahram began to cough in the middle of August, just as Butters was leaving on a trip to Normandy to inspect the yearlings bred at the Aga Khan's studs there. While he was away from home the trainer received daily reports that Bahram was still coughing but had no temperature. When he did shake off the attack the colt had to miss the race planned for him at Hurst Park. But he had lost little condition, and Butters was able to produce him at Doncaster perfectly fit to run in the St. Leger. The epidemic, on the other hand, had whittled down the St. Leger field so that Bahram had only seven opponents. There was however an alarm the day before the race when Freddy Fox, who had ridden him in all his races that year and in three of his five races as a two-year-old, had a crashing fall in a selling race and suffered such severe concussion that he was unable to ride again that season. Charlie Smirke was given the mount in his place and made no mistakes, riding Bahram out with his hands and heels after taking the lead two furlongs from the finish to beat Solar Ray by five lengths.

The St. Leger was Bahram's last race. There was talk of him being started for the Champion Stakes, but the idea was quietly dropped. It is fair comment that he earned his reputation cheaply. The other three-year-olds of 1935 were a sub-standard lot once Bobsleigh went out of circulation. Yet he won three of the most important two-year-old races besides the Triple Crown, proving himself a champion over distances from five furlongs to $1\frac{3}{4}$ miles, and there is no gainsaying the opinion of his trainer, who had an experience of top-class horses unsurpassed in his time, that he was never extended either at home or on the racecourse.

Bahram ought to have stayed in training as a four-year-old, ought to have been pitted against the best horses of another age group in order to establish his real merit. But the lure of a 500 guineas covering fee, the top fee in those days, was too strong for his owner to resist, and Bahram found himself at the Egerton Stud, Newmarket, for the 1936 season.

The story of Bahram's stud career is a sorry one. In 1940 the Aga Khan, beleaguered in Switzerland for the war years, sold him to an American syndicate headed by Alfred G. Vanderbilt and James Cox Brady for £40,000. Years afterwards the Aga Khan defended the sale of Bahram and his other Derby winners Blenheim and Mahmoud by saying that he needed the money to keep himself and his family during the war years. The American syndicate, disillusioned by Bahram's lack of quick success as a sire in the United States, sold him to an Argentine syndicate after the 1945 stud season for a sum reputed to be 130,000 dollars. He died in Argentina in 1956.

During his brief period at stud in England Bahram sired three top-class horses—the Two Thousand Guineas winner Big Game, the St. Leger winner Turkhan and the Coronation Cup winner Persian Gulf. Big Game and Persian Gulf both became top-class sires. In the United States his progeny began to win races in large numbers after he had departed to the Argentine, where he never really settled down. It is clear that the changes in climate and environment involved in his travels from England to the United States and from the United States to Argentina were beyond his powers of adaptation. If Bahram had remained in the British Isles his beneficial influence on the breed might have been immeasurably great. It is sad but true that, in the final computation, the record of his splendid achievements is clouded by the thought of what might have been.

Mahmoud (1933)

Only four greys have won the Derby since its inception in 1780. They are Gustavus (1821), Tagalie (1912), Mahmoud (1936) and Airborne (1946). By far the most distinguished of these four was Mahmoud, who not only won the Derby in record time, a record that still stands today, but was subsequently a highly successful sire in the United States.

Mahmoud was bred and owned by the late Aga Khan and was by the Aga Khan's first Derby winner, Blenheim, a son of Blandford, out of Mah Mahal, a grey by the wartime Triple Crown winner Gainsborough out of the famous Mumtaz Mahal, by The Tetrarch.

Mumtaz Mahal was unquestionably one of the most brilliant two-year-olds seen on an English racecourse this century, and like her sire, she captured the imagination of the racing public. Known as "The Flying Filly", she won all her races her first season bar the last, the Imperial Produce Stakes at Kempton. She had been a bit off-colour before that event, but it was reckoned that her superiority was such that she could win this rich prize even if perhaps a shade below her best.

It was a risky decision, and to make the filly's task harder, the Kempton course rode heavy after overnight rain. To the consternation of her admirers, she was worn down and beaten by half a length by Mr. A. de Rothschild's Arcade, a colt to whom she was conceding 7 lb. As a three-year-old she barely stayed six furlongs but was third in the One Thousand Guineas. She finished her career by victories in the King George Stakes at Goodwood and the Nunthorpe Stakes at York.

Mumtaz Mahal's daughters tended to atone for being indifferent performers on the racecourse by success at the stud. Mumtaz Begum, the dam of Nasrullah, conformed to this pattern and so did

Mah Mahal, the dam of Mahmoud. Mah Mahal won a single minor event and dead-heated in another of comparable insignificance, these modest successes earning the meagre total of £380. Besides Mahmoud, she bred Mah Iran, who won five races and became the dam of the Eclipse Stakes and Prix de l'Arc de Triomphe winner Migoli: and grandam of that superlative grey filly Petite Etoile, whose victories included the One Thousand Guineas, the Oaks, and the Coronation Cup (twice).

Mahmoud was bred in France and was foaled in 1933 at the Haras d'Ouilly, where Mah Mahal was visiting Pharos. From there he went to St. Crespin and, after weaning, to Etrehan, where the Aga Khan's yearling were usually reared. In August 1934 the Aga Khan sent a draft of yearling to be sold at Deauville. This draft included two colts by Blenheim, Mahmoud and Vanbrugh. Fred Darling wanted to buy one of the two for Mr. J. A. Dewar and preferred Mahmoud, but the reserve was so high that he contented himself with Vanbrugh. Mahmoud failed to reach his reserve and was sent to Newmarket to join Frank Butters's stable.

Mahmoud's first race was the five furlong Spring Stakes at the now defunct Newmarket Second Spring Meeting in May. He was still backward and accordingly featured among the "25–1 others". The race proved a total fiasco. Windsail, one of the co-favourites, gave a lot of trouble at the starting gate. When at last the gate went up, not all the horses started and the starter, Captain Allison, at once signalled that it was not a start. The jockeys on the horses that had started could not see this and unfortunately the man in the middle of the course, who could hardly have failed to see the warning flag, failed lamentably in his duty and took no action at all except to get out of the way. Most of the runners, Mahmoud included, completed the course but as there had been no start, the race had to be re-run. The majority of the horses, Mahmoud among them, were withdrawn and the field was reduced from fourteen to four—three that had never started and one that had finished the course.

Mahmoud, after this rather futile episode, began to make improvement and his next outing was the five furlong New Stakes at Royal Ascot. Staring at 10–1 in a big field of eighteen, he ran a race full of promise for the future to finish third, beaten half a length and three lengths, behind Miss Dorothy Paget's Bossover colt, later named Wyndham, and Allensford. Among the unplaced competitors was Vanbrugh.

5*

The following month Mahmoud and Vanbrugh met again, this time in the six furlong Exeter Stakes on the July Course at Newmarket. Mahmoud was receiving 4 lb., and favourite at 11–10, he won smoothly from Vanbrugh by three lengths. The pair met for a third time in the six furlong Richmond Stakes at Goodwood and Mahmoud gave ample proof of his continuing improvement by giving his rival 9 lb. and finishing four lengths in front of him.

The Richmond Stakes had shown that Mahmoud was one of the best two-year-olds in the country and he started favourite for the six furlong Champagne Stakes at Doncaster, in which among his opponents were the Bossover colt and a very promising youngster called Abjer that carried the colours of M. M. Boussac. Making all the running, Mahmoud won by three parts of a length from Abjer with the Bossover colt two lengths away third. It is true that the Bossover colt was hampered by Abjer in the closing stages, but he was under strong pressure at the time and the result was certainly not affected.

The same three colts met in the six furlong Middle Park Stakes at Newmarket in October. Mahmoud, who started favourite at 11–8, was on this occasion ridden by Smirke in place of Fox who had partnered him on previous occasions, Fox having been laid low by a crashing fall at Doncaster in September. Unfortunately Mahmoud lost ground at the start—at least two lengths, possibly rather more. He recovered the lost ground rapidly, slightly too rapidly in fact, and was in front racing down to the Dip, but the effort had taken too much out of him and in the end he was third, beaten two lengths and a head, to Abjer and the Bossover colt.

In the Free Handicap Mahmoud and Abjer were both given 9 st. 6 lb., 1 lb. less than the top weight Bala Hissar, a colt of the Aga Khan's that had won the Dewhurst Stakes. In general the critics, while recognizing Mahmoud's merits, found it difficult to visualize him as a likely winner of the Derby. Some thought he was lacking both in substance and in scope for future development; others, that there was too much sheer speed in the bottom half of his pedigree to entertain the probability of him ever becoming a top-class middle distance horse.

Mahmoud grew very little during the winter and as a three-year-old he stood no more than 15 hands 3 inches. In colour he was a very light and distinctive grey, while one of his more notable characteristics was his typical Arab-like head. He possessed plenty of power behind the saddle and a beautiful light action, eminently suitable for firm ground.

His first racecourse appearance in 1936 was in the 1 mile Greenham Stakes at Newbury on April 1st. He had to concede from 3 lb. to 16 lb. to his nineteen opponents and the going was heavy. Well placed early on, he ran out of steam in the last two furlongs and eventually finished fifth to his stable companion Noble King, who was receiving 13 lb. This failure seemed to many to confirm the view that he was a non-stayer, and some doubted his ability to last even a mile, let alone a mile and a half. The fact is that he was quite unsuited to the going and furthermore he was still an appreciable distance from attaining his physical peak. Those who knew him best were not unduly dismayed by his defeat.

The Aga Khan ran both Bala Hissar (Smirke) and Mahmoud (Donoghue) in the Two Thousand Guineas, Bala Hissar starting at 8–1, Mahmoud at 100–8. Midstream and Mahmoud were both rather unruly at the start and when the gate went up, Mahmoud lost a length. This in fact suited Donoghue as he planned to ride a waiting race on Mahmoud, believing, as did many others, that the grey might have difficulty in staying the stiff Rowley Mile.

Approaching the Bushes, Thankerton, Mahmoud and Pay Up were virtually in line with Rhodes Scholar hard on their heels. This was not precisely what Donoghue had intended. He had in fact tucked Mahmoud in behind his stable companion Bala Hissar, but Bala Hissar, who proved to be an extremely moderate three-year-old, compounded all too quickly and in consequence Mahmoud was uncovered sooner than Donoghue wanted.

Coming down into the Dip, Mahmoud dashed into the lead and he started the ascent to the winning post half a length ahead of Pay Up. Immediately, though, Pay Up put in a most resolute challenge. Both horses battled on with exemplary courage but Pay Up finished just the stronger to win a great race for Lord Astor by a short head. It is arguable that if Mahmoud could have been held up a little bit longer, he would have won. The fact that he was beaten after leading a furlong out did nothing to weaken the view that he did not really stay.

Pay Up was favourite for the Derby at 5–1. Second favourite at 6–1 was the Aga Khan's Taj Akbar, who was partnered by Gordon Richards and who had won over the course in April before proving his stamina by a victory in the Chester Vase. Mahmoud, ridden by the ever-confident Smirke, always at his best on the big occasion, was easy to back at 100–8. Taj Akbar was the smallest colt in the race, but Mahmoud was only taller than him by a quarter of an inch. The going, and this was to prove a very important factor, was as hard as a moneylender's heart.

There was some trouble at the start largely due to the antics of Abjer, the unfortunate Thankerton being kicked on the knee, while his jockey, Burns, received a painful blow on the mouth from another horse's head. When at last the gate went up, Carioca was the first to show in front but he was soon headed by Bala Hissar. At the top of the hill, though, Thankerton dashed into the lead and headed for home flat out, as if the winning post was a furlong away and not five.

At Tattenham Corner Thankerton was half a dozen lengths clear of Bala Hissar, and Mahmoud was lying about sixth. Thankerton showed not the slightest hint of weakening and Smirke had to make a swift decision. He had planned to hold Mahmoud up for a late run but now he felt the situation surely demanded a change of tactics and accordingly he set off in hot pursuit of the leader. With two and a half furlongs to go, he gave Mahmoud a single tap with the whip and Mahmoud at once bounded forward. Simultaneously Thankerton faltered. The result was, that with a quarter of a mile still to go, Mahmoud, the supposed non-stayer, was leading the field. For one very nasty moment Smirke thought he had made his effort too soon but Mahmoud showed not the smallest tendency to stop, and skimming over the hard ground with his light action that was so per- fectly suited to the conditions, he went on to win with the utmost ease by three lengths from Taj Akbar who never got close enough to put in an effective challenge. Thankerton was third, less than a length behind Taj Akbar. Thus the Aga Khan owned both the win- ner and the runner-up, an achievement in the Derby equalled only by the Duke of Bedford (1789), Lord Grosvenor (1790), Lord Jersey (1827) and Colonel Peel (1844).

There were some distinctly red faces after the race among those who had declared that Mahmoud would be quite unable to stay the distance and had no hope of winning at all. That redness tended to deepen when it became known that Mahmoud had won in the record time of 2 minutes 33·4/5ths seconds. This was 8·1/5th seconds faster than the great Persimmon's time on hard ground in 1896; no less than 26·1/5th seconds faster than the time taken by the famous Flying Dutchman in 1849.

The probability is that Mahmoud's time will never be beaten. In his era the Epsom track, after a dry spell, was liable to be very hard and bare and in some places bore a striking resemblance to the Cromwell Road. Nowadays the course is more carefully tended, and what with the heavy peat dressing and the lusher growth of grass, conditions may never again be as favourable for sheer speed as they were in Mahmoud's year.

Whether in fact Mahmoud was a genuine mile and half horse is a matter of opinion. Of course he had the great good fortune to find conditions entirely to his liking and advantage. Undeniably, he made brilliant use of the opportunity that came his way.

At the Royal Ascot meeting Mahmoud took the field in the 1 mile St. James's Palace Stakes but he had not fully recovered from his Epsom exertions and was well and truly trounced by a good horse in Rhodes Scholar, who was receiving 7 lb. and who had been prevented by sore shins from running in the Derby.

In August Mahmoud was afflicted by contagious acne, an infection commonly known as "heel-bug". His St. Leger preparation was interrupted at a vital stage but he nevertheless faced the starter at Doncaster. Smirke nursed him carefully and the pace was anything but a fast one, but nevertheless he failed to stay the distance and finished third to Boswell and Fearless Fox with the hot favourite Rhodes Scholar unplaced. Though defeated, Mahmoud had at least gained the by no means common distinction of having been placed in the first three in all the three Classic events for colts.

Mahmoud was still perfectly sound but the Aga Khan never liked keeping his best horses in training as four-year-olds and the grey was retired to the stud at a fee of 300 guineas. In 1940, though, he was sold for export to the United States for £20,000. The Aga Khan was of course entitled to his own views on the outcome of the war and to dispose of his bloodstock as he thought fit. He did the British bloodstock industry, however, a marked disservice by selling to the United States all his pre-war Derby winners, for Bahram and Blenheim were sold to the United States, too, Blenheim for £45,000, Bahram for £40,000.

Before he left England, Mahmoud sired Majideh, who not only won the Irish One Thousand Guineas and the Irish Oaks, but also became dam of the Oaks winner Masaka. In America Mahmoud proved an outstanding success as not only did he sire many winners, but his daughters proved admirable broodmares. He headed the sires list there on one occasion and he was also second once and third once. His best winners included First Flight, Monsoon, Mighty Story, Snow Goose, Vulcan's Forge, Mount Marcy and Oil Capitol. He was retired from stud duties in 1958 and was in his thirtieth year when he was found dead one morning at the C. V. Whitney Farm, Lexington, Kentucky.

War Admiral (1934)

The larger-than-lifesize bronze statue of Man o' War dominates a wide tract of the blue grass lands of Kentucky. Set on a granite plinth in the centre of a two-acre park, ringed with pin-oaks and sycamores, this memorial to America's greatest thoroughbred is an object of pilgrimage for thousands of horse-lovers every year. Man o' War, who died in 1947 at the age of thirty, is buried beneath the statue. Two of his most successful sons, War Admiral and War Relic, have been honoured by burial beside him. War Admiral, the subject of the present study, was easily the best racehorse he ever sired and, if lacking the panache and the brillance of Man o' War himself, was undoubtedly one of the genuine "greats" of American Turf history.

Samuel Doyle Riddle, the owner of Man o' War, was one of the most bizarre eccentrics ever to become deeply involved in the affairs of the Turf. He was completely besotted with the excellence of his champion. Man o' War was given a birthday cake with twenty-one candles on his twenty-first birthday, and when he died "Big Red", as the horse was nicknamed, was laid in state for three days in his stallion box at Faraway Farm, adjoining the memorial park. The local undertaker received the most extraordinary commission of his life, which was to build a coffin big enough to hold the massive thoroughbred and lined with satin in the black and gold Riddle racing colours. On the day of the funeral the coffin, covered by flowers and wreaths sent by admirers all over the United States, was loaded on a hearse and taken in solemn cortège to his resting place.

All this sentimental extravagance was harmless. The baleful aspect of Riddle's infatuation was the jealous hoarding of Big Red's services as a stallion. Man o' War was virtually a private stallion. He was confined to twenty-five mares a season, mostly Riddle's own mares and those of his nephew-by-marriage, Walter Jeffords. As this selfishly restrictive policy was accompanied by some capricious and often highly fanciful prejudices about the kind of mares suited to him, the wonder is that Man o' War did sire a horse as good as War Admiral in addition to numerous other top-class performers and that, a quarter of a century after his death, he was still very much a force to be reckoned with in international Classic breeding.

A large share of the credit for the breeding of War Admiral was owed to Jeffords, who bought War Admiral's great grandam Bathing Girl, then in foal to Swynford's brother Harry of Hereford, for 4,000 dollars to send to Man o' War in his first covering season in 1921. Bathing Girl bred nothing of note when mated to Man o' War and Annette K, the foal by Harry of Hereford, was unplaced in the only race in which she took part. However the purchase began to pay a worthwhile dividend when Annette K was mated to Man o' War and produced War Glory who, in September 1933, won the Lawrence Realisation over 1 mile 5 furlongs at Belmont Park, the American race corresponding to the St. Leger.

Annette K was small, measuring less than 15 hands 1 inch. The year before she was mated with Man o' War she visited Sweep and the produce was a filly Brushup, who when fully grown was an inch smaller than her dam. Brushup appeared on the racetrack three times, but could not overcome the disadvantage of her pony size. Nevertheless Riddle, who had bought Annette K privately from Jeffords, decided to keep Brushup for stud. Harrie B. Scott, who managed Faraway Farm at the time, had persuaded Riddle that Brushup was an ideal mate for Man o' War, because Man o' War was a scion of the male line of Australian, while Sweep combined the male lines of Bonnie Scotland and Eclipse (by Orlando and not to be confused with American Eclipse or the original English Eclipse foaled in 1764). Bonnie Scotland, Australian and Eclipse were all imported from England about the middle of the nineteenth century and by the nineteen-thirties the male lines they founded were among those with the longest history of continuous development on the North American continent.

This was just the kind of romantic notion likely to appeal to Riddle. He adopted it with such enthusiasm that he repeated the mating, after the initial experiment, no less than five times. These five subsequent matings resulted in five fillies, of whom one never

Plate 16 Cameronian

Plate 17 Brantôme

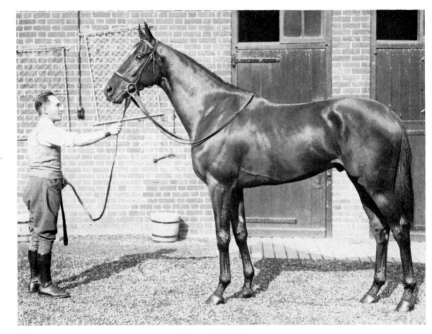

Plate 18 Bahram

Plate 19 Mahmoud

Plate 20   War Admiral

Plate 21   Sun Chariot

Plate 22 Bernborough

Plate 23 Citation

ran, three ran but failed to gain even a place, and one gained a single success at two years of age. There was no magic in the mating. But it did pay off, and at the very first time of asking, by producing a horse of the consummate ability of War Admiral.

War Admiral had the advantage of being trained by George Conway, who had been assistant to Louis Feustal in the days when the latter had charge of the preparation of Man o' War. Conway was appointed head trainer to Samuel Riddle's Glen Riddle stable in 1925, and in this capacity had had more sons and daughters of Man o' War through his hands than any other man. Thus he was thoroughly versed in all the idiosyncrasies of the Man o' War tribe. This was to prove an asset of decisive importance as the career of War Admiral developed.

War Admiral made his début at Havre de Grace, within easy reach of Riddle's training quarters on the eastern shore of Chesapeake Bay, on April 25th, 1936, and was successful. He then moved north to New York and won his second race at Belmont Park a month later. On June 6th he made his first appearance in "Stakes" company when he was third, two and a half lengths behind the winner Pompoon, in the National Stallion Stakes, and then finished second, one and a half lengths behind Fairy Hill, in the six furlong Great American Stakes. These defeats proved that he did not excel in precocious speed, but they showed equally that he was within measurable distance of the best of his generation in this respect. Pompoon went on to win that key race in the two-year-old championship, the Belmont Futurity, and Fairy Hill was the future winner of the Santa Anita Derby.

War Admiral was a victim of the coughing epidemic which swept through the eastern states in the summer of 1936, and was out of action for nearly three months after the Great American Stakes. When he returned to the track for the Eastern Shore Handicap at Havre de Grace on September 19th he met Maedic, who had won five consecutive "Stakes" races at the Saratoga meeting. Maedic was set to concede 8 lb. to War Admiral, a task which was altogether too much for him. Although he was drawn in the outside position in the field of fifteen, War Admiral was taken into the lead by his rider Charley Kurtsinger directly after the start and made all the running to win easily by five lengths, with Maedic unplaced. This performance earned War Admiral top weight for his final race as a two-year-old, the Richard Johnson Handicap at Laurel on October

10th, and he was beaten into second place, one and a half lengths behind Bottle Cap.

If War Admiral's two-year-old campaign had been unsensational, it had revealed him as a colt of solid merit with three victories, two seconds and a third to show from six starts. He was allotted 8 st. 9 lb., 5 lb. less than the top weight in the Experimental Free Handicap compiled by John B. Campbell, the official handicapper for the New York Jockey Club. He had not too wide an ability gap to bridge in order to become a champion as a three-year-old, and bridge it he did in no uncertain fashion. Before long it became evident that he had inherited many of the characteristics of his sire, not least the fire and the impatient temperament which made Man o' War such a redoubtable thoroughbred. But the influence of Man o' War was not exclusive. From Brushup he had inherited not only his brown colour, in contrast to the glowing chestnut coat of Big Red, but also his small stature. When fully grown he measured only 15 hands 2 inches, more than a hand less than Man o' War, and it was this limitation of physical size and scope which may be held to account for the difference between the sublime brilliance that put Man o' War with St. Simon, Ormonde and Ribot in the category of "all time greats", and the less egregious excellence of War Admiral.

Yet if the saying "a good big 'un will beat a good little 'un" has a fair degree of validity over the whole field of thoroughbred activity, the old saw received no endorsement from the three-year-old campaign of War Admiral. Like Hyperion, Northern Dancer and others before and after his time, War Admiral proved that a great little 'un will always beat the merely good big 'un, and he was invincible with eight wins from eight starts in his second season. He opened his campaign on April 14th with an effortless victory in an overnight race over six furlongs at his local track, Havre de Grace. The race was part of his preparation for the Chesapeake Stakes over eight and a half furlongs on the same track ten days later, when he gave the first sure sign that he had trained on into something out of the ordinary by jumping off in front and drawing steadily further ahead to win by six lengths from Court Scandal and Fairy Hill. As Court Scandal had won the Flamingo Stakes, then the most important race in Florida, and Fairy Hill the Santa Anita Derby, there was no denying the high merit of War Admiral's victory. Riddle was so elated that he made up his mind to break with his custom of omitting the Kentucky Derby from the programme of his best three-year-olds.

Even Man o' War had been held back from participation in America's premier Classic race at Churchill Downs, but happily War Admiral was given the opportunity to secure the Triple Crown honours which were denied to his illustrious sire.

The stunning performance of War Admiral in the Chesapeake Stakes had so captured the imagination of the racing public that there was a record crowd, estimated at 70,000 and including the Vice-President John Garner, on Derby day. War Admiral started favourite at 8–5, supplanting the winter favourite Pompoon whose stamina was under suspicion at that stage, in spite of the fact that he again was drawn on the outside of the field. This could have been an acute disadvantage because there were twenty runners but, as in the Chesapeake Stakes, War Admiral cancelled the disadvantage by his combination of impetuosity and quickness into his stride. Having taken an early lead, War Admiral was steadied by Kurtsinger, but drew further ahead gradually as he rounded the last turn and won, without being seriously challenged, by one and three-quarter lengths from Pompoon. Pompoon stayed the one and a quarter miles well enough—he finished eight lengths in front of the third horse Reaping Reward with the other runners far strung out—but was simply outpaced by a superior colt. War Admiral's time of 2 minutes 3·1/5th seconds was, up to that year, second only to the record of 2 minutes 1·4/5th seconds set up by Twenty Grand, also ridden by Kurtsinger, in the Derby six years earlier.

Pompoon made a closer race of it in the second leg of the Triple Crown, the Preakness Stakes at Pimlico a week later. War Admiral was the hot favourite at 2–5, with Pompoon, who had done a fast trial in mid-week, next in the betting at 5–1. The behaviour of War Admiral at the start was becoming worse with every appearance in public but, fractious though he was, he got away in front once more from a position on the outside of the field. Kurtsinger settled him about a length ahead of the main body of the field and made no attempt to cut across to the inside. In a shrewd tactical move, Wayne Wright shot Pompoon through on the rails at the turn into the straight, and in a few strides was racing neck-and-neck with the favourite. It was a close run thing throughout the last half furlong, but the issue was not really in doubt. Wright was plying his whip freely, whereas Kurtsinger was merely brandishing his to keep War Admiral going, and in the end War Admiral's margin of a head did not reflect his superiority truly. His time was only just outside the track record, and the other runners trailed in far behind Pompoon.

The scene shifted to New York for the last leg of the Triple Crown, the Belmont Stakes three weeks later. This was the occasion of War Admiral's most unruly display at the start. The 10–11 favourite, he allowed his eagerness to be off to get quite out of hand, dragging a starter's assistant through the gate repeatedly and causing a delay of eight minutes. Fortunately the officials were more patient than he was, and a fair start was achieved in the end. Caught half off balance, War Admiral leapt forward, stumbled and, as he struggled to recover, sheared through the wall of the hoof of the off-fore foot with his hind foot, cutting away a piece an inch square. Blood spurted from the wound with such force that his belly was sprayed with it. However the horse can have felt little in the heat of action. He moved up to and past the leaders in a few strides and was three lengths clear after a quarter of a mile had been covered. None of his opponents was able to reduce his lead, and he passed the winning post with the same margin to spare from Sceneshifter. Vamoose was ten lengths further back in third place and Pompoon, failing to stay and perhaps jaded by his previous defeats, was a distant fifth.

His Belmont Stakes victory, gained in adversity, was War Admiral's finest performance. His time of 2 minutes 28·3/5th seconds equalled the American record for one and half miles, and broke by one-fifth of a second the track record set up by his sire in the Jockey Club Stakes seventeen years earlier. The reverse of the coin was that his explosive over-eagerness at the start could easily have cost him the race and, if he had been in the hands of a trainer less skilful and experienced than George Conway, his career might have been in ruins. Conway had to give him four and a half months rest after the Belmont Stakes while a new hoof was grown. During this period a new star, the year older Seabiscuit, had captured the attention of the racing public. Seabiscuit had begun racing in the most humble circumstances. He ran fifteen times as a two-year-old before he gained his first success, and for the whole of that year and most of the next he was competing in claiming races. Then he was bought for 8,000 dollars by Charles S. Howard, who had made a fortune as distributing agent for General Motors in California, and began a meteoric rise to fame. He carried all before him in California in the spring of 1937, then moved east to win such important races as the Brooklyn Handicap, the Massachusetts Handicap and the Continental Handicap, and earn the status of a popular hero.

After War Admiral had returned to action with an easy victory over the good older horse Aneroid in a small race at Laurel on October 26th, the talk in racing circles was all of a meeting between the Triple Crown winner and Seabiscuit. The prospect had immense appeal, for War Admiral could be billed as the representative of the purest racing class and Seabiscuit as the protagonist of the aspiring equine middle classes steeled in the fire of handicap competition. There were hopes that the meeting would come about in the Washington Handicap over $1\frac{1}{4}$ miles on October 30th, but the image of Seabiscuit was tarnished somewhat when he was withdrawn after heavy rain had softened the track. War Admiral profited from his absence to give weight and a beating to other good older horses, and expectations of a meeting that year had to be abandoned when, four days later again, War Admiral won the inaugural running of the Pimlico Special and retired into winter quarters at Glen Riddle Farm.

The Pimlico Special was one of the most dramatic races in which War Admiral was involved. That winning was considered a mere formality for him was shown by the fact that he started at odds of 1–20 but, after his usual display of bad manners had caused him to lose ground at the start, he found himself sandwiched between Masked General and War Minstrel. He was badly buffeted, dropped back behind the leaders and seemed to be faced with inevitable defeat when he came under the whip half a mile from the finish. Masked General approached the last turn with a commanding lead but, happily for War Admiral, ran wide and became unbalanced. Hugging the inside rail, Kurtsinger drove War Admiral through the gap for all he was worth, and War Admiral responded with spirit to win, quite decisively in the end, by two lengths.

Considering that he was conceding 28 lb. to Masked General and was having his third race within nine days, War Admiral had acquitted himself in the manner of a champion and was fully entitled to a rest. He had not been beaten as a three-year-old, had proved himself unquestionably the best of his age and had outclassed reputable older opponents. There could be no demur when he was voted "Horse of the Year".

The demand for a match between War Admiral and Seabiscuit revived in the spring of 1938 when both horses showed that they had kept their form. Seabiscuit campaigned successfully in California, War Admiral in Florida. War Admiral won a small race over seven furlongs at Hialeah on February 19th, and the Widener Handicap, the principal race of the meeting, two weeks later, when he carried 9 st. 4 lb. and conceded at least 13 lb. to each of his twelve opponents. The Belmont Park executive then stepped in with a proposal for a match between the two horses to be held on Memorial Day, May 30th. The match was to be over $1\frac{1}{4}$ miles for 100,000 dollars, winner take all. Both sides accepted, but shortly before the date Howard withdrew Seabiscuit, declaring that the horse was suffering from knee trouble and was in no condition to race. A week later War Admiral, who had not run for three months, turned out for the Queen's County Handicap, and gained his eleventh consecutive victory by beating the Suburban Handicap winner Snark and the Metropolitan Handicap winner Danger Point, to each of whom he was conceding a good deal of weight, with plenty in hand.

The Queen's County Handicap came at the beginning of a triumphant summer campaign which was marred only by an upset in the Massachusetts Handicap at Suffolk Downs, in which he could finish only fourth behind the three-year-old Menow. This defeat was explained by the fact that he was trying to give weight away all round in fetlock-deep mud. At Saratoga he won in succession the Wilson Mile, the Saratoga Handicap and the Whitney Stakes over $1\frac{1}{4}$ miles, and the Saratoga Cup over $1\frac{3}{4}$ miles, leading all the way on each occasion. He then moved on to Belmont Park and gained another easy victory in the Jockey Club Gold Cup over 2 miles.

Despite earlier setbacks, plans for a match between War Admiral and Seabiscuit had been shelved only temporarily. The realization of the dream was not facilitated by the insistence of Howard that the match should take place only on a good surface, and the insistence of Riddle that the match should be started from a barrier, not from stalls. At last Alfred G. Vanderbilt, the vice-president of Pimlico, hit on a simple formula to solve the difficulties. The track was to provide only 10,000 dollars, in contrast to the 100,000 previously offered by the Belmont executive, but Howard and Riddle were to put up 5,000 dollars each, the whole stake to be forfeit on withdrawal. The race was to be run over nine and a half furlongs at Pimlico on November 1st, from a barrier start, and each horse was to carry 8 st. 8 lb.

After an early morning inspection of the track, the match was declared "on", and a capacity crowd assembled to witness the eagerly awaited clash of champions. Seabiscuit was ridden by

Georgie (Ice Man) Woolf, War Admiral by Charley Kurtsinger. As they went down to the start Kurtsinger was palpably nervous, whereas Woolf, true to his nickname, was completely self-possessed. When the starting flag fell Woolf, in an opportunist stroke, whipped Seabiscuit into the lead and Kurtsinger and War Admiral, accustomed to making the running, were obviously caught unawares. After half a mile Seabiscuit was four lengths in front. War Admiral closed the gap under the whip and got his head in front approaching the last turn, but he had never been on good terms with himself, and Seabiscuit regained the lead in the straight to win by three lengths in the track record time of 1 minute 56.3/5th seconds.

Much publicized matches between rival champions can be relied on to fire the enthusiasm of the crowds, but more often than not they end in anti-climax. Like the famous matches between Zev and Papyrus and between Nashua and Swaps, the War Admiral/Seabiscuit encounter failed as a spectacle and as a credible test of ability. In races of this kind too much depends on the tactical skill of the riders, and at Pimlico Woolf clearly outmanœuvred Kurtsinger. Moreover War Admiral had to come back from racing over two miles to nine and a half furlongs, while Seabiscuit had been racing over distances similar to that of the match.

On balance War Admiral was the better horse, as his odds of 1–4 at the start of the match indicated. Moreover he had proved himself invincible in the supreme tests of the thoroughbred as a three-year-old, whereas Seabiscuit was struggling in claiming races at the corresponding stage of his career. At least War Admiral's racing life did not end in humiliation. Two weeks after his defeat he scored a convincing victory in the Rhode Island Handicap and so was reinstated in popular esteem.

War Admiral was kept in training as a five-year-old, and on February 19th won a minor race at Hialeah in preparation for an attempt to win the Widener Handicap for the second time. Unfortunately he ran a temperature two nights before the big race and had to be withdrawn. Back in training in May, he injured a fetlock joint and, with no prospect of an early return to racing, he was retired to Faraway Farm.

War Admiral was a worthy stud companion, and later successor, to Man o' War. He was leading sire of winners in 1945, when his daughter Busher was "Horse of the Year". He was leading broodmare sire in 1962 and 1964. Although none of his sons was able to continue the dynasty, he exerted an enduring influence through his daughters, who bred such celebrities as the dollar millionaire Buckpasser and the Derby winner Never Say Die. In the late nineteen-sixties and early seventies he was emerging as one of the most effective means for channelling the influence of the mighty Man o' War to future generations, just as he had been the best of Man o' War's progeny on the racecourse.

Sun Chariot (1939)

The year 1942 saw the turn of the tide in the Second World War—the battle of Alamein, the Anglo-American landings in North Africa and the catastrophic German defeat at Stalingrad. In a more parochial sporting sense, it also brought the summit of the fortunes of the British National Stud and of King George VI as owner when Big Game and Sun Chariot galloped their way to victories in four of the five Classic races. Big Game won the Two Thousand Guineas and proved himself a colt of brilliant speed, but Sun Chariot won the One Thousand Guineas and the Oaks and then trounced the Derby winner Watling Street in the St. Leger to earn the right to be numbered with Sceptre, Pretty Polly and Petite Etoile as one of the truly great English-trained racemares of the twentieth century.

The National Stud came into being in 1916 when Lord Wavertree offered to the nation his entire stud of thoroughbred horses on condition that the Government purchased his breeding establishments at Tully in County Kildare and Russley Park in Wiltshire. For half a century, first at Tully and after 1942 at Gillingham in Dorset, it operated in parallel with the principal commercial studs supplying yearlings to the market until, with the move to brand-new quarters at Newmarket, its function was radically altered and it became an establishment for owning and boarding stallions only. The list of top-class or influential horses that it bred would be the envy of most studs, private or commercial. Its best products included Blandford, the foremost Classic sire of the period between the two world wars: the St. Leger winners Royal Lancer and Chamossaire; the Oaks winner Carrozza; the Grand Prix de Saint Cloud winner Hopeful Venture; and the two brightest jewels in its crown of achievements, Big Game and Sun Chariot.

From time to time the National Stud leased animals, mostly fillies but more rarely colts, that might be required back at the stud for breeding purposes at the end of their racing careers. The lessees were at first the "Yellow Earl" Lord Lonsdale, and later King George VI and his daughter Queen Elizabeth II. This system enabled the stud to retain such valuable horses as Big Game, who became a leading sire, Sun Chariot, Carrozza and Hopeful Venture; it also, ironically enough, helped to destroy the credibility of the stud as a supplier of high-class thoroughbreds to the yearling market and caused such a disastrous slump in demand for its products that a drastic change in policy became inevitable. But no presentiment of the eventual outcome was felt in 1942, and if any doubts about the wisdom of the leasing policy had been expressed at that climactic period of the war they would have been swept aside by the flood of patriotic emotion released by the sheer appropriateness of four Classic victories being placed to the credit of the nation and the monarch in a single season.

Like many great racehorses, Sun Chariot began inauspiciously. The practice was for the National Stud-leased horses to be trained by Fred Darling at Beckhampton on the Wiltshire Downs. Darling, who trained seven Derby winners, was one of the most gifted members of his profession, but he was also irascible and intolerant, and he felt that patience was out of place with moderate animals in the restricted conditions of wartime racing. So when Sun Chariot was backward and showed little sign of latent ability at the time he tried to slip some fast work into her in the early spring of 1941, he decided that she must be sent home to Tully. Fortunately, wartime conditions also required the issue of an export permit for the transport of a horse to Ireland and, a few days before this arrived at Beckhampton, Sun Chariot went well enough in a gallop to cause a rapid about-turn in the trainer's plans.

Big Game was much quicker to come to hand and, as the unnamed Myrobella colt, had run and won three times before Sun Chariot made her first appearance in the Acorn Plate, a five furlongs race for two-year-old fillies, at Newbury on June 6th. The stable jockey Gordon Richards had broken his leg just above the ankle when he was kicked at the start of a race at Salisbury a month earlier, an accident which put him out of action for the rest of the season. Harry Wragg stepped into his shoes as rider of the Beckhampton horses and as a result ended up as champion jockey for the only time in his career. Sun Chariot, who like Big Game was unnamed at that

stage in her career and was running as the Clarence filly, gave Wragg
an incident-free ride as she raced to victory two lengths ahead of
Trouble, an easy winner of her previous race at Salisbury, and the
favourite Perfect Peace, whose high reputation was justified by
subsequent events.

The considerable ability of Perfect Peace was demonstrated when
she and Sun Chariot met again in their next race, the Queen Mary
Stakes, a substitute for the normal Royal Ascot race and run at
Newmarket at the beginning of July. The Newmarket July course,
flanked on one side by the famous Ditch and on the other by the
dark mass of the Plantation, has a gentle downhill gradient for the
first half mile of the straight five furlongs, but has a sharper uphill
stretch for the last furlong to the winning post. Sun Chariot got
unbalanced quite early on, and did not begin to stride out properly
until she met the rising ground. She was really travelling in the last
hundred yards and got up in the last stride to beat Perfect Peace by a
short head. Perfect Peace had been in front a long way from home
and wandered a bit near the finish. As the race was run Perfect Peace
may have been unlucky to lose, but events before and after proved
that she was flattered by her proximity to Sun Chariot.

Sun Chariot had a ten lengths win over second rate opposition at
Salisbury at the end of July. Big Game won the substitute Coventry
Stakes at Newmarket on the same day as Sun Chariot won the Queen
Mary Stakes, and in August won the substitute Champagne Stakes
at Newbury by a short head after a terrific duel with Watling Street.
Darling decided that Big Game had done enough for the season after
the Champagne Stakes, and Sun Chariot was given the responsi-
bility of representing the stable in the Middle Park Stakes at
Newmarket on October 9th. Her opponents were the three high-class
colts, Watling Street, Ujiji and Gold Nib, but they caused her no
trouble at all. Watling Street threw away any chance he may have
had by losing several lengths at the start, and Sun Chariot beat
Ujiji easily by three lengths.

In the Free Handicap of 1941 two-year-old Sun Chariot was given
top weight of 9 st. 7 lb., 1 lb. more than Big Game—or 4 lb. more
taking sex allowance into consideration. At that stage Sun Chariot
was low but lengthy. She stood only 15 hands $2\frac{1}{2}$ inches, but had any
amount of scope and range, beautifully moulded quarters and
immense strength in her back, loins and hindlegs. Unfortunately she
also had an extremely nervous and irritable temperament. When

Gordon Richards resumed riding out at Beckhampton early in 1942, he found that Sun Chariot's mental approach had deteriorated sadly since the previous spring. She used to refuse to start in her gallops, spinning round and round in circles instead. Richards never knew whether he would be able to persuade her to work or not. When the time came for her to have her first outing in the Southern Stakes over six furlongs at Salisbury on April 25th Darling told Richards to keep her back well behind the leaders in the early stages and try to settle her down. The experiment turned out badly. As soon as Richards tucked her in on the heels of the leaders she dropped her bit and refused to take any further interest in the proceedings, with the result that she finished a poor third behind Ujiji, whom she had out-classed over the same distance in the Middle Park Stakes, and Mehrali. Richards concluded that Sun Chariot had a mind of her own and would brook no interference from her jockey. He let her have her own way in the rest of her races.

The Southern Stakes marked the nadir of Sun Chariot's career. The career of Gordon Richards also was at a low ebb. He was having great difficulty in getting going, and as the winners failed to come the more wolfish of the critics began to say that his accident had destroyed his nerve and judgment. Inevitably his confidence suffered. But at last the luck turned, as it was bound to turn. When she ran again at Salisbury in the seven furlong Sarum Stakes on May 2nd Sun Chariot, allowed to run her own race, won in style, and the two other Beckhampton stars, Big Game and the previous year's Derby winner Owen Tudor, gained easy victories in their respective races. The winners were flowing again for Gordon.

The two races for the Guineas were run on successive days, Tuesday and Wednesday, May 12th and 13th, and resulted in spectacular triumphs for the Royal owner, Darling, Richards and the two products of the National Stud. Big Game cantered in from Watling Street in the Two Thousand Guineas on the first day. On the second day Sun Chariot, though a little restive at the start, did nothing really wrong in the One Thousand Guineas, took up the running at half-way and raced away to beat her old rival Perfect Peace easily by four lengths. Even the normally impassive Fred Darling had a smile on his face as she returned to the winner's enclosure. Sun Chariot had behaved well at Newmarket, but she was becoming less and less tractable at home. She got on better with her lad Warren than with anyone else, and he was kept on her for most of her work. However there was one morning between the One Thousand Guineas and the Oaks when Gordon Richards had to ride her, and that was when the King, who had been prevented by public duties from seeing the One Thousand Guineas, came down with the Royal Family to see her work at Beckhampton. Sun Chariot was in her ugliest mood, and stubbornly refused to start. At last the head lad Templeton went behind her and gave her a tap with his hunting whip. Sun Chariot promptly took off and bolted into the middle of a ploughed field, where she went down on her knees and roared like a bull. In his reminiscences *My Story* Gordon Richards, commenting on the incident, wrote that he had seen a colt do this, but never a filly before. In the end Sun Chariot did consent to work, but she was a real handful that morning.

All the wartime Classic races, with the exception of the first two St. Legers, were run at Newmarket, so Sun Chariot had to return to the July course for the Oaks. She was unwilling to join the other runners and spoiled the starter's first three attempts to get them into line. She was facing the right way the fourth time and the starter let them go. But instead of moving off up the course she darted off to the left and lost lengths before she caught sight of the others streaming away into the distance and made up her mind to follow them. The start of the $1\frac{1}{2}$ miles race on the July course is out of sight from the stands behind the Plantation, so the spectators had no idea how Sun Chariot, a 4-1 on favourite, was faring. But to Gordon Richards the position seemed hopeless until Sun Chariot, her competitive instincts thoroughly aroused, began to overtake the rest of the field hand over fist. She went wide at the bend into the straight, but was galloping so resolutely that Richards did not try to stop her. She caught up the tail of the field with half a mile to go and began to pick off her opponents one after another. She reached the front going into the Dip, but then considered she had done enough and began to ease up. The gallant Afterthought was running on strongly, and Richards had to keep her going vigorously in the last furlong to win by a length.

Sun Chariot had made nonsense of the racing adage that you can give away weight but you can't give away distance. Her Oaks performance was one of the most extraordinary in Turf history, for Afterthought was a genuine top-class stayer. Sun Chariot was as demure as a choir girl when the King, in air force uniform, led her in, but at that moment neither he nor any of the spectators could have known how nearly her temperament had cost her the race.

Big Game was at 6–4 on to complete the big Classic double the next day but he faded in the last quarter of a mile and finished sixth behind Watling Street, Hyperides and Ujiji. It is tempting to comment that he let the side down, but that would be unfair, because he simply lacked the stamina to beat high-class opponents over one and a half miles.

Racing was regionalized in 1942. There were few valuable races for the best horses to aim at, and only a handful of Classic and other prestige races at Newmarket were open to horses from all the regions. After the Oaks there was only one worthwhile target for Sun Chariot, and that was the St. Leger run over 1 mile 6 furlongs and 150 yards on September 12th. As the autumn approached so did her behaviour improve, a phenomenon often found in fillies. She made no difficulties about starting in her gallops. For her final work Darling borrowed the $1\frac{3}{4}$ miles Barton gallop at nearby Manton and galloped her with her usual companions Massowa and Bakhtawar, who was a first rate four-year-old stayer. A fast pace was set, but in the last furlong Sun Chariot, ridden by Warren, sailed past Gordon Richards on Bakhtawar to win easily, a performance which left no doubt that she was in splendid trim for the St. Leger.

On the day before the St. Leger Bakhtawar was beaten by a short head and a head by Afterthought and High Table in the Jockey Club Cup, which redoubled confidence in Sun Chariot. The market on the St. Leger, however, preferred the winner of the Derby to the winner of the Oaks, because Watling Street was favourite at 2–1, while Sun Chariot was at 9–4. In the paddock Sun Chariot was cool, sensible and self-assured, and looked perfectly trained. The parade did not upset her, and she remained completely unperturbed when Watling Street, who had become a terror at exercise on Newmarket Heath, played up at the start. In the race, too, she was a model of deportment as she settled down at the rear of the field and tracked Watling Street. As Watling Street moved up so did she. Watling Street took the lead half a mile from home, but Sun Chariot was still cantering and went past him in effortless fashion when Richards gave her a little rein. Sun Chariot outclassed the best colts of her generation as she drew away to beat Watling Street by three lengths, with Hyperides five lengths further behind in third place. She must have been a great filly to beat the Derby winner and second so summarily, and Gordon Richards was adamant that she was much the best of her sex he ever rode. In the Free Handicap of three-year-olds she was allotted exactly the same weight as Big Game, which meant that she was considered his superior by 3 lb. after adjustment for sex allowance.

However wilful she may have been at times, Sun Chariot always had a wonderful constitution. She took all her work and all her races without turning a hair. On the other hand Big Game, who redeemed himself with a splendid victory in the Champion Stakes, was much more delicate and was distressed even after a fast gallop. Sun Chariot's temperamental improvement, so evident at the time of the St. Leger, persisted when she went to stud. She was easy to handle and was a model parent. Some critics have asserted that her breeding record was disappointing. It is true that she did not produce a Classic winner, but she did produce a high proportion of good class performers. She was barren three times, slipped her foal three times, and had one colt who died young. This left her with eleven surviving foals, of whom ten ran and seven won a total of eighteen races. The unbeaten Blue Train won the Newmarket Stakes; Gigantic won the Imperial Stakes; Landau won the Rous Memorial and the Sussex Stakes, and became a successful sire in Australia; and Pindari won the King Edward VII and the Great Voltigeur Stakes and was third in the St. Leger. Altogether, this was a record of which any mare could be proud.

Big Game, Sun Chariot's comrade in arms, also did notably well at stud. He was a good sire of winners, getting the Classic winners Ambiguity and Queenpot, and a better sire of broodmares. Like Sun Chariot, he remained the property of the National Stud until he died, again like her, in 1963. Indeed it is fair to say that seldom in the history of the thoroughbred can the antecedents and the careers of two brilliant horses have touched at so many points. Sun Chariot and Big Game were the same age, and they died within a few weeks of each other. They were both bred at the National Stud, and Dolabella, the grandam of Big Game, and Blanche, the great grandam of Sun Chariot, were in the original group of mares presented by Lord Wavertree to the nation. They went into training with Fred Darling at the same time, and were leased to the King. They were ridden by Harry Wragg as two-year-olds and by Gordon Richards as three-year-olds. They were assessed officially as being of practically equal merit in each of their racing seasons. They both won Classic races. They retired to the National Stud at the same time, and they both left a mark on the progress of the thoroughbred by their achievements there.

And if there are not coincidences enough in that catalogue, one more can be extracted from the pedigree of Sun Chariot herself. For when her sire Hyperion, the brilliant Derby and St. Leger winner of 1933, gained his initial success in the New Stakes at Royal Ascot as a two-year-old, the runner-up was none other than Nun's Veil, the grandam of Sun Chariot.

Bernborough (1939)

Bernborough, the pride of Australian racing in 1946, was one of the most extraordinary great racehorses ever to grace the Turf. In the early days of the thoroughbred, when horses had to carry heavy weights over long distances, it was accepted that a racehorse could not reach maturity until he was six years old; but many equine generations of selective breeding for precocity had changed all that and by the middle of the twentieth century, when Bernborough was foaled, an entire horse who had not thrust his way into the upper crust of flat racing competition by the time he was three or four was unlikely ever to get the chance to do so. Bernborough, whose amazing sequence of fifteen victories on leading Australian courses overlapped his six-year-old and seven-year-old seasons, put the clock back, albeit temporarily, about two hundred years.

Bernborough's tardy breakthrough may be attributed to two causes. One was his gigantic size—he stood 17 hands 1 inch when fully grown—which slowed down the development of strength and physical maturity: the other was the peculiar circumstances of his early career which had nothing to do with his potential as a racehorse but denied him proper outlets for his talents.

A bay horse bred by Mr. Harry Winten at the Rosalie Plains Stud in the Dalby district of Queensland, Bernborough was one of the first crop of foals by Emborough, who had been imported from England in 1938. Emborough was a product of the English National Stud and was by Gainsborough, a Triple Crown winner during the First World War, out of Embarras de Richesse by Phalaris. Embarras de Richesse was a granddaughter of Tillywhim, one of the most famous of the National Stud mares and the ancestress of the remarkable Levmoss, winner of the Prix du Cadran, the Ascot Gold Cup and the Prix de l'Arc de Triomphe in 1969. Emborough

6

was bought by the South Wales shipping magnate Lord Glanely, then one of the most lavish spenders at the yearling sales, for 1,500 guineas at the Newmarket July Sales in 1933. He did not come to hand quickly, but as a three-year-old won the Harewood Handicap over a mile at Doncaster and wound up the season by winning the Liverpool Autumn Cup under 6 st. 12 lb. He gained the most important success of his racing career in the Manchester Cup over $1\frac{1}{2}$ miles as a four-year-old.

On pedigree and performance Emborough could be adjudged just the type of horse to succeed as a stallion in Australian conditions. The credentials of Bernborough's dam Bern Maid did not look so promising. Her dam Bridesmaid, by the July Cup and Prix du Conseil Municipal winner Best Man, had been imported from England as long ago as 1907, but the family had still to achieve anything of note in Australia. Bern Maid herself was bred at the Hobartville Stud in New South Wales, but so little was thought of her that she was sold for the give-away price of $42\frac{1}{2}$ guineas as a yearling and was sent to Queensland. She showed no ability in the few races she contested and failed to make her name as a broodmare until, at the advanced age of eighteen, she produced Bernborough.

The early history of Bernborough was extremely involved. When he was a foal at foot he and his dam were sold at Oakey, in the Darling Downs, for 155 guineas, but they changed hands again later the same year for £140. Later again Bernborough was leased to the Queensland trainer J. Roberts, but the Queensland Turf Club, which controls the racing in Brisbane, refused to register the colt for racing purposes. The Club reserved to itself the right to ban horses without assigning a reason, and no official explanation of the exclusion of Bernborough was ever given. It was generally believed that the QTC authorities had doubts about the validity of the sales and the current ownership of Bernborough but, fortunately for the colt's career, the Downs and South-West Racing Association, based in Toowoomba seventy-five miles west of Brisbane and having the status of an independent authority, took a more lenient view of the transactions and raised no objection to registering him.

Thus Bernborough was confined to the so-called "bush meetings" at Toowoomba from two till five years of age. Prize money at that track was minimal. Victory in his first race, the Toowoomba Maiden Handicap over five furlongs, earned a prize of £10, and seven further victories and a second as a two-year-old and three-year-old brought in a total of £291. His two outings as a four-year-old were unsuccessful, but he returned to form with victories in the Toowoomba Spring Handicap over seven furlongs, the Toowoomba Flying Handicap over six furlongs and the Toowoomba Park Handicap over nine furlongs as a five-year-old. He was second once and unplaced four times the same season. By that time prize money had improved, and his three victories were worth a total of £840.

Bernborough carried 10 st. 3 lb. when he won the Toowoomba Park Handicap. After that his handicap mark went through the roof and he was set to carry weights up to 11 st. Clearly he had outgrown bush meetings in stature and ability and, on the expiry of the lease to Roberts, a decision was made to send him to Sydney for sale at public auction. While awaiting sale he was stabled with the Randwick trainer Harry Plant who, on giving him some work one morning, was astounded to find that he had clocked 1 minute 12 seconds for the distance of six furlongs. That fast time showed that Bernborough was no ordinary horse from a bush track, and Plant advised his patron, the Sydney restaurant owner Mr. A. O. Romano, to buy him, adding: "When you stop bidding, let me know, and I'll continue for myself." Romano took the hint and bought Bernborough for 2,600 guineas, a high price for a virtually unknown six-year-old horse in those days, but a price at which Bernborough was to prove a magnificent bargain. The Australian Jockey Club accepted the validity of the sale and Bernborough was registered for racing in New South Wales.

Bernborough made his New South Wales début in the Belmore Flying Handicap at Canterbury on December 8th, 1945—Australian horses have their official birthdays on August 1st—but encountered a lot of interference in running and finished unplaced. Exactly two weeks later he reappeared in the 1 mile Villiers Stakes at Randwick and gained the first of the unbroken chain of victories that were to come his way in a period of less than ten months. Athol Mulley, a leading Australian jockey who also rode winners in England, had the mount on Bernborough in the Villiers Stakes and was his constant partner in all his subsequent successes. By the end of January Bernborough had added victories in the Tatt's Club Carrington Stakes and the Australia Day Handicap to his initial success, and then he moved south for some of the rich races in Victoria.

Already Mulley and Bernborough had perfected a distinctive and sensational style of racing, which was to drop right out to the back of the field immediately after the start and swoop down on the leaders with a short, sharp, irresistible burst of speed at the finish. Bernborough's first race in Victoria, the seven furlong Caulfield Futurity Stakes, left the spectators rubbing their eyes in amazement. There were some high-class Victorian horses in the field including Versailles and St. Fairy, who the previous year had won the Caulfield Cup and been third in the Melbourne Cup, two of the most sought-after prizes on the continent. Ron Hutchinson, who was to have a distinguished career as a jockey in England but was then an aspiring local rider aged eighteen, made the running on True Law. Bernborough was practically tailed off in the early stages, but accelerated with devastating effect in the straight and swept into the lead to win by five lengths from St. Fairy. "He was still pulling so hard when he came past me a furlong from home that Mulley's legs were stuck out in front of him like a pair of shafts," said Hutchinson years later, adding: "That was the way he used to do it—come from a long way back and mow them down."

A week later he was set to carry 9 st. 13 lb. in the six furlong Newmarket Handicap at Flemington, the biggest sprint handicap in Victoria. On this occasion he dwelt at the start and gave himself a seemingly impossible task. With a quarter of a mile to run he was ten to fifteen lengths behind the leaders and his supporters were in despair. Then he slipped into top gear and was away. He flew past one rival after another as if they were standing still and, in one of the most dramatic finishes ever seen in the State, got up in the last stride to beat Four Freedoms, to whom he was conceding 2 st., by a short head.

Back in New South Wales, Bernborough continued on his victorious way in the Rosehill Rawson Stakes over nine furlongs, the 1¼ mile Chipping Norton Stakes and the one mile AJC All-Aged Stakes during April. In the meantime, the QTC, following the acceptance of Bernborough in other States, had finally lifted the ban and Bernborough was free to run on the principal courses in his native state. He was given a hero's welcome when he turned out for the Doomben Ten Thousand (T. M. Ahern Memorial Handicap) over 6 furlongs and 127 yards on June 1st, and lived up to his reputation by storming up in the last furlong to win the race in the same manner as he had the Newmarket Handicap. That victory incurred a 10 lb.

penalty for the Doomben Cup a week later, which meant that he had to carry 10 st. 11 lb. over 1 mile 2 furlongs and 198 yards, a distance longer than he had ever attempted before. But Bernborough once again was equal to the occasion and his familiar tactics enabled him to win from Tea Cake, to whom he was conceding 38 lb.

Bernborough opened his seven-year-old campaign with victories in the Warwick Stakes, the Tatt's Club Chelmsford Stakes and the Rosehill Hill Stakes on New South Wales tracks during August and September. His performance in the Hill Stakes, in which he gave 9 lb. more than the sex allowance and a beating to the six-year-old mare Flight, must rank as one of his best, because Flight was regarded as one of the best of her sex ever to appear on the Australian Turf and set up a new prize money earnings record for her sex of £31,429.

A return visit to Victoria in October brought him quick successes in two weight-for-age races, the mile Melbourne Stakes at Flemington and the nine furlong Caulfield Stakes at Caulfield. The second of those victories brought his winning sequence to fifteen and, although he had been allotted the crushing weight of 10 st. 10 lb., few followers of racing would consider the possibility of defeat in the Caulfield Cup, always one of the most hotly contested races in the Australian Calendar, the next Saturday. He had acquired an aura of invincibility and many punters followed him blindly, however short the odds, in the firm belief that a small profit was certain. His popularity was not based purely on form. He seemed to assert a complete mental dominance over his rivals, while his terrific speed, his superb physique, massive size and profile sharply chiselled like that of a Parthenon horse all combined to capture the imagination of the public.

Bernborough's fans flocked to Caulfield racecourse in their tens of thousands on Cup day. The print of 70,000 programmes was sold out well before the first race, and after the second race there were still long queues at the turnstiles waiting to get into the track. Most of those who did get inside were jammed in solid masses behind and under the stands and had to be content with listening to the race commentaries. The crowd was officially counted at 108,123 and so many of them believed in the ability of Bernborough to defy his great weight that he started a hot favourite at 7–4.

Disillusionment followed. From the start of the 1½ mile Cup race Bernborough was in trouble. Although he had overcome difficulties often enough in the past, this time he never looked like recovering and further interference on the last turn finally wrecked his chance. He did make some progress in the straight, but at the finish he was no nearer then fifth behind Royal Gem, Columnist, Two Grand and Carey, beaten by about three lengths by the winner. Royal Gem, a high class four-year-old who had previously won the important Toorak Handicap on the same course, carried 9 st.—24 lb. less than Bernborough.

Mulley had to face a storm of criticism for the way he had handled Bernborough. As one Australian writer understated it: "Nobody was much impressed with Mulley's riding." Certainly the jockey failed to ensure a clear run for his mount. Nevertheless Caulfield is a sharp tricky course, with a straight run-in to the finish of only 1 furlong and 140 yards. Since Bernborough's day the safety limit of the Caulfield Cup field has been reduced progressively and in 1970 was fixed at eighteen. Bernborough had no fewer than twenty-six opponents. It is clear that no very high degree of incompetence on Mulley's part was required to result in Bernborough, with his habitual style of running, getting boxed in and battered.

Whatever the rights and wrongs of the case may have been, Mulley was sacked from the job of riding Bernborough after the Caulfield Cup. Billy Briscoe was given the mount in the L.K.S. Mackinnon Stakes at Flemington a fortnight later, but the new partnership was ill-starred. Bernborough started at 5–1 on, but got no further than the last turn, where he faltered and stopped as suddenly as if he had been shot. He was found to have shattered the sesamoid bones in his near foreleg. His breakdown left a suspicion that the wear-and-tear of many hard races under heavy weights may have been taking effect by the time he ran in the Caulfield Cup, and that neither misjudgment nor interference may have been the main cause of his defeat in that race.

Fortunately the veterinary surgeons were able to save Bernborough. Towards the end of the same racing season an announcement was made that Romano had sold him to the Hollywood tycoon Louis B. Mayer, and he went to stand at Spendthrift Farm in Kentucky. He proved a successful sire. The best of his progeny, Berseem, won twenty-one races and 189,000 dollars. He also sired the top-class fillies Gainsboro Girl and Parading Lady, and many of his progeny excelled on grass in the United States. His son Hook Money did well as a sprinter and sire in England.

Bernborough was a great weight carrier—in this respect one of the greatest horses that have ever lived. His consistency, his powers of acceleration, his determination, his powerful and outsize frame, the strange twists of his career as it unfolded: all these aspects helped to make him a unique phenomenon among thoroughbreds. Mr. E. W. Wood, one of the vets who attended him after his leg injury, summed him up in this lapidary phrase: "When one looks at him and sees his splendid head with such a fearless eye, it is little wonder that he was a great horse."

Citation (1945)

Few thoroughbreds have been honoured by having their life-size statues on public display, and in this respect Citation is well worthy of his inclusion in the same category as Man o' War, Gladiateur and Hyperion. The bronze statue of Citation stands on a marble plinth in a lily pond behind the stands at Hialeah, and is a prominent feature of that exotic Florida track, along with the flamingo fountain, the aquarium, and the aviary of brightly plumaged tropical birds. It was at Hialeah that Citation opened the glorious three-year-old campaign that was to cause pundits to compare him with Man o' War himself, and to label him one of the two greatest American racehorses of the twentieth century. Although his later career tailed off to some extent as a result of injury, he now has a double claim to lasting fame: he was the last American Triple Crown winner and the first equine dollar millionaire.

The production of Citation was the supreme achievement as breeder of the baking powder tycoon Warren Wright and of Calumet Farm, the stud near Lexington in the blue grass lands of Kentucky which Wright built up during the nineteen-thirties and forties. Between 1936 and Wright's death in 1950 Calumet bred the winners of nearly 2,400 races and more than ten million dollars, and one of the few causes for regret was that his owner-breeder did not live long enouth to see Citation push his earnings above the million dollar mark the following year.

The decisive event in the making of the fortunes of Calumet Farm was the purchase of Bull Lea for 14,000 dollars as a yearling in 1936. Bull Lea was not quite top class on the racecourse. He won the Blue Grass Stakes, the Derby trial run at Keeneland, but was unplaced in both the Kentucky Derby and the Preakness Stakes. On the other hand there was no doubt about his class when he retired to stud at

Calumet, where he became one of the most successful sires of the century, heading the winning sires list five times and getting such progeny of rare excellence as Armed, Bewitch, Coaltown, Iron Liege, Hill Gail and Twilight Tear. At the Newmarket July Sales in 1941 Warren Wright bought, through the British Bloodstock Agency, the three-year-old filly Hydroplane for £2,940. Hydroplane had been of little account on the racecourse, and the best she had been able to do in six races was to be second twice in modest company, but her pedigree combined some of the best Classic strains of Lord Derby's stud, and she was by the Derby and St. Leger winner Hyperion out of the Oaks winner Toboggan. Three years later Hydroplane, to whose name the roman numerals II had been added for American registration, was mated to Bull Lea and as a result produced Citation, destined to become the finest of all Bull Lea's sons and daughters, on April 11th, 1945.

Citation was remarkably quick to mature. He was not a particularly tall horse, but was lengthy, deep through the heart and equipped with tremendously powerful quarters. His hocks were a little away from him in a manner characteristic of the progeny of Bull Lea, but there was no mistaking the strength and the propulsion in his hind-legs. A bay with black points and only two small rings of white above the coronets of his hind feet, he could not be called a thoroughbred of striking elegance, but he was a supremely efficient racing machine. Unlike Man o' War, who was a physical giant and imbued with superabundant nervous energy, Citation was neat in build and equable in temperament, using up no more energy than was strictly necessary for each of his racing tasks. His trainer Ben Jones considered his unusual intelligence one of his greatest assets. From the outset his physical maturity, his self-control and his intelligence, allied to brilliant speed, marked him out as a racehorse of quite extraordinary gifts.

His early racing was in Chicago, in the summer of 1947, when he won his first five races and set up a new course record of 58 seconds for five furlongs at Arlington Park. The only race of more than passing moment that he contested during this period was the Elementary Stakes. His first important venture was in the Washington Park Futurity on August 16th. The Calumet policy was to spare no effort to win important races, and Citation was accompanied in the Washington Park Futurity by his stable companions Bewitch and Free America. The filly Bewitch was just a little bit more precocious

6*

even than Citation, and it was she who was the winner by a length from Citation, with Free America a head away third, to give Calumet a notable one-two-three.

It was Citation's turn when he and Bewitch moved to New York for the Belmont Futurity, in which Bewitch was hampered in the early stages and could finish only third behind the colt, who won by three lengths from Whirling Fox. Citation went on to win another of the top two-year-old races, the Futurity at the Pimlico track in Baltimore, Maryland. With a victory in a minor race to eke out his earnings, Citation ended his first season with eight victories in nine races and a prize money aggregate of 155,680 dollars. Bewitch, with 213,675 dollars, was the highest earner among the 1947 two-year-olds, but Citation headed the colts in this respect. He was also given pride of place in the Experimental Free Handicap, in which the handicapper John B. Campbell allotted him 9 st., 3 lb. more than the next colts Better Self and Relic and 5 lb. more than Bewitch, the leading filly.

It was as a three-year-old that Citation came into his own and demonstrated his true greatness. The racing community was impressed not only by the manifest improvement in relation to his contemporaries which caused Campbell to reckon him 15 lb. superior to the next best at the end of the year, by his overwhelming victories in the Triple Crown Classic races (the Kentucky Derby, the Preakness Stakes and the Belmont Stakes), by earnings of 709,470 dollars which were a record for an individual horse in a single year, and by his unanimous acclamation as "Horse of the Year" in the voting conducted by Triangle Publications, but also by the marvellous vitality and constitution which enabled him to contest twenty races during a campaign which lasted from February to December and win nineteen of them. During that year alone he ran only one less than Man o' War ran in his whole racing career, covering two years, a quarter of a century earlier.

Most top-class American three-year-olds do not take on their seniors until after the Triple Crown series of Classic races is concluded in mid-June. Citation was thrown straight into the deep end of all-aged competition when, after only a brief winter intermission, he reappeared in the Ground Hog Purse over six furlongs at Hialeah on February 2nd and won rather cleverly by a length. Nine days later he again met his elders in the more important Seminole Handicap and again won by a length from Delegate, with his talented seven-year-old stable companion Armed in third place, covering the seven furlongs in the fastest time recorded at Hialeah that year. As he was not foaled until April 11th, he had thus beaten older horses twice before he was actually three years old.

After this unconventional but dramatically successful opening to his three-year-old campaign, Citation reverted to his own age group to gain easy victories in the Everglades Handicap and the Flamingo Stakes, the latter being a race with semi-Classic pretensions. He then moved north to Maryland where, at Havre de Grace on April 12th, he suffered his sole defeat of the year at the hands of Saggy in the Chesapeake Trial. Al Snider, who had ridden him in his previous races that year, had been drowned while on a fishing trip off the Florida Keys at the end of March, and Eddie Arcaro rode him for the first time in the Chesapeake Trial. However there was no suggestion that the handling of an unfamiliar jockey was responsible for the defeat, which was caused simply by the fact that he was carried wide by a tiring pacemaker on the final bend. Saggy got first run and Citation, though closing the gap at the finish, failed to catch him by a length.

Saggy was to make Turf history in one other respect. That was when, in the course of a generally undistinguished stud career, he sired Carry Back, the wonderful little Florida-bred colt who won the Kentucky Derby and the Preakness Stakes in 1961. There was no suggestion that Saggy might repeat his fluke Trial victory when he encountered Citation for the second time in the eight and a half furlong Chesapeake Stakes five days later. The public rejected the evidence of the Trial so unequivocally that Citation started at 5–1 on, odds that were justified when he won easily by four and a half lengths, with Saggy, who finished lame, in last place.

It was Citation who made the Turf history in the immediate future. Having won the Derby Trial at Churchill Downs, Louisville, at the end of April, he spent May and the first half of June securing the Triple Crown. For the Kentucky Derby he was joined by his stable companion Coaltown, who was rather overshadowed by the illustrious Citation during his three-year-old campaign but was a good enough horse to have won the Derby more years than he was beaten. The Calumet pair dominated the Derby situation to such an extent that no place betting was allowed on the race, and expectations were fulfilled when Citation won by three and a half lengths from Coaltown, with the rest of the field well behind. This was

Warren Wright's third Derby victory, as Whirlaway had won the premier Classic race for him in 1941 and Pensive in 1944.

Citation had an even easier time in the other two Triple Crown races, winning the Preakness Stakes by five and a half lengths and the Belmont Stakes by eight lengths. The Triple Crown programme is completed in five weeks, but Citation took so little out of himself when winning the Classic races that he was able to fit in the Jersey Stakes between the Preakness Stakes and the Belmont Stakes, winning this race by eleven lengths in record time for the $1\frac{1}{4}$ miles at Garden State Park in New Jersey.

From New York, where he won the Belmont Stakes, Citation moved west to Chicago, where he had one of his hardest races of the season to win the Stars and Stripes Handicap on July 4th. Although his margin was a decisive enough two lengths at the finish, Arcaro had to hit him with the whip several times, whereas he had required no vigorous urging in most of his races. The reason for this comparatively lustreless performance was probably that he pulled a muscle in his hip during the race, an injury which forced him to miss his planned engagement in the Arlington Classic, but he was back in action at the end of August to win a minor race and then the so-called American Derby at Washington Park.

Citation returned to New York to give two performances alike in their brilliance but contrasting in distance. First he won the Sysonby Mile, producing a sizzling burst of finishing speed to come from a position lengths behind the leaders to score in fast time, and then he was subjected to America's supreme test of stamina, the Jockey Club Gold Cup over 2 miles, which he won by seven lengths. Stamina was also at a premium in his next race, the 1 mile 5 furlong Empire City Gold Cup, which he virtually killed as an intended international race by a masterful style of winning highly discouraging to potential foreign challengers in the future.

The end of Citation's long and triumphant campaign was approaching. He would probably have been given a winter's rest after his walk-over in the Pimlico Special if he had not been within striking distance of the career earnings record of 918,485 dollars set up by Stymie in recent years. He was despatched to California in pursuit of the record, but early in December, after victories in two races, including the Tanforan Handicap, which took him within 50,000 dollars of Stymie's total, he developed osselet trouble and had to be sent home to Kentucky to be fired.

If Citation had been sent to stud at the end of 1948, as the large majority of horses would have been in the circumstances, he would have been acclaimed without reservation as one of the ten greatest racehorses ever to grace the Turf in any country. In terms of quality of performance, versatility, intensity of effort and duration, his three-year-old achievements were incomparable. But the Calumet policy-makers decided that he should be brought back to racing at all costs in an attempt first to beat Stymie's record and then to break the million dollar barrier. He was off the racecourse for the whole of 1949, while Coaltown came into his own and won twelve of his fifteen races, but was nearly fit by the end of the year and travelled to California with the rest of the Calumet horses for the opening of the 1950 season. On January 11th, just thirteen months after his last public appearance, he stepped back into the limelight with a victory in a six furlongs allowance race at Santa Anita.

So far so good, but subsequent events were to reveal unmistakably that his recovery of form was not complete and that, while still a top-class horse, he had lost his former supremacy over all other horses of his time. A long series of defeats followed his initial win. First he was beaten by the South American-bred horse Miche in an overnight handicap, then succumbed by a length to his stable companion Ponder in the San Antonio Handicap. The third horse in the race was Noor, who was to be his scourge for the next four months. Indeed the San Antonio Handicap was the only race in which Citation finished in front of his persistent rival. Their second meeting was in the Santa Anita Handicap over $1\frac{1}{2}$ miles on February 25th, when Noor, in receipt of 22 lb., won by a little more than a length. For their next meeting in the $1\frac{3}{4}$ mile San Juan Capistrano Handicap, which is the closing feature of the Santa Anita season, the weights had been adjusted in Citation's favour so that he had to concede 13 lb. This assessment resulted in one of the unforgettable duels of racing history. The two principals joined issue on the bend more than a quarter of a mile from home and were locked together, stride for stride and drawing ever further ahead of their struggling rivals, all the way up the straight. At the winning post only the camera could separate them, and the photograph showed that Noor had prevailed by a nose.

The San Juan Capistrano was the climax of the rivalry of the two horses. Thereafter Noor asserted himself more definitely. In the Forty Niners Handicap at Golden Gate Fields on June 17th the difference in the weights was reduced to 5 lb., but Noor won by a neck; and in their final encounter in the Golden Gate Handicap a week later Noor actually had to give 1 lb. to Citation but gained his easiest victory of the series, crossing the finishing line with three lengths to spare.

The Citation versus Noor series provoked a great debate. Was Noor improving all the time, or Citation suffering a progressive decline? As Citation was second on all four occasions and the relative changes in the weights were obtained by Noor moving up in the handicap rather than Citation moving down, it is reasonable to deduce that Noor was on the upgrade. This explanation made sense to those who had known him racing in England, for he was a gangling, immature colt when he was third to My Love in the 1948 Derby. Strong supporting evidence for this view is that Noor broke the track record when he won the Santa Anita Handicap and established new world record times in his remaining three races against Citation.

Nevertheless it is difficult to escape the impression that Noor gained a psychological domination over his famous opponent, and that Citation mentally accepted Noor's superiority after their epic duel in the San Juan Capistrano Handicap. Citation suffered other reverses that year, but he himself was still capable of breaking a world record, as he proved when he won the Golden Gate Mile on June 3rd in 1 minute 33·3/5th seconds.

Citation had a sprained fetlock after the Golden Gate Handicap and had to be sent home to Calumet. This was another obvious opportunity to retire him, for he had passed Stymie's earnings total. However he was still more than 60,000 dollars short of the million goal, and Warren Wright, who died before the end of the year, had expressed a strong wish that he should become a millionaire if possible. So Citation was nursed back to soundness again, and was in action once more at Bay Meadows, California, on April 18th, 1951, when he was third in a six furlongs allowance race. From then on he struggled towards his million dollar goal almost as laboriously as the celebrated Australian horse Tulloch struggled towards his £A100,000 target ten years later. At last, in June, he struck a rich vein of form which enabled him to wind up his racing career in a blaze of glory with three successive victories in the Century Handicap, the American Handicap and the Hollywood Handicap. His final success took him comfortably past the million mark, and, with his two famous stable companions of the same age, Bewitch and Coaltown, he retired to Calumet in state.

Seldom has any owner possessed three such great horses, all home-bred, of the same age at the same time. Although Calumet Farm continued to dominate the racing and breeding scene in the United States for another decade after the retirement of Citation, Bewitch and Coaltown, and was leading owner for the twelfth time in 1961, their joint careers really marked the summit of its achievement. In 1947, when Citation and Bewitch were the champion two-year-olds of either sex, Calumet was not merely the first owner ever to earn a million dollars in a single year but passed that mark by a massive 402,436 dollars—and proceeded to earn more than a million dollars in each of the next two seasons just for good measure.

It has been argued that Citation ought to have been retired when he had his first bout of leg trouble at the end of his exceptionally strenuous three-year-old campaign, and that even if he had been allowed one comeback he ought to have been taken out of training for good when he went lame for the second time as a five-year-old. On the other hand the tendency of many other owners has been to retire their top-class horses too soon, seeking to avoid defeat at all costs and oblivious of the fact that the function of a thoroughbred is to race. Citation was a world-beater as a three-year-old. He was never a world-beater again after his first injury, but he was always a supremely courageous performer in top flight competition, and he never gave any overt sign of loss of will-to-win. His last three races revealed him in exuberant victory mood and surely justified the protraction of a racing career which embraced thirty-two successes and only one failure to reach the first three in forty-two starts.

Much of the credit for the egregious success of Calumet Farm as owner and breeder may be attributed to the direction of Warren Wright, who applied the same thoroughness, the same detailed planning, and the same rigorous control to his thoroughbred as to his business affairs. But all the planning skill in the world could not guarantee that Bull Lea, purchased for racing, would prove a great stallion and sire Citation, Bewitch and Coaltown. Nor could the same planning skill prevent Bull Lea, a marvellous begetter of winners, from being a poor sire of sires, so that the supremacy of Calumet was being undermined just as it appeared to be most secure.

Unhappily Citation, like other top-class racing sons of Bull Lea, was relatively a failure at stud. He did sire a Classic winner in Fabius, who won the Preakness Stakes. He did sire ten other "Stakes" winners and the earners of 3·5 million dollars. These figures give an air of respectability to his stud record. But William Robertson exposed the underlying inadequacy of the figures when he pointed out in Citation's obituary notice in *Thoroughbred Record* that whereas Citation's runners had average earnings of 16,000 dollars, the mares who produced those runners had offspring from matings to other stallions who averaged 25,000 dollars. In relation to opportunity, Citation did not come to scratch as a stallion.

Citation will always be remembered as a racehorse who at three showed brilliance worthy of comparison with that of Ormonde plus a durability really beyond compare. He will be remembered as a top-class racehorse who made not one, but two successful comebacks after injuries that might have ended his career. He will not be remembered as the founder of a dynasty.

Abernant (1946)

Only in Great Britain do sprinters enjoy a status amounting to an estate of the thoroughbred realm. Even in the United States, where precocious speed is cultivated to a degree unknown elsewhere and six furlong races for horses of all ages abound, older horses are expected to run a mile or a furlong or so more in order to force their way into the big leagues, and are consigned to an inferior grade if they cannot do so. In Great Britain the sprinter, the horse who excels at five and six furlongs and is unable to race effectively at longer distances, is accepted and honoured in his own right, and the category of sprinter embraces some of the famous names in Turf history.

Among sprinters few horses have ever achieved a supremacy to compare with that of Abernant, or have conveyed a stronger sense of greatness in the context of the thoroughbred population as a whole. His trainer Noel Murless once described Abernant as one of the best horses he had ever trained, and this was high praise indeed from the man who developed the brilliance of Petite Etoile and prepared the Derby winners Crepello, St. Paddy and Royal Palace. He was beaten in only three of the seventeen races he contested, and there were extenuating circumstances in each case. In the vast majority of his races his superior speed and class settled the issue within the first few hundred yards.

Bred by Major (later Sir Reginald) Macdonald-Buchanan of Cottesbrooke Hall in Northamptonshire, Abernant was sent into training at the celebrated Wiltshire stable, Beckhampton, as a yearling in the autumn of 1947. A big change was impending at Beckhampton at that time. The choleric Fred Darling, who had trained seven Derby winners there, was about to retire on grounds of ill-health and to be succeeded by Noel Murless, a man in his middle thirties who had made a name for himself by his skill in sending out horses from his small stable at Hambleton, near Thirsk, to take on and often to beat the representatives of the powerful stables in the south. That year he had won the Stewards Cup, the most coveted sprint handicap of the season, at Goodwood with Closeburn.

It is no easy transition for a trainer to adjust his methods from the second-class animals that made up the strength of the Hambleton stable to the animals of Classic breeding and aspirations that gave the Beckhampton stable its distinctive character. Murless showed his professional genius by carrying on precisely where Darling had left off, and was leading trainer in his very first season at Beckhampton. Although his most resounding triumphs came after his subsequent move to Warren Place, Newmarket, his ability to extract the best from horses of the highest class was apparent from his earliest days at Beckhampton.

Indeed Murless was within a foot or so of landing the Guineas double in his first season at Beckhampton, when Queenpot won the One Thousand Guineas and The Cobbler was beaten by a head by My Babu in the Two Thousand Guineas. While Queenpot and The Cobbler were taking care of the stable's interests in the shorter Classic races, an exceptionally talented team of two-year-olds was preparing to carry on the good work. At the end of the season the Beckhampton colts Abernant, Royal Forest and Faux Tirage occupied three of the first four places in the two-year-old Free Handicap, and Murless was responsible for no fewer than five of the leading twenty two-year-olds.

While Abernant carried the colours of Major Macdonald-Buchanan, Royal Forest was owned by his wife, the daughter of the late Lord Woolavington, a wealthy whisky distiller who had been one of the principal Beckhampton patrons in the period between the two world wars. For most of the season Royal Forest had slight priority over Abernant in the esteem of their trainer because he was Murless's Derby hope for 1949; but events were to prove that Abernant was the more dependable colt and, whereas Royal Forest was able to finish only fourth behind Nimbus in the Derby, Abernant finally gained recognition as one of the greatest sprinters of all time.

Abernant made his first public appearance in the Spring Stakes over five furlongs at Lingfield on April 16th. Some horses seem to know instinctively what is required of them from the moment they set foot on a racecourse; others take a little time to familiarize themselves with the strange surroundings. Abernant was one of the latter. At the start he screwed round when the tapes went up, and then wandered along completely off balance for most of the race. It was not until they were approaching the last furlong that Gordon Richards was able to get him on an even keel and racing in earnest. Then Abernant began to eat up the ground in spectacular fashion, but the winning post came one stride too soon for him and he failed to catch The Potentate, who had made all the running, by a short head.

The extent to which the form of a two-year-old first time out may be false is stressed by the fact that, whereas Abernant was given top weight of 9 st. 5 lb. when the Free Handicap was compiled seven months later, The Potentate was not good enough to be included at all. It is true to say that The Potentate would not have been able to live with Abernant in any of his races after the Spring Stakes.

The Lingfield race had taught Abernant all he needed to know. When he appeared next in the Bedford Stakes at Newmarket a month later he cantered away from his two opponents, and in the Chesham Stakes at Royal Ascot he shot from the gate like a bullet and made all the running to beat El Barq by five lengths. His first searching test was in the National Breeders Produce Stakes at Sandown Park in July, when he met Star King, who had won the three races in which he had run in scintillating fashion and by margins of at least five lengths. Odds of 2–1 were laid on Abernant, with Star King at 9–4 and the other three runners virtually ignored. Sam Wragg took Star King off in front from the start. After three furlongs Gordon Richards called on Abernant for his effort and the colt responded immediately with a burst of acceleration which took him to the front in a few strides. The race looked over, but Star King began to run on with determination under the whip and suddenly the struggle became really tense. Abernant edged to the right under pressure, and Star King got closer with every stride. Only the judge could tell which had won as they flashed past the post together, as the five furlong winning post is set at an awkward angle to the stands, and he awarded the verdict to Abernant by a short head.

The waiting tactics adopted at Sandown Park had not seemed to suit Abernant. Like many horses endowed with brilliant speed, he preferred to get on with the job and race in front from start to finish. From that time on he was allowed to run his races his own way and on only one other occasion, in heavy going at Royal Ascot as a four-year-old, was he waited with—and then was beaten.

Abernant was running over six furlongs for the first time when he reappeared in the Champagne Stakes at Doncaster in September. Only two horses opposed him, but one of them was Nimbus, who had run Royal Forest to a head in the Coventry Stakes at Royal Ascot. The race showed just what a horse of Abernant's brilliance can do to a reputable opponent. Abernant set off at such a blistering pace that Nimbus was taken off his legs and was soon sprawling, and Abernant raced home practically alone to win by six lengths.

Two weeks later Royal Forest gave his first sign of fallibility by suffering a sensational defeat by Burpham in the Clarence House Stakes at Ascot, for which he had been considered such a certainty that he started at 25–1 on. The plan had been for Royal Forest to wind up the season by running in the Middle Park Stakes, but the Ascot fiasco led to a revision and Abernant was substituted. Again Abernant had no more than two rivals, Decorum and the French colt Targui, owned by Marcel Boussac, and Abernant strode right away from Targui up the final hill to win by five lengths.

In the Free Handicap Abernant was given 1 lb. more than Star King, who won the Gimcrack Stakes after his Sandown defeat, and 4 lb. more than Royal Forest, who had repaired his damaged reputation by winning the seven furlong Dewhurst Stakes at the Newmarket Houghton meeting. Star King, incidentally, won three of his five races as a three-year-old and afterwards became one of the most successful stallions of all time in Australia, where he was leading sire of winners five times. In Australia he was re-named Star Kingdom.

Abernant had proved that he could stay six furlongs well as a two-year-old, but his ability to stay much further as a three-year-old was in doubt. His favourite style of running precluded long distance running, and his pedigree did not generate confidence in his stamina. It is true that he was by Owen Tudor, who had won a wartime Derby for Mrs. Macdonald-Buchanan in 1941, but the pedigree of his dam Rustom Mahal was strongly biased towards speed. Rustom Mahal was by Rustom Pasha out of the flying Mumtaz Mahal, whose parents, The Tetrarch and Lady Josephine, have been two of the most potent influences for pure speed in the modern thoroughbred. Students of breeding did not fail to note that the other brilliant but non-staying son of Owen Tudor, Tudor Minstrel, also traced his pedigree on his dam's side back to Lady Josephine. Abernant inherited his grey coat from The Tetrarch via Mumtaz Mahal and Rustom Mahal.

His ability to stay a mile was put to the test in the Two Thousand Guineas. He had an easy reintroduction to racing in the seven furlong Somerset Stakes at Bath on April 6th, when one of the other two runners was his stable companion Kinlochewe. Despite the all-round strength of the three-year-old team at Beckhampton, Abernant was so superior to the others in short distance work at home that Murless was able to make an early announcement that the grey colt would be the stable's only runner in the first of the Classic races. Star King, who had won the Greenham Stakes at Newbury, was considered his most dangerous rival at Newmarket, but Abernant started a hot favourite at 5–4. Gordon Richards adopted the tactics that suited him best, allowing him to bowl along in front from the start. The pace was too hot for most of his opponents and, as he began the descent into the Dip with Star King already beaten, it seemed that he was going to come home alone. But then Nimbus, ridden with nice judgment and grim determination by Charlie Elliott, started to whittle down his lead. Abernant was still clear in the Dip, but his stamina began to ebb away as he met the rising ground and in the last hundred yards Nimbus got to grips and finally inched in front to win a thrilling race by a short head. The third horse, Barnes Park, finished four lengths away.

A storm of criticism broke about the ears of Gordon Richards immediately afterwards. The critics asked two questions: why had he tried to make all the running on a doubtful stayer? and why had he been content to sit and suffer without drawing his whip when Nimbus was challenging? Gordon himself gave the answer in his autobiography *My Story*. Having recalled that some people had said that he should have won the Guineas on both The Cobbler in 1948 and Abernant the next year, he explained: "I think The Cobbler was unlucky not to win, but only because he could not have the advantage of the tuning-up which a preliminary race provides. But there is no excuse for Abernant, who would never have got so near to Nimbus again over a mile. They would both have petered out just the same if I had waited on them. They were just sprinters; wonderful sprinters, but with no real staying power, as was afterwards proved in each case. I stick to my contention that in straight races at Newmarket you must let your horse run at his own speed and not pull him about, providing of course that he is running well within himself and that you have the confidence to ride such a race."

The jockey's apologia received the whole-hearted endorsement of Noel Murless. Indeed the trainer went much further and claimed that Gordon rode one of his greatest races on Abernant in the Two Thousand Guineas. "If Gordon had moved a muscle on him in the last furlong Abernant would have fallen to pieces," said Murless years later. Gordon Richards excelled in the difficult art of riding on the Rowley Mile at Newmarket. He won one Classic there, the One Thousand Guineas on Queenpot, which he was not entitled to win, and he very nearly did the trick again on Abernant.

The ways of Nimbus and Abernant parted after the Guineas. Nimbus went on to win the Derby, but Abernant's capabilities were realistically assessed and he found his vocation in sprinting. He was not beaten again that season as he swept aside the opposition in the King's Stand Stakes, the July Cup, the King George Stakes and the Nunthorpe Stakes. The only cause for regret was that he did not meet Solonaway who, after winning the Irish Two Thousand Guineas, raided England to win the Cork and Orrery Stakes and the Diadem Stakes, both run over six furlongs at Ascot. There is no doubt that he was the best sprinter to run in England that year apart from Abernant, and an encounter between them would have produced fireworks.

Abernant ran through a similar programme as a four-year-old. He was hardly extended as he won the Lubbock Sprint at Sandown Park on his first appearance and after that the July Cup, the King George Stakes and the Nunthorpe Stakes. The only check to his progress occurred in the King's Stand Stakes at Royal Ascot. The going was soft at the end of a wet Ascot meeting and Abernant had to give 23 lb. (14 lb. more than the weight-for-age allowance) to the three-year-old Tangle, who had won his previous two races easily. Gordon Richards argued that it would be courting disaster in the conditions to adopt his usual tactics and that he must hold him up. In the event, however, the champion jockey fell between two stools, neither permitting Abernant to stride along in the hope of taking his two opponents off their legs nor saving his speed for a late run. Though in front at half-way, he failed to shake off Tangle, who challenged strongly in the last two furlongs and exploited his weight advantage to win by half a length. There is no doubt that Abernant was a better horse on firm than on soft ground, but faulty tactics certainly contributed to his downfall in the King's Stand Stakes.

Murless's opinion of Abernant has been given already. Gordon Richards, too, thought the world of him. Independent confirmation of their views was offered by that most experienced and professional of journalists and watch-holders James Park in the authoritative *Bloodstock Breeders Review*: "I am a believer in the watch when it comes to sprint races. Usually they go out of the gate and hop along as merrily as they can. I know what to expect on the various courses and I want to put it on record that my watch revealed Abernant as the fastest horse in post-war years. Even as a two-year-old he kept coming up in times that frankly astonished me."

Apart from his hocks, which were rather away from him, Abernant was a lovely specimen of a thoroughbred sprinter. He had a lean head of great quality, tremendous power in his quarters and shoulders, and excellent depth through the body. And if he was an aristocrat in looks, he was also a true gentleman in character. No kinder horse has ever lived. One afternoon Murless's daughter Julie, in later years well known in the racing community as the successful trainer's wife Mrs. Henry Cecil but then a mischievous little girl, was found in Abernant's box. She had managed to scramble up onto the horse's back, and he was entering happily into the spirit of the game. Gordon Richards recorded that on one occasion at York Abernant's attention became riveted by a group of children playing on the ground near the starting gate, and he made it perfectly plain that he wanted to join in.

Abernant was always quiet as an old hack until he began to line up at the start. Then his whole demeanour changed in an instant, and he was all eagerness to be off.

Abernant spent his stud career at Mrs. (afterwards Lady) Macdonald-Buchanan's Egerton Stud at Newmarket, where he had to be put down at the age of twenty-four in July 1970. He transmitted a lot of his own speed to many of his progeny and sired Abermaid, winner of the One Thousand Guineas, in addition to fast animals like Zarco, Liberal Lady, Abelia, Favorita and Gwen. His daughters have bred the One Thousand Guineas winners Caergwrle and Humble Duty. If speed is the primary and essential asset of the thoroughbred, then Abernant served both to exemplify and to propagate it.

Tulyar (1949)

A certain degree of controversy has always surrounded the reputa-
tions of two of the late Aga Khan's most famous winners, Bahram
and Tulyar. Bahram won the Triple Crown and was never defeated;
Tulyar had a somewhat undistinguished record as a two-year-old
but was unbeaten at three years of age when his victories included
the Derby, St. Leger, Eclipse Stakes and King George VI and
Queen Elizabeth Stakes.

Despite these glittering achievements, it is not uncommon to hear
both Bahram and Tulyar devalued by describing them as merely the
best of their age in markedly poor years. Yet Bahram won from five
furlongs to a mile and three-quarters, and though at times somewhat unimpressive, was never in serious danger of defeat. Marcus
Marsh, trainer of Tulyar, never rated Tulyar in the same lofty
category as his first Derby winner Windsor Lad, but the fact remains
that no rival really got to the bottom of him during his second
season.

Tulyar was bred by the Aga Khan at his stud in Co. Kildare and is
by Tehran out of Neocracy, by Nearco. Tehran, by the 1938 French-
bred Derby winner Bois Roussel, won the 1944 St. Leger and ran
second to Ocean Swell in the Derby and the following year in the
Ascot Gold Cup. As a sire he was far from being consistently successful, his most notable winners besides Tulyar being Amante
(Irish Oaks), Mystery IX (Eclipse Stakes) and Raise You Ten
(Goodwood Cup and Doncaster Cup). In 1952 he was champion
sire, thanks to Tulyar, but never subsequently did he figure in the
leading ten.

Neocracy, who won two races as a two-year-old worth £2,562, was
out of Harina, who won £4,128 in stakes and was by Blandford out
of the late Mr. W. Barnett's famous mare Athasi. Athasi, by Farasi

whose stud fee at one time was the modest sum of £5, was little, if anything better than a selling plater and at one period of her career she was competing with scant success over hurdles. Nevertheless, she proved an outstanding broodmare, her offspring winning 28½ races worth over £51,000. Among them was Harina's full brother Trigo, who won the 1929 Derby and St. Leger. Neocracy herself was also the dam of Saint Crespin III, winner of the Prix de l'Arc de Triomphe and the Eclipse Stakes and sire of the One Thousand Guineas and Oaks winner Altesse Royale.

Tulyar was a May foal and as a yearling so small and backward that he was retained in Ireland for an additional six weeks after the rest of his owner's yearlings had been sent to join Marcus Marsh's stable at Newmarket. As a two-year-old he offered no hint at all that he was ever likely to reach Classic standard. He was unplaced in the Spring Stakes at Newmarket in May; third in the Virginia Water Stakes at Ascot in July; and unplaced in the Acomb Stakes at York in August. However, he then showed signs of making a useful stayer by winning two one-mile handicaps of no particular significance, the Buggins Farm Nursery at Haydock Park and the Kineton Nursery at Birmingham. He finished the season by running second in the Horris Hill Stakes at Newbury. Charlie Smirke, who rode him, afterwards reckoned he might have won that Newbury race if he had waited with Tulyar a bit longer. In the Free Handicap Tulyar was given 8 st. 2 lb., 19 lb. less than the top weight Windy City. On what he had accomplished so far, he looked like making a fair sort of staying handicapper.

Brown in colour, Tulyar stood no more than 15 hands 3 inches as a three-year-old and though by no means a dominating individual, he was nevertheless a difficult horse to fault. By temperament he was placid and indolent, so indolent in fact that he was misleadingly liable to appear indifferent in his work at home. He was quite happy to stand for hours at a time, often balanced on three legs, gazing contentedly into space. He was easy to handle and apparently without vice. When he did choose to extend himself, his stride was of remarkable length for a horse of his size.

The atmosphere in Marsh's stable in the spring of 1952 could hardly be described as happy one. The prospects of victory in the major races looked remote in the extreme and both the Aga Khan and his son Prince Aly Khan, accustomed to success, were beginning to show signs of dissatisfaction. The Aga was becoming old and feeble and much of the control lay in the hands of Prince Aly Khan. In fact, unknown to Marsh, Prince Aly Khan had already arranged for the bulk of the horses to be transferred to Noel Murless at the end of the season. With reprehensible lack of frankness, he never told Marsh of this arrangement and Marsh only heard of it quite by chance at Goodwood from the Aga Khan's stud manager, Mr. Nesbit Waddington. The irony of the situation lay in the fact that the 1952 season was to prove a record one for Marsh.

Tulyar was soon busy in 1952 and on April 5th he won the Henry VIII Stakes of seven furlongs at Hurst Park, beating King's Bench, who had been rated 10 lb. above him in the Free Handicap, had won the Coventry Stakes and the Middle Park Stakes, and who, shortly after this defeat, was runner-up to Thunderhead II in the Two Thousand Guineas. This race indicated that Tulyar had made considerable improvement but Marsh, while naturally well satisfied, took the view that King's Bench had been badly in need of a race. Tulyar missed the Two Thousand Guineas partly because it was thought at the time that he needed a lot of give in the ground to be seen at his best; partly because Marsh reckoned him to be far better suited to the Derby and the St. Leger.

Tulyar next ran in the 1¼ mile Ormonde Stakes at Chester, where the going was really heavy after several days of rain. Carrying 7 st. 9 lb. and ridden by Doug Smith as Smirke of course could not hope to do the weight, Tulyar stayed on gamely in the mud to win by a length from Nikiforos. He had certainly shown resolution and stamina but as the critics were quick to point out, the form really amounted to very little. In fact Nikiforos, who later became a useful long-distance hurdler, failed to win a race of any sort that season.

Far more convincing was Tulyar's performace in the Lingfield Derby Trial shortly afterwards. Patiently ridden by Smirke, he was not in the leading six with a furlong and a half to go but then accelerated in great style to win decisively by two lengths. Even after this, though, there remained a reluctance to admit he was a top-class colt and as late as the morning of Derby day it was possible to back him at more than double the price at which he eventually started.

There was a spell of warm, dry weather after Lingfield and the going everywhere became firm. This was thought detrimental to Tulyar's chance and there was even talk of Smirke being switched to Marsh's other Derby runner, Sir Humphrey de Trafford's Indian

Hemp. However, five days before the Derby Tulyar did a really good final gallop. Smirke was able to tell Marsh that Tulyar was at least as good on fast ground as on soft, while Marsh informed Prince Aly Khan that Tulyar represented a cast-iron each-way bet.

The going was still very much on the firm side at Epsom. Tulyar started favourite at 11–2, a huge volume of late money having forced his price down from 100–8. Joint second favourites were the French pair Silnet and Argur, while there was plenty of support, too, for Worden II, Thunderhead II and Faubourg II. Tulyar was in fact the only English runner among the first half dozen in the betting.

At the top of the hill the Newmarket Stakes winner Chavey Down led from Monarch More, Caerlaverock, Bob Major, Thunderhead and Tulyar. Approaching Tattenham Corner, Gordon Richards drove Monarch More into the lead, while H.V.C. improved and Thunderhead II fell back beaten. In the straight Monarch More still led with Bob Major, Tulyar, Chavey Down and H.V.C. in line abreast roughly a length behind him. Monarch More soon cracked and Chavey Down and Bob Major did not last much longer. This left Tulyar in front considerably sooner than Smirke really desired. Tulyar's burst of acceleration put him two lengths clear and it was then just a question of whether he could maintain his advantage to the end. The final stages are best presented by Marsh's own description in his entertaining book of reminiscences *Racing With The Gods*: "Inside the final furlong Lester,* on Gay Time, was definitely beginning to gain ground on the wide outside and once again I had cause to be glad that I had Charlie up. Sensing the danger, he switched his whip to his left hand and went over to join Gay Time, performing what I have always regarded as the most brilliant of all race-riding manœuvres, stealing another horse's ground. He came just close enough to make Gay Time break his stride and yet not close enough to be accused of interfering in any way—and there is a perilously narrow dividing line between the two."

Tulyar won by half a length from Gay Time with Faubourg II a length away third. Piggott wanted to object but was dissuaded from doing so by Gay Time's owner, Mrs. J. V. Rank. After passing the winning post Gay Time had slipped up, unseated Piggott and had galloped away. Piggott returned to the unsaddling enclosure on foot and Gay Time, apprehended by a mounted policeman at the

* Lester Piggott.

Durdans, only arrived at the unsaddling enclosure twenty minutes after the race was over.

The Aga Khan was not well enough to lead Tulyar in and that office was performed by Prince Aly Khan. It was the fifth and last of the Aga Khan's five Derby triumphs and the third of Smirke's four victories in that race. In the opinion of some of the more experienced jockeys, it had been a deplorably rough race. Marsyad broke a fetlock and had to be destroyed. Prince Aly Khan, who had done his level best the previous winter to sell Tulyar for £70,000, won £40,000 in bets but even so was inclined to be querulous on the grounds that Marsh had been unreasonably slow to recognize Tulyar's true merits.

After the Derby Tulyar went from strength to strength. Starting at 3–1 on, he won the Eclipse Stakes at Sandown with the utmost ease by three lengths. A week later he took the field in the King George VI and Queen Elizabeth Stakes at Ascot, winning cleverly by a neck and a length and a half from Gay Time and Worden II, to both of whom he conceded 2 lb.

The Eclipse Stakes earned Tulyar £9,636; the King George VI and Queen Elizabeth Stakes, in which Smirke, after some drastic wasting, still had to put up 2 lb. overweight, £23,302. Among the horses defeated by Tulyar at Ascot were Worden II, subsequently winner of the Washington International at Laurel Park; Arbele, who was to win the Prix Penelope and the Prix Jaques le Marois; Niederlander, winner of the German Derby; Nuccio, who had won the Coronation Cup and was to win the Prix de l'Arc de Triomphe; Mat de Cocagne, winner of the Prix du Cadran; Zucchero, who had just won the Princess of Wales's Stakes and was a really good horse on his day; Sybil's Nephew, second in the 1951 Derby; and Fraise du Bois II, winner of the Irish Derby. It can hardly be argued that Tulyar only beat equine nonentities.

Tulyar was favourite for the St. Leger at 11–10 on and won very easily by three lengths from Kingsfold, despite having to be checked and switched to the outside with just over a furlong to go. That race concluded his three-year-old career and there was general satisfaction when it was announced that he would remain in training as a four-year-old. However, bearing in mind the Aga Khan's record with his previous Derby winners and his relish for a deal in horseflesh, only the more simple-minded members of the racing world were really surprised to hear during the winter that the Aga Khan had sold Tulyar to the Irish National Stud for £250,000. Needless to say, Marsh had not been informed of this change of plan and the first he heard of what was singularly unwelcome information for him was in a news bulletin on the boat bringing him back from a holiday in South Africa. It was reasonable to suppose that Tulyar would have won a lot of prize money in 1953, a percentage of which would have gone to Marsh. Marsh suggested that under the circumstances he was entitled to a percentage on the sale, but the Aga Khan, a realist, to put it in civil terms, over money matters replied that he had never given a percentage on a sale and had no intention whatsoever of commencing that practice.

During his two seasons in training Tulyar had won £76,417 10s. in stakes, thereby beating the record of £57,455 established by Isinglass who had raced until he was five. Tulyar's total was surpassed a few years later by that of Ballymoss and the record is now held by Mill Reef—the record, that is to say, for a horse trained in England or Ireland. As a three-year-old Tulyar had won from seven furlongs to a mile and three-quarters and on going varying from rock hard to mud. He was rarely spectacular but the fact remains that no opponent that year ever really got to the bottom of him. He was one hundred per cent genuine and a great favourite with the racing public.

It was always Marsh's opinion that Tulyar would never make a stallion, based on the theory that he was not a sufficiently dominating type to stamp his stock. Certainly Tulyar's offspring in England and Ireland were disappointing, the best being a filly called Ginetta that won the Irish One Thousand Guineas. In 1955 Tulyar was sold by the Irish National Stud to an American syndicate headed by the Claiborne Farm, Kentucky. Unfortunately, soon after his arrival in the United States, he became gravely ill and for a long period there seemed little hope for his recovery. He did pull through in the end but it is probable that this serious illness contributed towards his failure to make any real mark as a sire.

Never Say Die (1951)

There was a long gap of seventy-three years between the first American-bred Derby winner, Iroquois, and the victory of the second one, Never Say Die, in 1954.

Never Say Die was bred and owned by Mr. Robert Sterling Clark, who had been born in New York and derived much of his wealth from the Singer Sewing Machine Company. His brother, Mr. F. Ambrose Clark, was for many years a popular and familiar figure in English hunting and steeplechasing circles, his wife winning the 1933 Grand National with that great Aintree jumper Kellsboro' Jack.

Mr. Robert Clark was particularly interested in the breeding side of racing and if he betted at all, it was on a very small scale indeed. He began racing in the United States in the nineteen-twenties and had a stud at Sundridge, Upperville, Virginia. He first registered his colours for English racing in 1930 and soon afterwards purchased a stud of 120 acres at La Lisière in Normandy. This stud was rendered unusable for bloodstock owing to the depredations of German occupation and the damage done to it in the battle for Normandy in 1944. In 1946 Mr. Clark decided to give up racing in the United States completely, followed a dispute with the New York Jockey Club, which refused to register for racing purposes the produce of some Arab mares that he owned.

Never Say Die is a chestnut and is by that temperamental race-horse but outstanding sire Nasrullah out of Singing Grass, by War Admiral, a great American horse that stood only 15 hands 2 inches, out of Boreale, by Vatout, winner of the French Two Thousand Guineas and sire of the 1938 Derby winner Bois Roussel. Singing Grass was trained in Yorkshire by Harry Peacock and won seven minor races worth £1,879, her main success being in the Stockton

Stewards Handicap. When her racing days were over she went to the Beau Parc Stud in Ireland, where Mr. Clark kept some of his mares. She was covered firstly by Combat, and the following year, 1950, by Nasrullah who was then standing in Ireland. She was safely in foal to Nasrullah when she was shipped to the United States and it was there that Never Say Die was foaled on March 26th, 1951. He was reared and partially broken at the stud of Mr. John A. Bell before being sent to England with a number of other yearlings in the autumn of 1952.

When Mr. Clark's yearlings arrived in England, it was the custom of his trainers to toss up to decide who had first pick. On this occasion Harry Peacock won the toss, but although Never Say Die was clearly the best of the bunch on looks, Peacock declined to have him as he did not care for Nasrullah's stock. It did in fact take Nasrullah an appreciable time to overcome the prejudice that existed against him due to some of his own performances on the racecourse. Peacock chose Flying Wedge, who won three races the following season, and Joe Lawson, who had never trained a Nasrullah horse before, got Never Say Die, whose grandam Boreale was a half-sister to Galatea II. Trained by Lawson, Galatea II had won the One Thousand Guineas and the Oaks for Mr. Clark in 1939.

During his first season in training Never Say Die offered no clues to suggest future greatness. Altogether he ran six times and his solitary success was in the Rosslyn Stakes at Ascot in July. Previously he had been sixth in a big field of twenty-five in the May Maiden Stakes at Newmarket on April 28th and he had then run reasonably well to finish sixth to Hydrologist in the New Stakes at Ascot. It was because of the promise he displayed in the New Stakes that he started a 9–4 favourite for the Rosslyn Stakes.

Because of Never Say Die's hot Nasrullah blood, Lawson was extremely careful not to hurry him and to bring him along gradually. The policy seemed to be succeeding but Lawson confessed to a feeling of disappointment that Never Say Die did not appear to make any appreciable improvement after his Ascot win. At Goodwood he was a moderate third of six behind that very fast Irish colt, The Pie King, in the Richmond Stakes. At Sandown he looked exceptionally well, and was soundly backed, too, when he turned out for the seven furlong Solario Stakes, but he could do no better than finish fifth to Barton Street. Finally, in the seven furlong Dewhurst Stakes at Newmarket in October, he was third of five, receiving 8 lb., behind Infatuation, who finished four and a half lengths in front of him.

In the Free Handicap he was given 8 st. 3 lb., 18 lb. less than the top weight, The Pie King. When the 1954 Classics came under discussion, his name was never mentioned.

Never Say Die thrived during the winter. However, he looked distinctly big and backward when he turned out for the Union Jack Stakes at Liverpool in the very first week of the flat-racing season. He ran well but was beaten by Tudor Honey, who was giving him 5 lb. He was confidently expected to improve next time he ran and was in fact made favourite for the seven furlong Free Handicap at Newmarket on April 8th. Ridden by Piggott, he finished down the course and was clearly outpaced in the second half of the contest. Time was to show that he really needed a considerably longer distance than this, which was strange as his sire was certainly not deficient in speed, while Singing Grass was a middle distance performer that never won beyond eleven furlongs.

Never Say Die was not asked to take part in the Two Thousand Guineas, won by Darius, and his next race was the ten furlong Newmarket Stakes at Newmarket in May. In a close finish he was third behind Elopement and Golden God, beaten half a length and a head. The race was run at a muddling pace and Never Say Die would certainly have preferred a stronger gallop. "Manny" Mercer, who rode him, had been told to ride a waiting race but perhaps slightly overdid his patient tactics as he was last of the eleven runners at the Bushes. At that point, two furlongs from home, he asked Never Say Die for his effort and Never Say Die responded to such effect that he actually struck the front coming into the Dip. In so doing, though, he became a little unbalanced and was headed as he met the rising ground.

The critics were unanimous about the race. It was, they declared, a moderate field and the result had no bearing on the Derby. One of the most attractive things about racing, however, is that the alleged experts are wrong so much more often than they are right. The field for the Newmarket Stakes included horses that finished first, second, fourth and fifth in the Derby.

The element of chance enters so often into racing, even in races of primary importance, that it is worth recording an incident that occurred immediately after the Newmarket Stakes. Mr. Clark's racing interests in England were managed for him by a well-known veterinary surgeon, Mr. Gerald McElligott who was also a director of the British Bloodstock Agency. In the Newmarket Stakes Never Say Die had tended to hang to the left when he became unbalanced. Unfortunately Mr. McElligott was informed that the colt had hung to the right. Now a tendency to hang to the right would be singularly unhelpful on a left-handed track like Epsom, so Mr. McElligott wrote to Mr. Clark suggesting that Never Say Die missed the Derby and went for the King Edward VII Stakes at Ascot instead. Mr Clark cabled back agreeing with that proposal. In the meantime Mr. McElligott luckily discovered that he had been misinformed. He at once communicated with Mr. Clark, and Never Say Die was permitted to take his chance at Epsom. In racing, as in other aspects of life, the ability to distinguish between left and right is sometimes essential.

The Derby, run on excellent going on a typical English summer afternoon with unbroken grey cloud and a searing wind from the east, was generally regarded as an extremely open race. Joint favourites at 5-1 were the north-country colt Rowston Manor and Ferriol, the hope of France. Darius, despite doubts of his ability to stay the distance, was soundly supported at 7-1. The big backers paid scant attention to Never Say Die, on offer at 33-1, but small punters all over the country entrusted him with their shillings, partly because his name appealed to them; partly because he was ridden by Lester Piggott, then only a boy of eighteen but already the idol of the rank and file of the racing public.

Rowston Manor, a fine big chestnut, led round Tattenham Corner, closely followed by the Queen's colt Landau, a son of the famous Sun Chariot. Darius was third, Blue Sail, the mount of the American jockey Johnnie Longden, fourth, and Never Say Die, going very easily, fifth. With three furlongs to go Rowston Manor, who had run all too freely, was in trouble and a great cheer went up as the royal colours were seen to be in front. Landau, though, did not stay a mile and a half and soon afterwards his stride began to shorten. From then on the issue was between Darius and Never Say Die. Darius battled on courageously but he did not really quite stay the distance and he simply could not match the acceleration of Never Say Die, who ran on to win with impressive ease by two lengths. Second was Arabian Night, who finished strongly to deprive Darius of second place close home. The time was the good one of 2 minutes 35·4/5th seconds. Unfortunately Mr. Clark was ill in New

York and thus missed seeing the greatest triumph of his career as breeder and owner.

At the time of this success Never Say Die stood 15 hands 3½ inches. He was certainly a good-looking, well-proportioned colt but he had attracted no particular attention in the paddock. Those who fancied him, though, had noted with satisfaction his placid demeanour and the undoubted strength of his back and loins. It was Joe Lawson's thirteenth Classic success but he had never won the Derby before. He was in his seventy-fourth year at the time.

Never Say Die had taken so little out of himself in the Derby that it was decided to run him in the mile and a half King Edward VII Stakes at Ascot. Piggott was again in the saddle. The race turned out to be the most sensational and least agreeable of the entire season, with Never Say Die and Derby runner-up Arabian Night both unplaced.

At this stage of his career Piggott had unfortunately not yet learned to temper his brilliance and courage with discipline and restraint. There were times when his total lack of fear, combined with his determination to win at all costs, degenerated into sheer recklessness that endangered not only his own neck, but the necks of his fellow jockeys as well. Because of this, his brushes with the authorities were anything but infrequent. The public freely forgave Piggott these lapses, feeling that they were caused solely through his zeal to win. They regarded him as fundamentally on their side, reserving their resentment and contempt for certain riders they reckoned were just a bit too crafty and occasionally too economic in effort. As he grew older, Piggott learnt to respect the Rules of Racing, and the safety of the other jockeys, without forfeiting his resolution or his boldness.

The King Edward VII Stakes was duly won by Rashleigh by a length from Tarjoman, with Blue Prince II close up third. Never Say Die was fourth and Arabian Night fifth. It was an ugly race to watch and few, if any, of the jockeys concerned emerged with much credit. It seemed more of a trial of strength, in fact, between the riders than anything else, and in the course of the race only one of the four clauses of Rule 140 of the Rules of Racing was not broken. Piggott was suspended for the rest of the meeting and in due course the Stewards of the Jockey Club informed him that "they had taken notice of his dangerous and erratic riding both this season and in previous seasons, and that in spite of continuous warnings, he continued to show complete disregard for the Rules of Racing and for the safety of other jockeys". A statement was then issued that before any application for a renewal of Piggott's licence could be considered, he must be attached to some trainer other than his father for a period of six months. He accordingly joined Jack Jarvis's stable at Newmarket. Many people thought the Stewards had been unduly harsh, but in fact this long suspension marked a turn for the better in Piggott's career.

Piggott had thus to miss Never Say Die's final race, the St. Leger, in which he was partnered by that irrepressible veteran Charlie Smirke. Favourite at 100–30, Never Say Die proved conclusively that the further he went, the better he was. He treated his fifteen opponents as if they were weary hacks from a seaside riding school and won as he pleased by twelve lengths from Elopement with the French colt Estramadur four lengths away third. It was a great performance by a magnificent stayer, and Mr. Clark, not surprisingly much moved, was overwhelmed with congratulations.

Never Say Die was unquestionably one of those very rare horses that combine apparently boundless stamina with notable power of acceleration. Had he been kept in training as a four-year-old, he would surely have proved a superb Cup horse. Mr. Clark, though, was an elderly man in indifferent health; in fact he died two years later at the age of seventy-nine. He decided to retire Never Say Die at the peak of that horse's fame and any disappointment at that decision was mitigated when, as a token of his regard for English racing, he presented Never Say Die to the National Stud. As a mark of gratitude for this generous gift, Mr. Clark was elected an honorary member of the Jockey Club.

Never Say Die appeared to have all the attributes for success at the stud but it has to be admitted that after a highly auspicious start, he has proved progressively disappointing. In 1960, when his daughter Never Too Late II won the One Thousand Guineas and the Oaks, he was third on the list, while two years later, when his son Larkspur, aided by good fortune, won the Derby he was champion. Since then, though, he has been far less successful and all too many of his stock appear to lack the essential quality of speed. No doubt he was unlucky in 1967 when General Gordon broke his leg at exercise and had to be put down, as in the opinion of the late Sir Jack Jarvis, General Gordon was as good as, if not better than, his stable companion Pretendre, who was only just beaten in the Derby by Charlottown.

Petite Etoile (1956)

Petite Etoile belongs with Sceptre and Pretty Polly in the category of the most brilliant fillies ever to tread the British Turf. Although she had only two Classic victories, compared with the four of Sceptre and the three of Pretty Polly, she could do no more than win both the Classic races in which she started. Like Pretty Polly and Sceptre, she was put properly through the mill on the racecourse, and won fourteen of the nineteen races in which she took part; Pretty Polly won twenty-two of her twenty-four races and Sceptre thirteen of her twenty-five races. Like Pretty Polly, Petite Etoile won the Coronation Cup, the renowned all-aged race run over the Derby course at the Epsom Summer meeting, when she was four and five years old. Like Sceptre, she encountered the Derby winner of the previous year as a four-year-old and, whereas Sceptre was narrowly beaten by Ard Patrick in the Eclipse Stakes, she proved much too good for Parthia in the Coronation Cup.

The comparison with Sceptre and Pretty Polly thus is not unfavourable to the filly who was foaled more than half a century after them. But the comparison fails to indicate the dominant and distinctive asset which was the mainspring of Petite Etoile's greatness, for that was her sheer blinding speed. Petite Etoile was grey, and greyness in the thoroughbred has been closely linked with speed ever since The Tetrarch, the spotted grey wonder, outpaced and outclassed all the other two-year-olds of 1913. Petite Etoile inherited her greyness from The Tetrarch through her dam Star of Iran, and then back through the female chain of ancestry formed by Mah Iran, Mah Mahal and The Tetrarch's daughter, "The Flying Filly" Mumtaz Mahal. She was bred jointly by the Aga Khan and his son the Aly Khan, and Mumtaz Mahal, purchased for 9,100 guineas as a yearling in 1922, was one of the foundation mares of the stud which was to become one of the most powerful in the world. The Aly Khan, who unfortunately died when Petite Etoile was at the height of her racing form, was unwavering in his belief that she was not only the best filly that he and his father had bred, but was the best filly he had ever seen.

The essential qualities of The Tetrarch and Mumtaz Mahal pervaded the family. Petite Etoile's grandam Mah Iran was a three-quarters sister of the record-breaking Derby winner Mahmoud, and her dam Star of Iran, by the Derby winner Bois Roussel, was an own sister of the Eclipse Stakes and Prix de l'Arc de Triomphe winner Migoli. Closely allied branches of the family produced Nasrullah and Royal Charger, superbly fast horses who as stallions have exerted a profound influence on the progress of the thoroughbred.

Petition, the sire of Petite Etoile, reinforced the same qualities that she received from her dam. A top-ranking speed specialist when he was two, Petition grew in stamina and reputation as his career unfolded, and as a four-year-old he captured one of the richest middle distance prizes that British racing has to offer, the $1\frac{1}{4}$ mile Eclipse Stakes. Finally, the pedigrees of Petition and Star of Iran had a vital common factor in Lady Josephine, the dam of Mumtaz Mahal and the grandam of Petition's sire Fair Trial. No individual thoroughbred in the twentieth century, with the exception of The Tetrarch himself, has done more to promote and diffuse pure speed throughout the breed than Lady Josephine, and when The Tetrarch and Lady Josephine are duplicated and found in conjunction, the results are liable to be sensational.

So Petite Etoile was bred to run like the wind. She was a product of the Aga Khan's group of Irish studs centred on the Curragh, but the Aga Khan died when she was a yearling, so she raced as the sole property of his son, the Aly Khan, until he too died three years later. Most of their horses were trained by Alec Head at Chantilly, but a small number were kept with Noel Murless at Newmarket, and it was to Murless's Newmarket stable that Petite Etoile was sent when it was time for her to go into training. It is almost a cliché of racing history that the early careers of great horses tend to be clouded by circumstances or setbacks that put their whole futures at risk. In this respect Petite Etoile was no exception to the rule, for her first public performance was not calculated to raise exaggerated hopes. Murless sent her to Manchester at the end of May in her two-year-old season to make her début in the Prestwich Stakes, a modest race with a prize of £500. She had a single opponent, Chris, and a quieter or less nerve-racking introduction to the business of racing would be difficult to imagine. However Petite Etoile, always inclined to be skittish and temperamental, was completely overcome by the occasion. She got rid of Lester Piggott twice before the start, and when she did at last consent to line up she was in no state to do herself justice. She was beaten by the ignominious margin of eight lengths and, although Chris developed into a top-class sprinter and won the King's Stand Stakes at Royal Ascot, she gave no glimpse or hint of the excellence that was to come.

Inauspicious as her display had been, Petite Etoile had learnt a lot from her experience at Manchester, and she acquitted herself with credit in her three remaining races as a two-year-old. She was much too good for the second-rate opposition in the Star Stakes at Sandown Park in July, and in the Molecomb Stakes at Goodwood three weeks later was second to Krakenwake, a filly endowed with tremendous precocious speed and then at the height of her powers. Although she was beaten by two lengths, Petite Etoile finished much further in front of the rest in a race which always attracts some of the fastest of the two-year-old fillies. In her only other race that season, the Rose Stakes at Sandown Park in August, Petite Etoile, starting at 6–1 on, met the colt Belafonte on 10 lb. worse terms than weight-for-sex and beat him comfortably by a length.

Petite Etoile did not attempt a longer distance than five furlongs in her first season. She had shown that she possessed good speed, but had not proved herself one of the leaders of her sex and age group. In the Free Handicap she was given 8 st. 6 lb., 10 lb. less than the two best fillies, Lindsay and Rosalba, who had been first and second in the Cheveley Park Stakes. The handicapper may have underestimated her even on her two-year-old form. At any rate the Free Handicap, run over seven furlongs at the Newmarket Craven meeting, was chosen for her first outing as a three-year-old. The Australian jockey, George Moore, had recently arrived in France to ride for the Aly Khan there, and the Aly Khan asked Murless to find a few mounts for Moore in England so that he could gain some experience of English courses. Petite Etoile was one of only two horses the Aly Khan then had in training in England. As Murless had another runner in the Free Handicap, a filly called Short Sentence leased by the Queen from the National Stud, the logical arrangement was for Moore to have the mount on Petite Etoile and for the stable jockey Lester Piggott to ride Short Sentence. Neither of the Murless fillies figured prominently in the betting, but the result was an eye-opener as Petite Etoile raced to the front in the Dip and stormed up the final hill to give Moore an easy three lengths win on his very first mount in England.

The acceleration of Petite Etoile had been electrifying and her victory impressive, but not impressive enough to convince everyone that she was capable of winning Classic races. At the beginning of the season Collyria had been regarded as the main hope for the fillies Classic races at Warren Place, and Piggott chose to ride her in the One Thousand Guineas. Moore was to ride Paraguana, owned by the Aly Khan but trained by Alec Head. Accordingly Doug Smith was engaged for Petite Etoile, and so came in for a lucky chance mount. Rosalba, who had shown that she had wintered well by winning the Fred Darling Stakes, was favourite at 9–4, with Paraguana second favourite at 5–2 and Petite Etoile next in demand at 8–1. Murless's instructions to Smith were not to go to the front too soon, but when Smith asked the grey filly to improve her position after the Bushes he was astounded by the alacrity of her response. Petite Etoile simply shot to the front in a few strides and was three lengths clear in the Dip. Rosalba went after her and reduced the gap steadily in the last furlong, but Petite Etoile was too far in front to be caught and still had a length to spare passing the winning post. Paraguana was four lengths away third.

The One Thousand Guineas proved conclusively that Petite Etoile was an exceptional filly over a mile. Her time of 1 minute 40.36 seconds was more than two seconds faster than that of Taboun who, ridden by Moore, had carried the colours of the Aly Khan to victory in the Two Thousand Guineas two days earlier. Whether she could stay one and half miles was another matter, and many backers were inclined to doubt it. Although Piggott was on her back for the first time that season, Cantelo, who had won the Cheshire Oaks in a canter, and Mirnaya were preferred to her in the betting on the Oaks. The result of the race proved what few had been able to bring themselves to believe up till then, that Petite Etoile was indeed a great filly. Cantelo and Rose of Medina took up the running before reaching Tattenham Corner and forced the pace as best they could, but they could not get Petite Etoile at full stretch. The grey filly moved up on the bit two furlongs from home and, when Piggott gave her her head entering the last furlong, she swept past Cantelo to win as she liked by three lengths. Once again the watch confirmed visual evidence, for she had covered the distance in 1/5th of a second faster time than Parthia in the Derby two days earlier.

Later evidence endorsed the excellence of the Oaks form, for Cantelo went on to beat the best of the colts, including Fidalgo, Pindari and Parthia, in the St. Leger. Two days earlier Cantelo herself had been beaten by Petite Etoile's stable companion Collyria, who was at last fulfilling the expectations that she would become a top-class filly, in the Park Hill Stakes over the St. Leger course, but the winning margin of Collyria was a hard-earned one and half lengths, not the hard-held three lengths of Petite Etoile in the Oaks.

Petite Etoile went through her three-year-old season without defeat. She toyed with the opposition in the Sussex Stakes over a mile at Goodwood, for which her starting price was a prohibitive 10–1 on, and in the Yorkshire Oaks her two opponents played into her hands by going no gallop for more than half of the distance of one and a half miles and allowing Petite Etoile to conserve her speed. Her last race of the season, the Champion Stakes at Newmarket in October, was a different story. As in the Yorkshire Oaks, she had only two opponents, and on any past form she was bound to beat the Irish St. Leger winner Barclay and the French candidate Javelot without the slightest trouble. However Lester Piggott gave the filly's admirers a hair-raising experience by getting boxed in in a field of three on the wide expanses of Newmarket Heath. She was still in the trap with no apparent chance of escaping as they ran through the Dip, but when they met the final furlong of rising ground Javelot edged away from the rails and left a small gap. That was enough for Petite Etoile, and she shot through to beat Barclay by half a length, with Javelot a neck away third. Piggott's tactics had been dictated by the laudable intention to give Petite Etoile as easy a race as possible, and they generated a more exciting finish than anyone had dared to predict, but only luck saved them from causing a disaster.

The decision of the Aly Khan to keep Petite Etoile in training as a four-year-old caused great satisfaction in racing circles, as did the parallel decision of Sir Humphrey de Trafford to persevere with Parthia. The exciting prospect for 1960 was of the first clash between a Derby winner and an Oaks winner as four-year-olds since the unforgettable confrontation of Ard Patrick and Sceptre in the

Eclipse Stakes in 1903. The encounter was billed for the Coronation Cup from an early stage of the season. Unhappily her owner-breeder, the gay and charming Aly Khan, did not live to see the race, as he was killed in a motor accident in the suburbs of Paris a few days after Petite Etoile had made her first appearance of the season in the Victor Wild Stakes at Kempton Park and outclassed her two rivals. The Aly Khan's racing interests were taken over by his son, the Aga Khan.

The eagerly awaited race for the Coronation Cup ended in anti-climax. Once again there were only two other runners, Parthia and his stable companion, the Queen's colt Above Suspicion. Appreciating that a slow run race could benefit only Petite Etoile, Cecil Boyd-Rochfort, the trainer of her rivals, instructed Harry Carr on Parthia and Doug Smith on Above Suspicion to set a strong pace the whole way. The jockeys carried out their orders, but they could not get Petite Etoile off the bit. Piggott kept Petite Etoile behind until well inside the last furlong and then pounced. The race was all over in a few strides as she shot past to win by one and half lengths.

The next objective for Petite Etoile was the King George VI and Queen Elizabeth Stakes, Great Britain's most valuable race for three-year-olds and older horses, run over one and a half miles at Ascot in July. The going, affected by heavy rain earlier in the week, was softer than she was accustomed to, and her opponents were more numerous than in any of her races since the Oaks. The field of eight included Aggressor, who had beaten Parthia in the Hardwicke Stakes at Royal Ascot, besides Parthia himself. Nevertheless few of the spectators had any premonition of disaster as Petite Etoile went down to the start at a price of 5–2 on. In the race Piggott tucked her in at the back of the field in accordance with his invariable practice, but there were a few rumours of alarm when he still had her in last place at the final turn. It is difficult to make up much ground in the short, uphill straight at Ascot. Two furlongs from home a gap appeared on the inside rail and Jimmy Lindley sent Aggressor, who revelled in the yielding ground, through it and went hard for the winning post. Piggott, trying to follow through several lengths behind him, found the gap closed and had to switch to the outside. Petite Etoile quickened and, with a furlong to go, she was clear of the others and only Aggressor was in front of her. But when Piggott called for the final effort to clinch matters there was nothing there.

7*

Petite Etoile came off the bit for the first time for over a year, but she could make no impression on Aggressor, who kept galloping on relentlessly to beat her by half a length.

At the time probably ninety per cent of the critics were inclined to blame the defeat on Piggott, arguing that he had thrown the race away by delaying his effort too long and giving her too much to do in the last two furlongs. Murless took the opposite view. He was already aware that Petite Etoile did not truly stay one and a half miles in testing conditions against top-class opponents on a course where stamina really counted. He knew that nothing Piggott could have done would have enabled her to beat Aggressor in the circumstances.

The plan was for Petite Etoile to run in the Queen Elizabeth Stakes and the Champion Stakes in the autumn, but she was a victim of the coughing epidemic in the autumn and was unfit to take part in either of those races. However an announcement was made, to the surprise and delight of racegoers, that she would remain in training for another campaign in 1961. Sceptre and Pretty Polly had both run as five-year-olds, but it had become increasingly rare for top-class fillies to stay in training after the age of four. On the other hand the Aga Khan's stable cupboard looked like being rather bare of top-class talent in 1961, and he was strongly advised that Petite Etoile must be called on if he wished to win some of the most important races.

The decision was understandable. The Aga Khan was a young man who had had little interest in racing up to the time of his father's death, and Petite Etoile was just the horse to kindle his enthusiasm. Neverthless the experiment of running her as a five-year-old was not an unqualified success. She had always been highly strung, and as a five-year-old she became so restive in training as to be almost unmanageable at times. One of her whims was to refuse to go out on to Newmarket Heath for training sessions unless she was following another grey horse. Fortunately Murless had two grey three-year-olds, Eddy and Dolgelley, in his stable that season and, although neither of them won a race, they did yeoman service by leading Petite Etoile.

All went well in her first three races, the Coronation Stakes at Sandown Park, the Coronation Cup at Epsom and the Rous Memorial Stakes at Royal Ascot. However it was noted that she was sweating profusely and was reluctant to parade in front of the stands at Epsom, and needed some persuading to come into line at the start. In the race Sir Winston Churchill's four-year-old Vienna set a hot pace, and although Petite Etoile beat him by a neck in the end, Piggott did not look quite as blissfully confident as he had done in most of her races. The lesson was not lost on Vienna's trainer, Walter Nightingall, and when he saddled Sir Winston's other good four-year-old, High Hat, against Petite Etoile in the Aly Khan Memorial Gold Cup in July, he instructed Duncan Keith to set a blistering pace from the start. The race, with a £10,000 prize subscribed by friends of the Aly Khan, was run over one and a half miles on a sunlit evening at Kempton Park. Keith obeyed his orders to the letter. High Hat went a tremendous gallop with Petite Etoile tracking him. The other four runners were shaken off long before they reached the straight but, when it came to the crunch and she was asked to challenge the pacemaker, Petite Etoile was found wanting in stamina, and High Hat had no difficulty in staying ahead and winning by two lengths. The young Aga Khan was a disconsolate figure as he stood with Murless in the unsaddling enclosure surveying his beaten mare.

Petite Etoile was seen in public once more, when she was beaten by the Irish four-year-old Le Levanstell in the Queen Elizabeth II Stakes over the Ascot Old Mile in September. She only just succeeded in keeping the three-year-old Eagle out of second place. Her lack-lustre display proved beyond doubt that she had lost the keen edge of her ability and her love of racing and she was due for retirement.

Petite Etoile in her prime was a beautifully balanced specimen of the thoroughbred, with exceptional propelling power in her hindlegs. Her rather small eyes were her only fault. If her reputation was a little tarnished in her last two seasons, and if the ease of her earlier victories over one and a half miles was shown to be an illusion based on Piggott's sleight of hand, she was undoubtedly a filly and mare of outstanding brilliance, and had winnings of £73,002, a record for a member of her sex, to prove it.

Petite Etoile retired to the Aga Khan's studs at the Curragh. It would be pleasant to be able to give an account of the triumphs of her offspring, but unhappily her career as a broodmare has been a practically unmitigated disaster. In her first nine stud seasons she was barren six times and once produced twin fillies, neither of whom survived. She had only two offspring, both colts, to run, and of those

Afaridaan alone won races, gaining his successes in French races of the humblest class. An unkind Fate seemed to preside over her destiny at stud, and it is by her deeds on the racecourse that she will be remembered.

Kelso (1957)

Geldings, for the cogent reason that they remain in training as long as they keep their health, soundness and running ability, tend to win more secure places in the affections of the racing public than even the most brilliant entire horses and mares, who are liable to be transferred to lucrative stud duties at a relatively early period of their lives. Familiarity breeds feelings of admiration that deepen with the years. This aptitude of geldings for inspiring affection found its exemplar in Kelso, who in the course of an active racing career lasting from 1959 to 1966 won the hearts of many thousands of American enthusiasts as he advanced from triumph to triumph, shattering records, both in respect of race times and otherwise, and proving himself a truly great racehorse not only by the standards set by other geldings but by the standards of the breed as a whole. "King Kelly", as he was nicknamed, richly deserved the legend engraved on a plaque set in the outer wall of the box he occupied in his retirement at Woodstock Farm, Maryland: "The most durable horse in racing history". The same plaque proclaimed that Kelso was voted "Horse of the Year" for five successive years from 1960 to 1964, a record that will surely stand for ever—as will his achievement in winning the Jockey Club Gold Cup, the supreme test of stamina in the United States, in each of the same five years.

Kelso was fortunate to be bred and to race in the United States. No other country offers such splendid opportunities for profitable employment to geldings of his particular gifts. In most other leading racing countries geldings are debarred from many of the principal events, including the world's richest race the Prix de l'Arc de Triomphe. Moreover the American Triple Crown races (the Kentucky Derby, the Preakness Stakes and the Belmont Stakes) account for a much lower proportion of the total prize money distribution than the Classic races do in countries like Great Britain, where the scales are loaded heavily in favour of entire colts and fillies who excel as three-year-olds. Instead the numerous valuable races, mostly but not exclusively handicaps, open to horses of all ages enable horses to continue earning at a uniformly high rate as long as they remain in training and keep their form. Kelso, gelding though he was, finally retired at the age of nine with career earnings of 1,977,896 dollars as a result of thirty-nine wins, twelve seconds and two thirds from the sixty-three races in which he had taken part. His earnings, a world record, were over 200,000 dollars more than the total attributed to the leading entire horse, Round Table. Two other geldings, Native Diver and Fort Marcy, were among the ten "dollar millionaires" of racing history up to the end of 1970, while another gelding, Armed, had been the top stakes earner of American turf history during the nineteen-forties.

No gelding racing on the flat in Great Britain, except Brown Jack, had ever been able to hold a candle to Kelso's achievements; and indeed the only gelding of whatever nationality worthy of serious comparison with Kelso in point of all-round class was the great Australian horse Phar Lap, who for a time was the highest prize money earner ever bred in the British Commonwealth.

Kelso was bred in 1957 by Mrs. C. duPont at A. B. Hancock's Claiborne Farm, Kentucky, where she kept her mares at the time, though they were later transferred to Woodstock Farm. Mrs. duPont was a well-known horsewoman and Master of the Vicmead Fox-hounds in Maryland. His sire, Your Host, had won the Santa Anita Derby, but his dam Maid of Flight had been nothing out of the ordinary on the track and won only three of the nineteen races in which she ran at two, three and four years of age. In arranging this mating Mrs. duPont was motivated partly by a desire to blend high-class bloodlines. Maid of Flight was by the American Triple Crown winner Count Fleet, and her mating with Your Host meant that the progeny, namely Kelso, had Hyperion and Mahmoud, who estab-lished new record times for the Derby at Epsom during the nineteen-thirties, and America's greatest thoroughbred Man o' War as three of the four sires in the third generation of his pedigree. But in selecting Your Host she was also influenced by admiration for his courage, for he fell and broke a leg in his last race as a four-year-old and bore his suffering unflinchingly while the vets argued whether he could be saved for stud. When the leg did mend a syndicate was formed to acquire him for stud duty, Mrs. duPont expressed her admiration for his fortitude by taking a share. Her faith in the sterling character of the horse brought an exceedingly rich reward.

There was little to foreshadow the greatness to come when Kelso appeared for the first time in public to represent Mrs. duPont's Bohemia Stable at the Atlantic City meeting in September 1959. His début had been delayed by stifle joint trouble which was to affect him again later in his career, and in general physical development he was backward. There was nothing to catch the eye in his rather plain looks; his body was narrow and his neck was lean. Nevertheless he won a maiden race over six furlongs at the first attempt on September 4th, and was second to Dress Up and to Windy Sands in the two subsequent races which followed at ten-day intervals.

He was trained by Dr. John Lee for his two-year-old races, but was in the charge of the former jockey Carl Hanford for the rest of his career. His first appearance as a three-year-old was not until late June at Monmouth, New Jersey, and the races he took part in then and at the New York track, Aqueduct, nearly a month later were modest enough in class, though he could do no more than win on each occasion. However his first venture in high-class company was inauspicious, as he could finish no nearer than eighth behind T.V. Lark in the Arlington Classic on July 23rd. The Chicago track was not a lucky one for him, and any doubts about his ability to hold his own with the best raised by his Arlington Classic failure were swept away as he went through the rest of the year without another defeat. Back at Monmouth early in August, he gained his first important victory in the Choice Stakes over eight and a half furlongs, and followed up with victories in the Jerome Handicap over a mile and the Discovery Handicap over nine furlongs at Aqueduct in the first half of September.

These successes had proved that Kelso was a force to be reckoned with in good company at distances round about a mile, but his next race, the Lawrence Realisation at Belmont Park at the end of September, added a new dimension to his evolving career. Not only is the distance of the Lawrence Realisation 1 mile 5 furlongs, half a mile further than he had run before, but the race, though open to geldings, is regarded as the American equivalent of the St. Leger. In 1960 the top-class proven three-year-old form was represented by Tompion, the winner of the Santa Anita Derby, and Kelso gave an eye-opening performance by beating him by four and a half lengths and equalling the track record of 2 minutes 40·4/5th seconds set up by the mighty Man o' War in the same race exactly forty years earlier.

The Lawrence Realisation had provided convincing evidence of both Kelso's class and his stamina. He went back to 1¼ miles for the Hawthorne Gold Cup in Illinois less than three weeks later, and demonstrated his versatility by romping away with the 88,000 dollars first prize after escaping from a pocket between On-and-On and Manassa Mauler on the far turn. At the finish he had six lengths to spare from the second horse Heroshogala, and T.V. Lark, who had humbled him at Arlington three months earlier, was unplaced. This was sweet revenge for Kelso, but was not the last round in the struggle for supremacy between two fine thoroughbreds.

Kelso returned to New York for the Jockey Club Gold Cup at Aqueduct on October 29th. This race over 2 miles is the principal test of stamina in the American racing calendar, and is the race that Kelso was to make peculiarly his own. He was opposed by Bald Eagle, who had won the Washington D.C. International once already and was to win it again a fortnight later. Tooth and Nail was started as pacemaker for Bald Eagle, and took a long lead in the early stages. The South American-bred Don Poggio took up the running when Tooth and Nail faded at half-way, but Kelso moved easily into the lead in the straight and forged ahead to win by three and a half lengths from Don Poggio, with Bald Eagle a further ten lengths back in third place. Although the track was soft, Kelso lopped nearly three seconds off the American record for the distance by running the two miles in 3 minutes 19·4 seconds.

Kelso was taken to California with the intention of running him in the Malibu Stakes at Santa Anita on the last day of the year, but he wrenched a stifle on the morning of the race and had to be withdrawn. Nevertheless his advance during 1960 had been astonishing, and in the year-end handicap of the leading three-year-olds published in *The Bloodhorse* he was placed top 2 lb. above the Preakness Stakes winner Ballyache, 8 lb. above the Kentucky Derby winner Venetian Way and 10 lb. above the Belmont Stakes winner Celtic Ash.

His stifle injury kept him out of action until the middle of May in 1961, when he won a small race at Aqueduct. Critics were quick to note the improvement in his looks. In his earlier days he had been plain, light of his neck and rather weedy in general physique, but as

Plate 24   Abernant

Plate 25   Tulyar

Plate 26   Never Say Die

Plate 27   Petite Etoile

Plate 28 Kelso

Plate 29 Royal Palace

Plate 30   Nijinsky

a four-year-old he put on weight in all the right places and began to assume the looks as well as the air of self-confidence that befit a champion. He certainly sprang straight into championship form by winning the Metropolitan, Suburban and Brooklyn Handicaps, the three races that constitute the so-called "Handicap Triple Crown", at Aqueduct between the end of May and the middle of July. In between times he found time to win the important Whitney Stakes at neighbouring Belmont, though victory on that occasion came only on the disqualification of Our Hope, who came up on the outside and bored across into Kelso so badly in the last furlong that the left stirrup iron of his jockey Eddie Arcaro was buckled by contact with the running rail. Our Hope reached the winning post a head in front, but his fault had been so glaring that his disqualification was inevitable, and his rider Pete Anderson was suspended for ten days.

Kelso's performance in the last leg of the "Handicap Triple Crown", the Brooklyn Handicap over $1\frac{1}{4}$ miles on July 22nd, was one of the finest of his whole career, for he was carrying 9 st. 10 lb. and giving at least 14 lb. to each of the other nine members of a top-class field, yet won easily by one and quarter lengths. His victories in the three big Aqueduct handicaps, followed by his victory in the weight-for-age Woodward Stakes at Belmont at the end of September and his second Jockey Club Gold Cup victory the following month, led to his invitation to represent the United States for the first time in the Washington D.C. International at Laurel on November 11th. The other U.S. representative was T.V. Lark, and so the stage was set for a final clash between the two old rivals. From the start they completely dominated the six foreign horses in the field. The pair were locked in a close struggle practically the whole way, but in the last half mile T.V. Lark gradually asserted himself and, despite a despairing late rally by Kelso, T.V. Lark had three-quarters of a length to spare at the winning post. The best of the foreigners, the Venezuelan Prenupcial, was twelve lengths back in third place. Despite this defeat the year-end handicap of leading horses published by *The Bloodhorse* placed Kelso top with 7 lb. more than T.V. Lark and Kelso was voted "Horse of the Year" unanimously.

It would be both pointless and wearisome to catalogue all the performances of Kelso during an active career which was to continue in full flow for three more years and at a reduced tempo for yet another year. To convey an impression of a horse who reached the top and stayed there with a resolution and for a length of time seldom if ever equalled in any country in the history of the thoroughbred, it is necessary to pick out only those meaningful events that enhanced or limited his reputation. Perhaps the most significant aspect of his whole career was the way in which, year after year, he met one or more of the leaders of the Classic three-year-olds and beat them. He had beaten the diminutive Carry Back, the best three-year-old of the year, in the Woodward Stakes in 1961, though it is only right to add that Carry Back got his revenge in two of the 100,000 dollars handicaps, the Metropolitan and the Monmouth, in May and July of the next year.

However Kelso was probably not quite at his best in the first half of 1962. When the Woodward Stakes came round in September he again found himself opposed to one of the best three-year-olds, Jaipur, who had victories in the Jersey Derby and the Belmont Stakes to his credit. Jaipur swerved at the start and lost a little ground, but quickly recovered to pursue the headstrong Beau Purple, one of the year's most spectacular if inconsistent performers. As Beau Purple faded out of the front rank Jaipur took up the running on the approach to the final turn, but Kelso sailed past him more than a furlong from the finish to win very easily by four and a half lengths.

The story was the same in 1963, when Kelso overwhelmed Never Bend, who had been second in the Kentucky Derby and third in the Preakness Stakes and was to become the sire of the Derby winner Mill Reef, by three and a half lengths to win the Woodward Stakes for the third time.

Running like a thread through all the Kelso story is his sequence of victories in the Jockey Club Gold Cup. Some of those five victories were somewhat hollow, for he was apt to frighten away potential opposition over a distance which few American-bred horses are able to stay with comfort. He was given an ovation by the crowd on the way to the start of the race in 1963, the first time in living memory that such a thing had happened on an American racecourse, but the race itself was such a one-sided affair that he started at 20–3 on and won in effortless fashion. It was different when he won the Gold Cup for the fifth and last time a year later, for he was opposed by the two top-class three-year-olds, Quadrangle and Roman Brother, who had been first and second in the longest of the American Triple Crown races, the 1½ mile Belmont Stakes. Kelso had a tough assignment indeed, but the result was the same as in the past, since Kelso romped in by five and a half lengths from Roman Brother, and Quadrangle was relegated to third place six lengths further back. Ismael Valenzuela, who had replaced Eddie Arcaro as Kelso's regular partner, was looking over his shoulder for possible but non-existent dangers well before reaching the finishing line. Nevertheless the presence of the top-ranking three-year-olds had compelled Kelso to stir himself to such good effect that he cut 0·2 of a second off the American record for two miles that he had set up in the same race four years earlier.

Another and perfectly valid way of viewing the career of Kelso is as a gradual preparation for a final, climactic and crowning triumph in the Washington D.C. International. We have seen how he was second to T.V. Lark the first time he was picked to represent the United States in 1961. A year later he was left with no reserve of energy to repulse the late challenge of the French horse Match III after engaging in a mad duel with the tearaway Beau Purple for the first mile. In 1963 the finish was all-American, as Mongo and Kelso battled for the lead throughout the last half mile and Mongo prevailed by half a length in the end. Mongo had come a little wide round the final turn, carrying Kelso with him, and Valenzuela afterwards lodged an objection. This however was overruled, and Kelso's jockey was fined 100 dollars for a frivolous objection.

By the time Kelso lined up for his fourth International in 1964 he was approaching the end of his seventh year and there was a now-or-never air of desperation about his bid for victory. Moreover his appearance in the eight-horse field representing seven different countries was spiced by his rivalry with the other United States runner Gun Bow. Hailed as one of the best handicap horses seen for years apart from Kelso himself, Gun Bow had prevailed in the Brooklyn Handicap and the Woodward Stakes, Kelso in the Monmouth Stakes, in which they were both beaten by Mongo, and the Aqueduct Stakes. The International was regarded as a decider between two horses of exceptional ability, and Kelso seized the opportunity to decide the issue his way. Outclassing the foreigners, the two American horses had the race to themselves the whole way. On the last turn Gun Bow came out a little from the rail and brushed Kelso, and Kelso retaliated by rolling back and crowding Gun Bow on to the rail. From that moment Gun Bow was a spent force and

Kelso raced clear to win by four and a half lengths, with the rest of the runners straggling in far behind Gun Bow.

The objection by Gun Bow's jockey Walter Blum against Kelso was overruled. But although Gun Bow had suffered a decisive defeat, he had made Kelso run to the extent of covering the one and a half miles in 2 minutes 23·8 seconds, 2·4 seconds less than the previous course record held by T.V. Lark and 0·6 of a second less than the previous American record held by Pardao.

Kelso's International victory left him with no fresh worlds to conquer. Although he ran six times as an eight-year-old in 1965, won three races including the important Whitney Stakes at Saratoga and earned more than 84,000 dollars, he was in the twilight of his career. After one race as a nine-year-old in which he earned 500 dollars by finishing fourth, he retired to Mrs. Richard duPont's Woodstock Farm at St. Augustine, near Chesapeake City in Maryland.

Kelso went into retirement, but not to a useless and monotonous life of idleness. Mrs. duPont hunted him regularly with the Vicmead Hounds, and Kelso showed a love and flair for jumping which would probably have made him one of the all-time greats of steeplechasing if he had been foaled and reared in Great Britain or Ireland. At Woodstock he played host to thousands of visitors who marvelled equally at his charming manners and the aristocratic good looks that made nonsense of his plainness in his early days.

Tributes have been showered on him—none more fitting or more memorable than that written by Frank Talmadge Phelps in *The Bloodstock Breeders Review* for 1964: "And then there was Kelso—the ageless, the magnificent, the champion again for the fifth consecutive season. He has become a law unto himself, a *non-pareil*, the transcendent standard by which others may be measured and found wanting."

Royal Palace (1965)

Foaled in 1965, Mr. H. J. Joel's Royal Palace won top-class races at two, three and four years of age. But for misfortune, he might well have proved the first Triple Crown winner since Bahram in 1935. As a four-year-old he was undefeated, and it seemed an odd decision that he was not voted "Horse of the Year" that season, the distinction being awarded to the American-bred Sir Ivor, whom Royal Palace had defeated fairly and squarely on the only occasion that they met.

Bred by his owner at Childwick Bury, St. Albans, Royal Palace is a bay by Ballymoss out of Crystal Palace, by Solar Slipper. Ballymoss is too well known to need a lengthy description here. After finishing second to Crepello in the 1957 Derby, he won the Irish Derby, the St. Leger, the Coronation Cup, the Eclipse Stakes, the King George VI Stakes and the Prix de l'Arc de Triomphe. Crystal Palace was a good middle-distance filly that won the Falmouth Stakes at Newmarket and the Nassau Stakes at Goodwood. Solar Slipper, a half-brother to the dam of the Derby winner Arctic Prince, won the Champion Stakes and was third in the St. Leger.

Crystal Palace's dam, the Borealis mare Queen of Light, won the Falmouth Stakes, and among her offspring was Chandelier, who bred the good winner and successful sire Crocket, and who was sold at the 1964 December Sales for 37,000 guineas. Queen of Light was out of the One Thousand Guineas winner Picture Play and came from a family that has been at the Childwick Bury Stud for a great many years.

Royal Palace was sent to be trained by Noel Murless at Newmarket and there was therefore not the slightest danger of him being either hurried or over-raced as a two-year-old. In fact his two-year-old programme was typical of the methods of his trainer when dealing with the potential winner of a Classic. The race selected for Royal Palace's first appearance was the six furlong Coventry Stakes at Ascot on June 14th. Ridden by Breasley, he was little fancied and ebbed quietly from 10–1 to 100–7 in the betting. There were fifteen runners and a hot favourite at 6–4 on was the Irish colt Bold Lad, trained by Paddy Prendergast. Bold Lad, by the leading American sire Bold Ruler, was so precociously mature that he seemed like a powerful adult condescending to take part in a game with boys.

Bold Lad duly won by four lengths whereas Royal Palace did not finish in the leading six, but what was pleasing about Royal Palace's performance was the speed that he displayed and the fact that he was able to hold his place among the leaders for four furlongs. He was still backward at the time and lack of condition told its tale in the final stages, but all in all it was a very encouraging performance by a colt that was bred to stay. His next appearance was awaited with considerable interest.

In fact Royal Palace did not run for two months and he looked noticeably fitter when he took the field for the six furlong Acomb Stakes at York on August 16th. Ridden by Lester Piggott and second favourite at 4–1, he took the lead just before half-way and when challenged by the favourite, Imagination, he stayed on stoutly to win by two lengths. The opposition was not of great account and this performance of Royal Palace was perhaps more workmanlike than spectacular. All the same, it was eminently satisfactory bearing in mind that he was by a St. Leger winner out of a mare that had won over a mile and a quarter so that in all probability he would be seen to better advantage over a longer distance.

Royal Palace's final race in 1966 was the 1 mile Royal Lodge Stakes at Ascot on September 23rd. Favourite at 6–4 and ridden by Piggott, he faced four opponents among whom were Starry Halo, an unbeaten colt by Aureole, and Slip Stitch, an attractive filly by Parthia that had won both her races. Royal Palace did not misbehave at the start but he was caught flat-footed and lost every bit of half a dozen lengths. The pace was brisk and Royal Palace had to work hard to recapture the lost ground. He was still last on the final bend but at least he was in reasonably close touch with the leaders. In the straight he accelerated smoothly and to such purpose that he led with two furlongs still to go. At that point he seemed likely to win very easily but his exertions in the first half of the race had taken a good deal out of him and in the end he had only a length and a half to spare over Slip Stitch, Starry Halo was four lengths away third.

In the Free Handicap Bold Lad was top with 9 st. 7 lb. and then came Royal Palace with 9 st. 4 lb. and Ribocco, winner of the *Observer* Gold Cup by three parts of a length from Starry Halo, with 9 st. 3 lb. A good many critics reckoned that Royal Palace had been somewhat overrated and judged Ribocco to be the sounder Derby prospect.

In 1957 Murless had won the Two Thousand Guineas with Crepello, subsequently winner of the Derby, without giving him a previous race and the same plan was adopted for Royal Palace. Accordingly his appearance in the paddock before the Two Thousand Guineas on May 4th excited a lively interest. The paddock critics are seldom an easy body to satisfy and their reaction to Royal Palace was by no means entirely favourable. A well-balanced, strongly-made bay of medium size, he seemed distinctly short in the neck, a weakness that detracted from his quality. Though he had clearly done plenty of work, he was still noticeably backward in his coat. He was sweating slightly about his loins and in general he conveyed an air of nervous tension that was not altogether reassuring. However, there seemed to be plenty of confidence behind him and in the end he started joint favourite with the powerful Bold Lad, who was unquestionably the pick of the field on looks. There was a lot of money, too, for Taj Dewan, a Prince Taj colt that carried the hopes of France. Lester Piggott had elected at the end of 1966 to sever his long association with Murless's stable and Royal Palace was ridden by the experienced and highly-skilful Australian jockey, George Moore. It was the first occasion that starting stalls were used in an English Classic.

Royal Palace's task was rendered easier by the fact that Bold Lad, ridden by the Australian jockey, Lake, got very badly squeezed when up with the leaders just under two furlongs from home. He had to be snatched up and switched to a position further away from the rails and by the time this manœuvre had been completed, his chance had gone. He eventually finished fifth, roughly four lengths behind the winner. It is impossible to say what the outcome would have been had he enjoyed a clear run.

Royal Palace had been in a handy position from the start and racing down into the Dip, he joined the leader, Taj Dewan. The two had a terrific battle up the hill, both running on with exemplary courage.

Royal Palace obtained a very slight lead about a hundred yards from the post and maintained it to win a memorable race by a short head. In view of the fact that it was his first race since September and that he was bred to stay a mile and a half, this was a highly satisfactory performance.

Royal Palace did not run again before the Derby for which he started favourite at 7–4. Next in the betting came the Irish pair Royal Sword and Dominion Day. Piggott's mount Ribocco, whose form that spring had been very disappointing, was easy to back at 22–1. The going was perfect. There were twenty-two runners and starting stalls were used for the first time in the greatest race of the year.

In those days the starting stall handlers were still comparatively inexperienced and it took a long time before all the competitors were finally loaded and away. Royal Palace settled down smoothly in the middle of the field. He experienced not the slightest difficulty in negotiating the steep descent to Tattenham Corner and on the turn for home he was lying fifth behind four rather moderate horses—El Mighty, Belted, Privy Seal and Persian Genius. In the straight he soon established his superiority and a great cheer went up when he swept into the lead just over two furlongs from home.

From that point the only danger was Ribocco. Coming on the wide outside, Ribocco made remarkable progress from three furlongs out and with a furlong to go he had almost drawn level. Moore, however, then gave Royal Palace a single reminder with the whip and the favourite immediately responded to draw clear and win quite comfortably by two and a half lengths. Dart Board was third, two lengths behind Ribocco. The victory was a very popular one as apart from the not unimportant fact that Royal Palace was a heavily-backed favourite, Mr. Joel is one of the most modest and popular personalities in the racing world.

Royal Palace's victory was all the more pleasing to Mr. Joel as apart from having bred Royal Palace himself, the Derby winner came from one of the oldest of the Childwick Bury families. The late Mr. J. B. Joel's mare Absurdity, by Melton, was foaled in 1903 and came to Childwick Bury after an undistinguished racing career during which she won two minor events in three seasons. At the stud, however, she proved a very different proposition. The best colt she produced was the 1914 St. Leger winner Black Jester, by Polymelus. Of her daughters, Jest, by Sundridge, won the One Thousand Guineas and the Oaks in 1913. Jest was unfortunately a shy breeder and when she produced the future Derby winner Humorist in 1918, it was her first living foal in five seasons. She died a few weeks after Humorist's Epsom triumph.

Absurdity produced a three-parts sister to Jest by Sunstar and this filly was named Gesture. In due course Gesture went to the stud and bred three winners; she also bred a filly by Phalaris called Amuse, who was Royal Palace's fourth dam. When Mr. J. B. Joel died in 1940, Amuse's stud career had been as unrewarding as her record on the racecourse as she was thirteen years of age and had failed to breed a winner. Mr. Jim Joel might well have decided to dispose of her, but instead he had her mated with the Italian-bred sire Donatello II. The result of this union was Picture Play, who won the One Thousand Guineas and bred seven winners, including Queen of Light, grandam of Royal Palace.

After Epsom, it was decided that Royal Palace would miss the big mid-summer races—the Irish Derby, the Eclipse Stakes and the King George VI and Queen Elizabeth Stakes—and concentrate on winning the St. Leger, victory in which would earn him the Triple Crown. Unfortunately, just before the York August meeting, in which he was due to run in the Great Voltigeur Stakes, he rapped a joint. At that juncture he was an odds-on favourite for the St. Leger. The injury seemed to clear up satisfactorily but time was running short and much would obviously depend on the final gallop. In that test Royal Palace appeared to go well but very much to the surprise of the general public his name did not appear among the four-day declarations and on the Saturday before the Doncaster meeting began the following statement was issued on Mr. Joel's and Noel Murless's behalf: "Although Royal Palace's leg has gone on satisfactorily, the earlier stoppage in his work has now shown that there is insufficient time to get him to the degree of fitness necessary for such a race as the St. Leger and it is now the intention to run him in the Champion Stakes."

Royal Palace did run in the ten furlong Champion Stakes in October but he was nothing like the horse he had been on Derby day. He completely failed to show his true form, and favourite at 11–8 on, he finished a moderate third to Reform and Taj Dewan. Reform was of course a really good horse and might even have beaten Royal Palace over this distance had Royal Palace been at his best, but the Derby winner certainly ought not, on previous form, to have finished so far behind Taj Dewan. Thus Royal Palace's three-year-old career ended on a distinctly low note and many of those who had praised him extravagantly at the time of his Epsom triumph now took the view that he was merely the best of his age in a very moderate year. Fortunately, though, for Royal Palace's reputation, Mr. Joel decided to keep him in training for another season.

Of Royal Palace's first three races in 1968 little need be said. The opposition in the Coronation Stakes at Sandown, the Coronation Cup at Epsom and the Prince of Wales's Stakes at Royal Ascot was negligible and Royal Palace won on each occasion without the slightest difficulty. His first real test came on July 6th in the 1¼ mile Eclipse Stakes at Sandown Park. Here he was opposed not only by his old rival Taj Dewan, who earlier in the season had won the £28,000 Prix Ganay, but also by Mr. Raymond Guest's brilliant American-bred three-year-old Sir Ivor, winner of the Two Thousand Guineas and the Derby. There were two other runners in the race, Frankincense and Franc Castel, but they were obviously outclassed and were friendless in the market at 50–1. The going was firm and Sir Ivor, despite his sensational defeat in the Irish Derby the previous week, was favourite at 5–4 on. Royal Palace was on offer at 9–4, Taj Dewan at 7–2.

This was probably the greatest race for the Eclipse since 1903 when Ard Patrick, winner of the Derby in 1902, won from Sceptre, who had won all the Classics the previous year bar the Derby, and Rock Sand, the Triple Crown winner of 1903. Not surprisingly there was an enormous crowd at Sandown and the atmosphere before the race conveyed that feeling of tension only usually found in the last few anxious minutes before the start of the Derby or the Grand National.

The pace was a good one throughout. Franc Castel led round the final bend followed by Taj Dewan, Royal Palace, Sir Ivor and Frankincense. Early in the straight Franc Castel dropped back beaten, whereupon Yves Saint-Martin on Taj Dewan, finding himself left in the lead, decided not to tarry but to head for home as hard as he could go.

These highly enterprising tactics seemed likely to succeed. At the distance Sir Ivor was being hard ridden by Piggott and was failing to produce that superb acceleration that was normally his strongest card. Royal Palace, partnered as in all his races in 1968 by young Sandy Barclay, was making progress but with Taj Dewan showing not the slightest hint of weakening, it looked as if he had been left with just a shade too much to do. In the final hundred yards, though, Royal Palace began to close the gap in earnest and the cheers of his supporters increased in volume. Both horses gave everything they had and as they flashed past the winning post they were inseparable from the stands.

As a matter of fact nineteen spectators out of twenty were of the opinion that Taj Dewan had just held on to win and a number of bold punters backed the French colt at 6–1 on, and even at 8–1 on, to secure the verdict. Saint-Martin was convinced he had won and so were all the French contingent. Barclay and Murless were noticeably less sanguine in respect of Royal Palace. Now it so happens that no English racecourse has a more deceptive finishing angle than Sandown and the photograph revealed that Royal Palace had won by approximately four inches.

To say that the connections of Taj Dewan were taken aback would be carrying understatement to excess. Among the more restrained comments were those of Robert Corme, Taj Dewan's trainer, and of Yves Saint-Martin who described the result respectively as "*incroyable*" and "*impossible*". Even a study of the photograph failed for a long time to convince some of the more excitable visitors from France. It was certainly an occasion that one was thankful for the existence of the camera. If there had not been one, and if the judge had given the verdict to Royal Palace, the French would have returned home convinced to a man that they had been robbed. It was the second time that Taj Dewan had been narrowly defeated by Royal Palace and those two near misses cost him prizes to the value of £77,000. To rub in the bitterness of Taj Dewan's defeat in the Eclipse, Royal Palace's stable companion Hopeful Venture won the Grand Prix de Saint Cloud the following day, defeating, among others, Vaguely Noble.

Three weeks after that dramatic race at Sandown, Royal Palace took the field in the King George VI and Queen Elizabeth Stakes at Ascot, starting at 7–4 on in a field of seven. The going was perfect. When, with a quarter of a mile to go, he took the lead smoothly from Ribero, he looked like winning with dignified ease, but a furlong from home he suddenly faltered and began to veer away to the left. Both Topyo, who had won the Prix de l'Arc de Triomphe the year before, and Felicio II, who had been last but one into the straight, began to close on the favourite. Felicio II in particular, with

Poincelet using the whip unsparingly, staged a tremendous late challenge but Royal Palace just hung on to win by half a length, with Topyo only inches behind Felicio II. Some of Royal Palace's more confident backers were in a cold sweat and tottered off the grandstand feeling that although they were still solvent, their expectation of life had been curtailed by several years.

It was soon all too apparent why Royal Palace had suddenly weakened as he was very lame on returning to the unsaddling enclosure. He had torn a suspensory ligament in the near foreleg. Only a horse of immense courage could have struggled on to win as he did and that desperate final furlong represented in some respects Royal Palace's finest hour. His racing career of course was at an end. His nine wins had earned him £163,950, a record at that time for a horse trained in England or Ireland. That total, though, was surpassed later in the year by Sir Ivor through his wins in the Champion Stakes and the Washington International

It is true to say that Noel Murless never rated Royal Palace quite as highly as he did Crepello, who had decisively defeated a really good horse in Ballymoss in the Derby. Royal Palace, though, was the sounder of the two and among his virtues were those of consistency and courage. In eleven races he was only twice beaten, the first time being when he was a backward two-year-old, making his initial racecourse appearance. As he grew older, he improved considerably in looks and he is now an exceptionally handsome stallion. One can only hope that he will transmit his admirable qualities to his offspring.

Nijinsky (1967)

On the face of the evidence, Nijinsky was the victim of the pernicious practice of rushing top-class thoroughbreds off to stud at the end of their three-year-old seasons and not testing them on the racecourse in the maturity of their four-year-old days. If he had had a limited three-year-old programme, so the case runs, based on the English Triple Crown, then a winter's rest followed by a four-year-old programme comprising the Prix Ganay, the Coronation Cup, the Eclipse Stakes, the King George VI and Queen Elizabeth Stakes and the Prix de l'Arc de Triomphe, he would in all probability have retired with his aura of invincibility intact and an imperishable reputation as one of the greatest horses ever to tread the Turf—or if he had been beaten once or more times as a four-year-old by Mill Reef, then defeat would have been honourable and sustained in decisive trials of strength with another vintage Derby winner. The goal, so seldom within reach, of direct confrontation between brilliant stars of different age-groups would have been achieved and a fascinating story of thoroughbred prowess would have unfolded. Instead, the attempt to cram two programmes into a single season, or more accurately to tag on elements of an all-aged programme after the capture of the Triple Crown, overtaxed his physical and nervous resources and was responsible for the humiliation of his defeats by inferior opponents in the Prix de l'Arc de Triomphe and the Champion Stakes. Consequently he retired, not as a conquering hero, but as a horse with a sadly deflated reputation and as one of the most puzzling enigmas in racing history.

This is the case for believing that the racing career of Nijinsky was misconceived after his two-year-old days. Will it bear critical examination? It is axiomatic that a horse intended for stud service of top-class mares should be tested for soundness, constitution, temperament and racing ability through three seasons if possible. Nijinsky was sound as a bell, and there was nothing the matter with his health when he finished racing in October 1970. If there were an impediment in his own make-up to racing as a four-year-old it could only be his temperament. Nobody who knew him would question that he was highly strung, and he was inclined to sweat profusely in nervous anticipation before his races. In the paddock before the Two Thousand Guineas the Newmarket trainer Noel Murless, who had been attending to his own runner Saintly Song, remarked to Vincent O'Brien that Nijinsky seemed perfectly cool.

"Yes," replied the Irish trainer. "I think he is going to be all right today."

Yet Nijinsky was awash with sweat by the time he was parading in front of the stands a few minutes later. The irony of it all was that his temperament improved during the summer and he was cool and relaxed both in the paddock and at the start before the St. Leger. If his racing activities as a three-year-old had terminated with the St. Leger and he had gone into winter quarters with a four-year-old campaign in view, few worries about his temperament would have been expressed.

If the diminution of Nijinsky's stature as a great racehorse was due to faulty planning, the blame cannot be laid at the door of Vincent O'Brien. A trainer may advise, but the decisions of policy concerning the duration of a horse's racing career and the timing of his removal from stable to stud are outside his competence. Nor should Nijinsky's owner Charles Engelhard, who survived the horse's second defeat by only five months, be held wholly accountable on this issue. Known as the "Platinum King", he was one of the world's richest men. It might be thought that he, of all people, should have been free to dictate the policy of his horses without interference. But in fact he was exposed to very strong commercial pressures within the racing and breeding industry, and circumstances made it very hard for him to resist the forces driving him inexorably to a decision to send Nijinsky to stud at the end of his three-year-old season.

Nijinsky was foaled on February 21st, 1967, at the stud of Mr. Edgar P. Taylor in Ontario, Canada. A brewing and industrial tycoon, Taylor had played a leading part in putting Canada on the map as a considerable bloodstock producing country; indeed his role in raising the standards of thoroughbreds in Canada had been comparable to that of Federico Tesio in Italy several decades earlier. The act which put him firmly on the road to success as a breeder was the importation, in 1953, of the English mare Lady Angela in foal to Nearco, the finest product of Tesio's Dormello Stud up to that time. The foal Lady Angela was carrying was Nearctic, who possessed great speed, courage and toughness, breaking track records in both Canada and the United States and winning twenty-one of the forty-seven races that he contested during four racing seasons. Nearctic was destined to be the grandsire of Nijinsky. Retired to Taylor's National Stud in Ontario, Nearctic was mated in his first stud season with Natalma, a three-year-old who had shown marked racing ability but had her racing career cut short by a chipped sesamoid bone sustained during her preparation for the Kentucky Oaks. The fortuitous result of that mating between two first season stud animals was Northern Dancer, the sire of Nijinsky.

Heredity often works in inscrutable ways. Nearctic and Natalma were extremely plain specimens of the thoroughbred. Nearctic was exceptionally long in the back, which was also slightly dipped. Natalma was notably lacking in quality, very straight in front and cow-hocked. Northern Dancer did not resemble either of his parents in the least. Neat, compact, deep through the body and short on the leg, he was the very picture of thoroughbred elegance, but stood barely 15 hands 2 inches. No doubt he was a throwback to Hyperion and Pharos, the grandsires of Nearctic. What he did inherit direct from his parents was their wonderfully placid temperament and good manners.

As Nijinsky was to put Canada on the map of the world as a thoroughbred producer, so did Northern Dancer put Canada on the map of North America in the same respect. He was far the best three-year-old of 1964 on the North American continent. He won the first two legs of the American Triple Crown, the Kentucky Derby and the Preakness Stakes, and was third in the final leg, the Belmont Stakes; and he took time off from his United States campaign to win the most important race in Canada, the Queen's Plate over $1\frac{1}{4}$ miles at Woodbine.

One of Northern Dancer's mates in his second stud season was Taylor's own mare Flaming Page. She too possessed first-class racing ability. Like Northern Dancer, she won the Queen's Plate, and she was second in the Coaching Club American Oaks, the premier American fillies Classic race. Unlike Northern Dancer, she was of rangy build and had a fiery temper. The produce of this mating was

Nijinsky, and it is clear that he inherited salient characteristics from each of his parents. He took after his sire in his noble head and his splendid limbs, but his length of body and leg and his nervous temperament may be attributed to the influence of his dam.

All yearlings bred by Eddie Taylor were for sale, at a price. If nobody wanted to pay Taylor's valuation for any individual yearling, he kept it and raced it himself. On the advice of Vincent O'Brien, Engelhard bought Nijinsky for 84,000 dollars at the Woodbine Sales in Toronto and sent him to O'Brien's stable at Ballydoyle, near Cashel in County Tipperary. Although he was a big, backward colt on arrival, his exceptional promise was unmistakable, and before long he was installed in the corner box recently vacated by Sir Ivor, the brilliant colt with whom O'Brien had won the Two Thousand Guineas and the Derby earlier the same year. Subsequent events were to prove him well worthy of the honour.

O'Brien found Nijinsky a very different subject to train from Sir Ivor. A horse of exquisite quality and well-nigh flawless make and shape, Sir Ivor possessed intelligence in a very high degree. From the moment he went into training he adapted himself to each successive stage of stable, training and racing routine immediately, almost as if he had done it all before in a previous existence. No such intimations of a former life could be drawn from the conduct of Nijinsky, who had to be educated in every aspect of his job the hard way. He was excitable and impatient, and would frequently whip round and stand up on his hindlegs on the way out to the gallops. He became very upset if he was not allowed to do his work first of the whole string.

Despite his size—he stood 16 hands 3 inches when fully grown—and his tendency to lankiness, Nijinsky did not take unduly long to develop the strength and co-ordination of his limbs that are essential for successful racing. His début was in the Erne Maiden Stakes over six furlongs at the Curragh on July 12th, 1969. His reputation had preceded him to the racecourse, so that he started at the unremunerative odds of 11-4 on. That was the only unimportant race he ever contested, and he won it by half a length from Everyday. He followed this initial success by winning three of the most valuable two-year-old races in Ireland, the Railway, the Anglesey and the Beresford Stakes, all run at the Curragh, before the end of September. Only in the Beresford Stakes, when Decies was his chief opponent, was he at full stretch. Decies, who was to win the Irish Two Thousand

Guineas the next year, had been beaten by five lengths in the Railway Stakes, but had improved immensely and had beaten Nijinsky's highly-esteemed stable companion Great Heron in the National Stakes in the meantime. In the Beresford Stakes he tried to make all the running and, when Nijinsky came up to challenge in the final stages of the mile race, fought back with such determination that Nijinsky was all out to win by three-quarters of a length.

In his first four races Nijinsky was ridden by the most polished and experienced Irish jockey, Liam Ward, who had a contract to ride O'Brien's horses in Ireland. When he was sent over to Newmarket for the seven furlong Dewhurst Stakes in mid-October for his last outing as a two-year-old he was ridden for the first time by Lester Piggott, the champion English jockey who was to be associated with most of his later triumphs, as well as his failures. The Dewhurst Stakes is the championship English two-year-old race over the distance, but on this occasion the opposition was sadly sub-standard. However the manner of Nijinsky's victory was so smooth and so authoritative that observers were left with a profound sense of his class; and the Jockey Club handicapper was equally impressed, placing him top of the two-year-old Free Handicap. Of course Nijinsky occupied top place in the corresponding handicap in Ireland.

The performance of Nijinsky in the Gladness Stakes, his preparatory race as a three-year-old, was sufficient to confirm that he had made the right progress. He beat the year older Deep Run, who had been second in the Irish St. Leger the previous September, in a canter. No other preparatory race in England, Ireland or France revealed a colt who could be seriously fancied to beat him in the first of the English Classic races, the Two Thousand Guineas. And on the day Lester Piggott kept him in the middle of the field for most of the distance, then allowed him to move up easily, take up the running a little less than two furlongs from home and cruise ahead to win by two and a half lengths.

Time was to show that Nijinsky had little to do in the Guineas, because not one of the five horses (Yellow God, Roi Soleil, Amber Rama, Joshua and Huntercombe) who followed him home most closely over the Newmarket Rowley Mile genuinely stayed the distance with the exception of Roi Soleil, and he needed very heavy going to produce his best form. Nevertheless the style of Nijinsky's victory was convincing. The opposition in the Derby was much stronger, including as it did two high-class colts from France, Gyr

8

and Stintino. Gyr was a big, awkward, temperamental colt, but so talented that his very shrewd trainer Etienne Pollet had postponed his own retirement for a year in the expectation that he would win the Derby; and Stintino had won the Prix Lupin, the valuable French semi-Classic race at Longchamp in mid-May, with a marvellous, swooping run that took him from last to first place in the short straight. A few critics expressed doubts about Nijinsky's stamina. More doubted his ability to maintain a balanced stride on the descent to Tattenham Corner, as they did also in the case of Gyr. They were forgetting that the Epsom gradients have never stopped a good horse winning the Derby, but are adduced year after year to explain the defeats of moderate horses. For all their size and lankiness, Nijinsky and Gyr negotiated the descent and the corner on perfectly even keels. In the straight Stintino, Gyr and the outsider Great Wall all had their moments of lively hope of victory, and Gyr was in clear command with a furlong and a half to go. But when Piggott drew his whip and gave Nijinsky a couple of sharp taps he evoked a dramatic response. Nijinsky accelerated and raced through the leading group with an unmatchable surge of speed that settled the issue just inside the last furlong and took him to a two and a half lengths lead over Gyr at the finishing line.

The Derby and his next two races, the Irish Sweeps Derby and the King George VI and Queen Elizabeth Stakes, represented the climax of Nijinsky's racing career. The excellence of his Derby performance is indicated not only by the fact that he beat two really good colts—Gyr confirmed his own prowess by beating Grandier, the six-year-old winner of the Prix Ganay, easily in the Grand Prix de Saint Cloud early in July—but also by the watch. His time of 2 minutes 34·68 seconds was much the best since Mahmoud established the existing record 2 minutes 33·8 seconds for the Derby thirty-four years earlier, and Mahmoud ran on an Epsom course that was hard and bare, ideal for fast times by horses who could cope with such conditions, whereas Nijinsky ran on a track that was well-grassed and resilient. When allowance had been made for this fact, and for the fact that Mahmoud's time was recorded before the days of mechanical timing, it seems fair to claim that Nijinsky's performance, timewise, had more merit than that of Mahmoud.

Significantly both Mahmoud and Hyperion, who had also set a new record by winning the Derby in 2 minutes 34 seconds three years earlier, appear prominently in the pedigree of Nijinsky.

In accordance with his contract, Liam Ward had the mount on Nijinsky in the Irish Sweeps Derby, and, finding the opposition of little account, indulged himself in a long, spectacular run up the inside rail in the straight to win in a canter from Meadowville, who had finished fifth nearly ten lengths behind Nijinsky at Epsom. The King George VI and Queen Elizabeth Stakes four weeks later brought Nijinsky face to face with a posse of older horses. Indeed no three-year-old was thought worthy of opposing him, and all the other five members of the field were his seniors. They were the four-year-olds Blakeney, winner of the Derby, Crepellana, winner of the French Oaks, and Caliban, winner of the Coronation Cup, and the five-year-olds Karabas, winner of the Washington D.C. International, and Hogarth, winner of the Italian Derby. Across the board they were a choice selection of international talent. Yet Nijinsky outclassed them, and that Blakeney made some progress in the final stages and held Nijinsky's lead to two lengths at the finish was due solely to the fact that Piggott was pulling up. This was a superb, breathtaking effort by Nijinsky.

The bids for Nijinsky as a stallion had begun to come in even before the Derby. The day after the Derby Peter Burrell, the director of the British National Stud, met Vincent O'Brien at Epsom and made overtures for the purchase of the horse. In the course of negotiations the National Stud offered a yard at the Newmarket establishment for the exclusive use of Engelhard's visiting mares if the transaction should be completed. There were two offers of £2 million each from Ireland, one from a syndicate headed by Captain Tim Rogers and another from a single individual. But American interests, with subtle persuasion and sheer weight of money to back them, were not to be denied, and the announcement was made in August that Nijinsky had been syndicated for 5,440,000 dollars (£2,266,666 at the then official rate) and would go to Bull Hancock's Claiborne Farm at Paris, Kentucky, where Engelhard's American mares boarded, at the end of the season.

Nijinsky's programme as originally planned had not included the St. Leger. However the attractions of the St. Leger forced themselves on his connections ever more strongly. The English Triple Crown still had a special prestige. Moreover the St. Leger would take little winning, since Nijinsky had already established supremacy among the three-year-olds, and the race came at a convenient time for the preliminary outing he would need before his autumn objective, the Prix de l'Arc de Triomphe. Unfortunately he succumbed to an attack of the skin disease ringworm, so severe that he lost all the hair from one flank, during August and was off work for weeks. He recovered in time to run in the St. Leger and beat his old and inferior rival Meadowville without apparent effort, but the disease had probably taken more out of him than anyone realized at the time.

Indeed hardly a voice was raised to express doubts concerning Nijinsky's ability to win the "Arc", though this was the world's richest race and a true European championship. So the shock of his head defeat by Sassafras, the winner of the French Derby but on the balance of his form rather an ordinary horse by Classic standards, was all the more shattering. What had caused the reverse? The most popular verdict immediately after the race was that Piggott had erred in his judgment of pace, had lain too far out of his ground and given Nijinsky too much to do in the short Longchamp straight. The next Sunday at Longchamp the patrol film of the "Arc" was shown to an audience of racing correspondents and other interested parties. The film showed every phase of the race in close-up and from three different angles, and allowed a complete picture to build up in the mind of the observer. It was evident that Piggott had Nijinsky some way behind the leaders and rather wide for the first few furlongs, as he was bound to according to French rules since he was drawn on the outside of the field of fifteen; that Nijinsky had advanced to a good position at the last turn and was not more than three lengths behind Sassafras when he launched his challenge: that he drew level with Sassafras 150 yards from the finish and would have won comfortably if he had maintained his run: that he then began to falter and, in the last few strides, veered very sharply to the left as Piggott wielded his whip in his right hand. He had had every chance but, when the crunch came, had lacked either the will or the ability to win. As the lights went up at the end of the film a senior French racing official exclaimed: "So you see, gentlemen, Piggott has nothing to reproach himself with."

Nobody demurred.

But if Nijinsky was well ridden in the "Arc", why was he beaten? His form in that race could not be reconciled with his form in the Derby and the King George VI and Queen Elizabeth Stakes, but the precise reason for his loss of form is difficult, though perhaps not impossible, to define. He had been manifestly upset by the overeager attentions of photographers in the parade ring before the "Arc"; he was at the end of a long and strenuous campaign which had involved a lot of travelling for a highly-strung animal; and he had suffered from an irritating and debilitating infection. It is probable that the combination of these factors was sufficient to make him vulnerable at the highest level of competition.

Any doubts whether Nijinsky was deteriorating in the autumn of 1970 were resolved when he ran again in the Champion Stakes at Newmarket thirteen days after the "Arc". On all form that he and his opponents had shown he should have won without effort, and the temptation to give him the chance to retire from the scene on a note of victory was irresistible. But the venture was exposed as ill-fated from the moment he set foot on the track. His nerves got the better of him before the race, and he was in a sorry state at the start. In the race all the old fire was missing, and Nijinsky, in front of 20,000 spectators who had flocked to see the most glamorous thoroughbred for many a year, crashed to ignominious defeat by Lorenzaccio, a five-year-old who had indicated time and again that he was merely on the fringe of the top class.

No joy is to be found in the contemplation of fallen idols. In two short weeks Nijinsky the invincible had become Nijinsky the twice beaten. But nothing could take from him the glory of his performances at Epsom and Ascot, or the fact that he was the first English Triple Crown winner since Bahram in 1935. It is still true that a three-year-old requires a very rare and marvellous combination of qualities to beat the best of his contemporaries over a mile in April, one and a half miles in June and 1 mile 6 furlongs and 127 yards in September, on courses of widely differing character. There is no question that Nijinsky was great; at the height of his powers he was probably one of the horses of the century.

General Index

Index of Horses